Teaching Students with Moderate to Severe Disabilities

USE OF RESPONSE PROMPTING STRATEGIES

D0080650

Mark Wolery
Allegheny-Singer Research Institute
Early Childhood Intervention Program

Melinda Jones Ault and **Patricia Munson Doyle**
University of Kentucky

Longman
New York & London

Teaching Students with Moderate to Severe Disabilities

Longman, 95 Church Street, White Plains, N.Y. 10601

Associated companies:
Longman Group Ltd., London
Longman Cheshire Pty., Melbourne
Longman Paul Pty., Auckland
Copp Clark Pitman, Toronto

Senior editor: Naomi Silverman
Development editor: Virginia Blanford
Production editor: Linda Moser
Cover design: Michelle Szabo
Text art: Burmar
Production supervisor: Richard Bretan

Library of Congress Cataloging-in-Publication Data
Wolery, Mark.
    Teaching students with moderate to severe disabilities: use of
response prompting strategies / Mark Wolery, Melinda Jones Ault,
Patricia Munson Doyle.
        p.   cm.
    Includes bibliographical references and index.
    ISBN 0-8013-0491-1
    1. Learning disabled children—Education.   2. Prompting
(Education)   I. Ault, Melinda Jones.   II. Doyle, Patricia.
III. Title.
LC4704.W64 1992
371.9—dc20   91-21208
                                                                              CIP

1 2 3 4 5 6 7 8 9 10-MW-9594939291

This book is dedicated to our parents, who taught us,
our spouses, who would love to teach us,
and our children, who continue to teach us.

Ruth, Delbert, Pete, Steve, Tim, Emma, Michael, and Emily—
thanks for your patience, love, and understanding;
we realize it didn't take just a few hours here and there.

Contents

Preface

This book is about teaching, specifically about teaching students with moderate to severe disabilities. It describes how to teach and discusses issues related to organizing instruction and extending its benefits to students' natural environments. The major focus is on a set of strategies called response prompting procedures, strategies that comprise most of the effective procedures used in teaching students with moderate to severe disabilities. This book includes much of what is known about how to use those strategies; particularly, it systematizes teacher assistance and prompts so that they can be effective instructional tools. The primary purpose of this text is to describe those teaching procedures so that readers will employ them when providing instruction to students with moderate to severe disabilities. Thus, this book is *about* teaching and is *for* teachers and students preparing to become teachers.

The book is designed to be a supplementary text for methods courses; it is appropriate as a supplemental text for courses with titles such as these:

Teaching Students with Mental Retardation
Teaching Students with Severe Handicaps
Educational Procedures and Practices in Mental Retardation
Education of Students with Moderate Mental Retardation
Teaching the Trainable Mentally Retarded Student
Curriculum and Instruction for Students with Mental Retardation
Curriculum and Instruction for Students with Severe Disabilities
Curriculum and Instructional Issues with the Severely Disabled

This text contains detailed information on instructional issues that is not contained in any other books on instruction of students with moderate to severe disabilities. Although other texts address instructional issues in a chapter or two, professors frequently must supplement these texts with articles. This text will be useful to professors who want their students to learn about instructional strategies. The book can also be used in practicum and student teaching courses as a means of having students acquire and apply instructional procedures. Finally, the text has potential as a core training manual for inservice and staff development programs. In fact, we have used selected chapters for this purpose (particularly Chapters 3–8).

This text is based on many assumptions, but in the interest of brevity, five are noted here. First, *students with moderate to severe disabilities should be recipients of the best available instructional practices and procedures.* We have come to this conclusion because we cannot find a defensible answer to the following question: "For which students and under what conditions is an inferior educational experience acceptable?" As a result, this book is about the best available instructional procedures and practices.

Second, *the research literature has much to say about how teachers organize and present instruction.* We accept this perspective because of the richness of instructional research literature and because of the challenges we have faced in attempting to provide instruction to students with moderate to severe disabilities. Thus, this book contains many references to the research literature, and we urge teachers to be regular consumers and contributors to that literature.

Third, *beliefs and values influence how instruction is implemented.* We have come to recognize that values shape much of what constitutes acceptable practice in most fields, and the education of students with moderate to severe disabilities is no exception. Therefore, this book contains such values, and we have tried to articulate them and base them on sound logic. The beliefs that families are major decision makers in their children's education, that students with disabilities should be integrated into their natural communities, that instruction should promote adaptive functioning and social competence, and that data should drive instructional decisions are examples of values we hold.

Fourth, *teams, and particularly teachers, are responsible for producing learning.* This assumption is based on the recognition that manipulations of environmental variables (particularly teachers' behavior) occur on a broad continuum and can produce subtle but distinct changes in students' performance and learning. It is also based on the recognition that many of those effects are specific and not as broad and enduring as we would like them to be. Thus, we argue for conceptualizing the products of instruction on a hierarchy of acquisition, fluency, maintenance, and generalization.

Fifth, *teachers are the pedagogical experts of interdisciplinary teams.* We have come to this conclusion after participating on teams and observing teams where most members are ill-informed of what and how to teach. We also have observed that educators frequently adopt the roles of implementing others' interventions and "pulling it all together." While these functions may be legitimate, we believe teachers should have a unique and specific body of knowledge that can influence other team members' views and practice. Thus, this book focuses on knowledge competencies teachers must have to fulfill the role of "pedagogical expert."

As with most texts on nearly all topics, we did not address many issues. Educating students with moderate to severe disabilities requires broad knowledge of many different issues and topics. For example, teachers must understand how to work with families, how to support them in achieving their goals, and how the disabilities of students influence their performance and their families. Teachers must also know how to address the physical and health needs and well being of students, how medications influence students' behaviors, and how to design environments to respond to the challenging behaviors of students. They must be skilled in how to negotiate and access services from the community, how to deal directly with ethical dilemmas, how to use the regulations of law to ensure adequate services, how to find learning and work placements for students, how to train others to provide useful experiences for students, and many other topics. The focus of this book on teaching does not minimize the importance of these issues. We believe that a competent educator of students with moderate to severe disabilities must be knowledgeable in these areas. However, we have not addressed these issues for two reasons. First, as noted above, teachers need information on how to teach. In this text we have tried to provide a centralized and systematic description of important information on teaching and on a set of procedures that will benefit students, teachers, and families. Thus, this book should be used in conjunction with others. It has more detail about how to teach than existing texts, and it should serve as a supplement to them. It also can be used as a resource for the practicing teacher. Second, we have chosen to focus on what we know and know well—that is, how to teach. The other topics have been and are best addressed by others who know those issues well. Rather than write in a cursory manner about all topics, we have focused our efforts on our areas of expertise.

This text is organized into ten chapters. The first two chapters provide background definitions, assumptions, and information about teaching. Topics include how to select and use reinforcers, the steps of systematic instruction, and general issues about promoting performance at different phases of the learning hierarchy. The next six chapters describe separate instructional procedures, describe how to use them, and illustrate that use with examples. The final two chapters are designed to pull the book together and provide a context for using the procedures described in its core. At the beginning of each chapter, key terms and questions about the content are provided. At the end of each chapter, exercises to encourage application of the content are included.

Acknowledgments

Upon completing this book, we must acknowledge the contribution of several individuals. David Gast and John Schuster have been our colleagues and our teachers for a number of years. They have contributed substantially to our personal and professional development, and we appreciate their efforts. We are grateful to Donald Cross, Chair of the Department of Special Education at the University of Kentucky, who encouraged us in our work and research. We also acknowledge others who have participated with us in our research, including Vince Winterling, Belva Collins, Ann Griffen, Jacqueline Farmer, Stacie Meyer, Catherine Cybriwsky, Lowry Morris, and many teachers in central Kentucky. Without the intelligence, work, and persistence of these individuals, much of what is described in this book would not be known. Thus, we are indebted to them for letting us describe their work. We are grateful to the families and students with moderate to severe disabilities who participated in our research. In addition, we appreciate the patience and contributions of Naomi Silverman of Longman Publishers; she had faith in the project from the beginning, despite the lack of speed with which the senior author executed his task. Finally, as many authors and investigators know, our greatest debt is to our families, and we dedicate this book to them.

CHAPTER 1

Introduction to Teaching and Instructional Practices

Chapter Overview

Defining Learning, Teaching, and Stimulus Control
Process of Providing Quality Instruction
Effective Teaching Practices
Phases of Performance and Implications for Instruction
Summary Comments
Exercises
References

Key Terms

Learning	Curriculum-Based Assessment
Teaching	Curriculum Catalogs
Behavior	Ecological Inventories
Target Behaviors	Acquisition
Stimulus Conditions	Response Prompting Strategies
Stimulus Control	Stimulus Modification Procedures
Differential Reinforcement	Aim Line
Positive Reinforcement	Fluency
Negative Reinforcement	Maintenance
Transfer of Stimulus Control	Generalization
Systematic Instruction	

Questions to Be Answered by This Chapter

1. How is teaching defined in terms of stimulus control?
2. What are the steps in systematic instruction?

3. What five functions characterize effective teachers?
4. What are some practices that exemplify each of the effective teaching functions?
5. What are the four phases of performance?
6. What are some instructional practices that appear to facilitate students' performance in each phase of performance?

We all have experienced teaching by attending school. Most of us have probably had good teachers and teachers who were not as good. Some of our teachers may have caused dramatic changes in our lives, while others may have been easily forgotten. Because we have had extensive experience with teachers, teaching, and going to school, we may believe that we know a lot about teaching and how to teach. However, the presence of students with moderate and severe disabilities in schools challenges many of our common notions about teaching. These students have taught us that teaching is neither a simple task nor an easy one. Students with moderate and severe disabilities prompt us to ask important questions, such as these: What is teaching? What should be taught? How is teaching best done? How do we know when teaching has been successful or unsuccessful? This text examines these questions. Specifically, the emphasis of this text is on how teachers can cause students to learn important skills. This text does not describe everything teachers of students with moderate to severe disabilities need to know. It recognizes that teachers have a unique role on intervention teams—they are the pedagogical experts. Teachers should know more than any other team member about how to teach, how to structure environments to promote learning, and how to extend learning beyond the instructional context. This role is exciting and challenging. An excellent teacher must acquire a large volume of knowledge, apply it, and learn from that application.

Chapter 1 defines learning and teaching and describes stimulus control—a mechanism for understanding, evaluating, and making adjustments in instructional activities. In addition, this chapter reviews the steps involved in providing systematic instruction and lists effective teaching practices. The chapter concludes with a framework for understanding children's learning and performance.

DEFINING LEARNING, TEACHING, AND STIMULUS CONTROL

Common definitions of teaching include imparting knowledge, causing students to come to know, and providing instruction. Some of these definitions (e.g., causing student to come to know) describe outcomes of teaching; that is, students know something new as a result of being taught. Other definitions describe what teachers do—provide instruction. This text deals extensively with the process of teaching, and it assumes that teaching is successful only when positive outcomes occur for students. It is important to note the difference between learning and teaching. **Learning** is defined as a relatively permanent change in performance as a result of experience. It does not refer to changes in performance that occur as a result of excitement, fatigue, or maturation. It refers to changes in behavior that are a result of experience. Learning can occur from experiences other than teaching. For example, children frequently learn a great deal about life simply by interacting with other children in their neighborhoods. However, learning is the ultimate outcome of teaching. **Teaching**, as used in this text, is the process of organizing experience so that children perform behaviors under new and/or different stimulus conditions.

This definition requires elaboration. First, it suggests that students' performance or behavior should be different after instruction. **Behavior**, of course, is a repeatable motor response that has a beginning and end and can be reliably measured by two or more individuals (Cooper, Heron, & Heward, 1987). Although learning may result in changes in what students know, how they perceive the environment, how they solve problems, and many other similar notions, this definition states that teaching must produce identifiable changes in their behavior.

Second, the definition suggests that the outcome of teaching should focus on specific behaviors called target behaviors. **Target behaviors** are any responses that have been identified by a team of professionals and the student's parents as being an important focus of instruction. Thus, in teaching, value is not assigned to any behavior change; rather, behavior change that improves students' lives is valued.

Third, the definition implies that the conditions or situations under which students' behaviors are displayed are known and understood. **Stimulus conditions**, as used in this definition, refer to the situations, others' behaviors, environmental variables, materials, and so on under which the target behaviors should be performed. If teaching is successful, students will be able to perform the target behaviors in situations in which those behaviors are needed. This implies that the goal of teaching is to cause students' behavior to be under the control of particular stimulus conditions, or under "stimulus control." What is stimulus control, how is it established, and what does it have to do with learning and teaching?

Stimulus control is defined as the reliable or predictable performance of a behavior when particular stimuli are present and the absence of that behavior when those stimuli are absent (Cooper et al., 1987; Wolery, Bailey, & Sugai, 1988). For example, when teaching a student to use a spoon, we want the stimulus conditions of hunger and the presence of food requiring the use of a spoon to result in spoon use. In other words, stimulus control means that a behavior will occur consistently when the stimuli that control it are present. For example, a father showing his daughter a picture of a dog while saying, "What's this?," causes her to say something like, "Doggie. Bow-wow." The presence of a green traffic light says, "Go or keep going," and we respond accordingly. When these stimuli are absent, the behaviors usually do not occur.

However, these stimuli do not "automatically" have this power. A child who has no experience eating with a spoon will not do so. A child may simply look at the picture of the dog if her father does not say, "What's this?" A person from a culture that does not use traffic lights will not comply correctly without experience or being told that "A green light means 'go.'" How, then, do stimuli get control of behavior?

In the most elementary terms, stimuli acquire control through **differential reinforcement**—reinforcement is delivered for the behavior when the stimulus is present but not delivered for the behavior when the stimulus is absent. Therefore, if the goal is to have a given stimulus control a behavior (i.e., have the behavior occur consistently when the stimulus is present), then reinforcement should be provided when the stimulus is present and should be withheld when the stimulus is absent. But what is reinforcement?

Actually, there are two types of reinforcement, positive and negative (Cooper et al., 1987; Wolery et al., 1988). **Positive reinforcement** is the process by which an event follows (occurs contingently upon) a behavior and produces an increase in the occurrence or the maintenance of that behavior (Cooper et al., 1987). The glass of juice quenches thirst (reinforcer) when it is drunk, and this reinforcement results in an increase in drinking. **Negative reinforcement** is the process by which an aversive event is removed contingent upon the occurrence of a behavior and produces an increase or maintenance in the occurrence of that behavior (Cooper et al., 1987). Turning on a fan on a hot day removes the aversive stimulus of heat. This removal results in an increase in "fan-turning-on" behavior when it is hot. When your supervisor or teacher nags you to get your reports written on time, the nagging can serve as an aversive stimulus. To remove it, you write and submit your reports on time, and the nagging stops. Both types of reinforcement can result in stimuli acquiring control of behavior, but positive reinforcement is used more frequently than negative reinforcement. If reinforcement is presented contingently and repeatedly for some behavior when a given stimulus is present, the stimulus begins to communicate (cue) to the learner that "If you do the behavior, you will probably receive reinforcement." When this occurs, we say that stimulus control has been established.

Thus, a major task for the teacher is to ensure that stimuli are present and to reinforce the target behavior when they are present and to withhold reinforcement for those behaviors when the stimuli are not present. But what if the behavior does not occur? This major problem does not allow the stimulus to acquire control of the student's responding. The teaching strategies described in Chapters 3–8 of this text are designed to deal with this problem. These strategies use "teacher help" (assistance or prompts) to get the behavior to occur in the presence of the target stimulus so that reinforcement can be provided for its occurrence. They also are designed to remove the assistance so that the behavior occurs only when the target stimulus conditions are present. Much of teaching is designed to shift the control of given stimulus conditions (teacher assistance) to other stimulus conditions (target stimulus). This process is known as the **transfer of stimulus control**. In a real sense, teaching could be defined as a process for establishing and transferring stimulus control. An almost endless number of environmental manipulations can be made to cause behaviors to occur, and there are different ways for providing and withholding reinforcement for the behavior when the stimulus is present or absent, respectively.

Establishing stimulus control should be viewed broadly. It involves deciding which behaviors should come under the control of which stimuli, how the schedule and physical and social dimensions of the environment should be ordered to cause opportunities for stimuli to acquire control, which materials are appropriate stimuli, how to ensure that children receive feedback for their behavior, and when to provide or withhold reinforcement when the stimulus is present or absent. Stimulus control also involves determining which teaching strategies will set the stage for stimuli to acquire the desired control, how opportunities for stimuli to acquire control can be organized throughout the day, how to monitor whether stimuli are acquiring the desired control, and how to make the control as broad as possible to ensure that all relevant stimuli will produce the desired behavior regardless of the context in which they occur.

This conceptualization does not suggest that stimulus control, as described here, accounts for all learning or that it explains the emergence of all behavior. Clearly, there are other types of learning and many different ways to conceptualize learning. Mercer and Snell (1977) review these different perspectives and draw implications for teaching. Also, many things clearly influence students' learning, such as maturation of the central nervous system; learning histories and social relationships; and health, biological states, and other individual characteristics. Stimulus control is probably the most useful means available for thinking about teaching and for planning, implementing, evaluating, and adjusting instruction. Further, not all learning is a result of external reinforcement. Many reinforcers are *not* delivered by the teacher. Reinforcers can come from the materials, the physical environment, peers, mastery and completion of tasks, and other sources.

Another important point related to defining teaching as organizing experience to establish stimulus control is that teaching is a process. *Process,* as used here, has two distinct meanings: The first refers to the process of establishing or transferring stimulus control, a process described extensively throughout this text; the second refers to the steps involved in identifying what to teach, deciding how the instruction should be provided, evaluating the effects of that instruction as it occurs, and determining whether students learned the behaviors that were targeted. This second meaning is described below.

PROCESS OF PROVIDING QUALITY INSTRUCTION

Providing quality instruction requires the use of systematic instruction. **Systematic instruction** involves a series of steps to identify the behaviors to be taught, plan instructional activities, implement those activities, evaluate their effects, and determine whether students' behavior changed as desired (i.e., whether stimulus control was established). Although various models of instruction place greater emphasis on some parts of this process than on others, most models include these basic functions (Wolery, 1989a).

The steps in providing systematic instruction include the following:

- Identify the content of the curriculum.
- Conduct ongoing, curriculum-based assessments.
- Involve an interdisciplinary team in program planning and implementation.
- Plan an individualized instructional program.
- Implement instruction and monitor the student's progress.
- Evaluate the student's overall progress at regular intervals.

Identify the Content of the Curriculum

The content of the curriculum refers to the behaviors and skills that are taught and should relate directly to the goals of education. For students with moderate and severe disabilities, several goals are generally accepted by these students' families, teachers and experts. These goals include the following: (a) increasing students' adaptive performance related to living and functioning in the community, (b) maximizing students' participation in community activities, (c) enhancing students' quality of life, and (d) helping ease families' care-giving responsibilities and stress (Sailor et al., 1988; Snell, 1987a). Since these statements are broad, they are made operational for each student through the systematic instruction process. To address these general goals, the content of the curriculum for students with moderate and severe disabilities includes the following general areas:

- *self-care skills,* such as eating and feeding, dressing and undressing, and toileting (Dever, 1988; Orelove & Sobsey, 1987; Snell, 1987b)
- *domestic living skills,* such as preparing meals, using a telephone, and doing household cleaning and laundry (Dever, 1988; Snell & Browder, 1987)
- *community living skills,* such as moving within the community and purchasing needed items and services (Dever, 1988; Snell & Browder, 1987)
- *leisure and recreation skills,* such as using radios and televisions, playing age-appropriate games, displaying appropriate social skills, and using community recreation facilities (Dever, 1988; Falvey, 1986)
- *vocational training,* including acquiring work skills and receiving actual on-the-job training (Dever, 1988; Falvey, 1986; Rusch, Chadsey-Rusch, & Lagomarcino, 1987)
- *communication skills,* such as making wants and needs known, conducting conversations, and using augmentative communication devices (Kaiser, Alpert, & Warren, 1987; Rowland & Stremel-Campbell, 1987; Miller & Allaire, 1987)
- *motor skills,* such as acquiring mobility and appropriate positioning (Bishop & Falvey, 1986; Campbell, 1987a, 1987b)
- *functional academics,* such as counting money, signing one's name, and reading community signs (Browder & Snell, 1987; Grenot-Scheyer & Falvey, 1986)

Other skills also are important. These skills include such things as trying again when the first attempt fails, seeking assistance from others, avoiding dangerous situations, cooperating with others in meeting a shared goal, understanding the perspectives of peers, and providing affection and assistance. In fact, any skill or pattern of responding that is important for a particular student is a legitimate target of instruction. However, competence in these general areas appears to provide a base from which students with moderate to severe disabilities can learn to live integrated and adaptive lives in their communities. With each student, the precise skills that are targeted for instruction are determined individually by the second step in systematic instruction: ongoing, curriculum-based assessment.

Conduct Ongoing, Curriculum-Based Assessments

Curriculum-based assessment is a process of gathering information for the purpose of determining what skills should be taught. As a result, it is different from traditional educational assessment that is designed to determine eligibility for services, diagnosis, and placement. Curriculum-based assessment involves comparing the student's performance to the objectives in a curriculum and/or to the demands of the unique ecologies in which that student lives. Since the curriculum for students with moderate to severe disabilities should focus on the areas listed above, each student's abilities and needs in these areas should be assessed. Two strategies are employed to accomplish this: the use of curriculum catalogs and the use of ecological inventories.

Curriculum catalogs are listings of common skills or activities by curriculum area (Wilcox & Bellamy, 1987). The student, her family, and relevant professionals review the curriculum catalog and select skills that are judged to be most important and useful to the student in functioning adaptively in her unique environment. The student is then assessed directly to determine the extent to which she can perform the identified skills when and where those skills are needed. **Ecological inventories** are individualized assessments of (a) the demands or requirements of specific activities within current and future environments and (b) the student's ability to complete those activities successfully (Browder, 1987; Nietupski & Hamre-Nietupski, 1987). Teachers of students with moderate to severe disabilities generally use curriculum catalogs and ecological inventories in conjunction with criterion-referenced measures (Browder, 1987). Direct testing (Browder, 1987), direct observation (Wolery, 1989b), and interviews (Winton, 1988) are used.

Involve an Interdisciplinary Team in Program Planning and Implementation

Appropriate education of students with moderate and severe disabilities, unlike that for students without disabilities, requires interdisciplinary team planning and intervention. The structure, function, and interaction of the team members is important (McCollum & Hughes, 1988). The *structure* refers to the relationships that exist among a team's members and who is on the team. In addition to family members, members from several disciplines—including special educators, physical therapists, occupational therapists, psychologists, nurses, speech and language pathologists, and social workers—are frequently found on interdisciplinary teams. Many teams will not include all of these, and other disciplines may be represented if needed. Besides having core team members who work regularly with the student or family, many teams include people who serve consultative roles. The *functions* of a team refers to the actions its members must perform and the tasks they must complete. Examples are conducting assessments to determine eligibility, to plan Individualized Educational Programs (IEPs), or to implement the educational services. The *interaction* between the team members is another way to think about a team. In a multidisciplinary team, little interaction occurs between disciplines; each member works in relative isolation and then joins other members to make decisions. In an interdisciplinary team, considerable interaction occurs between its members, but each member maintains the role related to his or her respective discipline. In a transdisciplinary team, the roles of different disciplines are blended, and there is mutual release and exchange of functions (Lyon & Lyon, 1980; McCormick & Goldman, 1979). While the structure, function, and interaction of different teams will vary, it is clear that appropriate education of students with moderate and severe disabilities is a team effort rather than one performed exclusively by the special educator. Teams can engage in several strategies to facilitate effective team practices. These strategies include (a) facilitating decision making and family participation, (b) developing and promoting communication skills, (c) establishing a team philosophy and setting goals for team performance, (d) establishing a structure for decision making, (e) disagreeing effectively, and (f) promoting effective leadership (Bailey & Wolery, in press).

Plan an Individualized Instructional Program

The instruction of students with moderate and severe disabilities must be individualized because of legal mandate and because such practices promote better outcomes. An individualized program is developed by the team carefully using curriculum-based assessment information to identify the skills a particular student needs to function adaptively in his environment. This, however, is only the beginning of an appropriate instructional program. The team also must identify high-priority skills, write long-term objectives, analyze those objectives, and write instructional objectives (Wolery, 1989a; Wolery et al., 1988). The team has to answer several practical questions, such as these:

- What is the basic intent of teaching this skill or activity?
- What materials or equipment, if any, are needed?
- Where will this skill or activity be taught?
- Who will provide the instruction?
- What instructional procedures will be used?
- What supports, assistance, and adaptations are necessary for teaching this skill or activity?
- How will the student's performance be monitored?
- Who will monitor the student's performance?
- What are the naturally occurring stimuli for this skill or activity?
- In what situations is the student most likely to need or use this skill or activity?

Answers to these questions are the starting points for meaningful instruction (Nietupski & Hamre-Nietupski, 1987). Careful consideration of these questions by the team, including the student's family, requires considerable time and effort.

Implement Instruction and Monitor the Student's Progress

After the instructional program is planned, it is implemented. However, plans are often inadequate to meet identified goals, and adjustments may be needed. As a result, the team should view each plan as tentative. If progress occurs as desired, then the program should be continued; if progress does not occur or occurs at a slow pace, then modifications and adjustments should be made. Monitoring students' progress helps (a) to determine whether progress is made and (b) to identify the modification that should be made if sufficient progress is not evident (Liberty & Haring, 1990). Ideally, progress should be monitored on a daily basis. Procedures for conducting such ongoing assessment, which have been described in detail in literature on the subject, include event sampling, time sampling, category sampling, levels-of-assistance data collection, and task-analytic recording procedures (Browder, 1987; Haring & Kennedy, 1988; White & Haring, 1980; Wolery et al., 1988). At a minimum, frequent probes of a student's progress should occur, and more frequent measurement should occur for a program in which progress is in question. Data decision rules are used for acting on instructional data to plan modifications (Haring, Liberty, & White, 1980; Liberty, 1988; Liberty & Haring, 1990).

Evaluate the Student's Overall Progress at Regular Intervals

In addition to frequently monitoring progress, the team should evaluate the student's overall progress at regular intervals. Public Law 94-142 requires yearly review of the IEP and a total reevaluation of progress every three years. However, the team should probably review the student's progress every 2–4 months. This will allow adjustments during instruction and will ensure that any new needs are addressed in a timely fashion.

The systematic instruction process requires careful consideration of several major steps: identifying the content of the curriculum, using appropriate curriculum-based assessment practices, involving a team in program planning and implementation, planning and monitoring the instructional program, and evaluating the effects of the program at regular intervals. Although this may seem like a fairly straightforward process, the actual implementation of these steps requires a competent and well-functioning team whose members communicate extensively with the student's family. In addition to this process, several practices have been identified in the literature that appear to make instruction effective; these are described below.

EFFECTIVE TEACHING PRACTICES

In recent years, considerable attention has been given to improving the quality and effectiveness of education for all types of learners (Bennett, 1986; Bickel & Bickel, 1986; Gagne, 1985; Paine et al., 1983; White et al., 1983; Wolery et al., 1988). Based on a review of much of this literature, White et al. (1983) identified five teaching functions that characterize effective teachers. These functions and examples of exemplary practices with each are shown in Table 1.1.

The first critical function is *managing instructional time*. It requires identifying the instructional priorities for each student, analyzing the time and resources that are available for instruction, and matching the instructional priorities to the time and resources available. The teachers, teaching assistants, and therapists who are available throughout the day or week and responsible for instruction must be identified, and each high-priority objective must be scheduled for instruction (Bailey & Wolery, in press; Helmstetter & Guess, 1987). In addition, teachers must be sure that each adult who provides instruction or therapy has the skills to do so, and that when the time arises, they are prepared. In almost all cases, the schedule set at the beginning of each school year requires modification many times as the needs of students change, as therapists' schedules change, as the available resources change, and as teaching assistants acquire more skill in implementing instruction.

To determine whether instructional time is being managed appropriately, the teacher can collect on-task, or engagement, data. Usually this is done by using a monetary time sampling procedure. The teacher observes all students at specific times (e.g., every 2 minutes) and records whether each student is engaged (on task, or doing what she is supposed to be doing), nonengaged (off task, or doing something other than what she is supposed to be doing, including behaving inappropriately), or waiting (e.g., waiting in line, for the materials, for her turn, or for the teacher) (Wolery et al., 1988). These three categories of behavior provide useful information about whether changes in the instructional context are needed.

TABLE 1.1. Teaching Functions and Effective Practices Associated with Each Function

1. *Management of Instruction Time*
   a. Teacher is prepared to initiate instruction when class is scheduled to begin.
   b. Teacher makes full use of the time allocated for instruction.
   c. Teacher maintains a high level of student time on task.

2. *Management of Student Behavior*
   a. Teacher instructs students in a clear set of rules and procedures for classroom behavior.
   b. Teacher observes student behavior continuously and stops inappropriate behavior promptly and consistently.

3. *Instructional Presentation*
   a. Teacher presents instructionally relevant lessons that match the students' current level of understanding of the topic.
   b. Teacher reviews lesson content and instructional tasks clearly.
   c. Teacher presents lesson content and instructional tasks clearly.
   d. Teacher makes instructional transitions quickly, smoothly, and effectively.
   e. Teacher presents instruction at an appropriately brisk rate.

4. *Instructional Monitoring*
   a. Teacher establishes reasonable work requirements and enforces them.
   b. Teacher regularly uses formal and informal assessment to determine the students' current level of understanding and progress.

5. *Instructional Feedback*
   a. Teacher provides consistent flow of performance feedback to students.
   b. Teacher gives appropriate feedback based on type of student response.

[From White et al. (1983, pp. 115–119).]

Successful management of student behavior is the second major function that characterizes effective teachers. These teachers have specific rules that students should follow, and they communicate those rules clearly to students (Paine et al., 1983). They also monitor students' behavior continuously and interrupt inappropriate behavior consistently and quickly. For many students, specific programs will be needed to decrease the occurrence of problem behaviors. When planning and implementing those programs, an instructor should use one of the available decision models (see Evans et al., 1985; Gaylord-Ross, 1980; Wolery et al., 1988). In each of these models, attention is given to determining whether the problem behavior should be changed, to carefully assessing the problem behavior, to developing a plan based on that assessment, to implementing the plan, and to evaluating its effects. These models also suggest that curricular modifications, environmental arrangements, and nonaversive procedures are the treatments of choice (Repp & Singh, 1990). Effective control of behavior problems is necessary for effective instruction; however, effective instruction frequently reduces behavior problems.

The third function that characterizes effective teaching is *careful presentation of instructional stimuli and procedures.* The teacher identifies appropriate skills to teach, plans the instruction carefully, provides review of previously learned behaviors, implements the teaching smoothly and clearly, presents the instruction briskly, and ensures that transitions from one activity to another are planned and executed smoothly. Thus, the stimulus to which control is to be transferred is identified, and instruction is designed to ensure that stimulus control is established. A large portion of this text focuses on how to do this.

The fourth function displayed by effective teachers is *frequent monitoring of students' performance.* Frequent monitoring identifies programs that are not working and suggests potential changes. For each of the instructional procedures described in this text, a number of ways are described to collect data on students' performance.

The fifth function that effective teachers employ is *frequent use of instructional feedback.* Feedback is important in establishing stimulus control. The procedures described in this text use frequent feedback for students' performance. In many cases, the feedback includes not only whether the response is correct or incorrect but also how to perform the response correctly.

In summary, effective teaching is characterized by appropriate management of instructional time, successful management of student behavior, clear presentation of instructional stimuli, frequent monitoring of student progress, and frequent use of instructional feedback. In many classrooms for students with moderate and severe disabilities, more than one adult will be involved. Thus, all the adults in the program should use effective teaching practices, and monitoring of everyone's teaching may be needed to ensure consistency.

PHASES OF PERFORMANCE AND IMPLICATIONS FOR INSTRUCTION

The goals of instruction with students who have moderate and severe disabilities is to assist them to live, function, and participate in the community and to ensure an appropriate quality of life as defined by themselves and their families. The outcomes of teaching should be evaluated in terms of the extent to which they improve students' lives. Thus, effective instruction will produce changes in students' behavior outside of school. Students' performance is frequently conceptualized as occurring in four phases: *acquisition, fluency, maintenance,* and *generalization.* The following sections define these phases, describe the strategies for facilitating each, and propose methods for detecting learning problems.

Acquisition

Defining Acquisition. **Acquisition** refers to initial learning, or learning how to perform the basic requirements of a behavior or skill (Wolery et al., 1988). Haring et al. (1980) present a technical definition of acquisition: "Acquisition is the period of learning when if performance falters, changes designed to provide information to the learner about how to perform the desired response have a higher probability than other strategies of promoting pupil progress" (pp. 171–172). Thus, the goal of teaching is to help students perform the desired behavior correctly. When most individuals think about teaching, they think about this phase of performance. In fact, much of teachers' time is spent helping students learn new behaviors. The importance of the acquisition phase of learning is readily apparent. Students' acquisition of adaptive behaviors is central to safe, independent, and competent performance in the community.

Procedures for Facilitating Acquisition.   Promoting acquisition of target behaviors is a primary function of teachers; it is establishing new stimulus control. Three basic issues must be addressed when attempting to promote acquisition of behaviors. First, students must attend to the relevant stimulus. *Attention* is defined as "a sense of alertness of reception of stimuli" (Gagne, 1985, p. 246). Stimulus control cannot be established (i.e., students will not learn when and where to perform target behaviors) if students do not attend to the relevant stimuli. Attention can be secured in a number of ways. The relevant stimulus can be made more obvious, it can be separated from other stimuli, and teachers can call students' attention to it. To ensure that students are attending, they can be asked to indicate that they are ready to start at the beginning of an instructional session. With many students, more frequent monitoring of their attention will be necessary and must occur on each trial. Sometimes this is done by determining whether each student is looking at the stimulus before a trial is presented. In other cases, students are asked to indicate more directly whether they are attending by touching the target stimulus, matching the stimulus, or performing some other active response that shows they are focusing their attention on the target stimulus.

Second, students should receive feedback about the correctness of their responses to stimuli. Feedback occurs in many different ways; the teacher can provide it, the natural environment can provide it (e.g., a child who pulls a door open gets feedback on his pulling behavior), and materials can provide it. Two types of feedback are described below: feedback for correct responses and feedback for incorrect responses.

Positive reinforcement is used to provide feedback for correct responses. As defined earlier, positive reinforcement is an event that follows a behavior and increases the probability that the behavior will occur again (Cooper et al., 1987). Also, as noted earlier, differential reinforcement is the mechanism by which stimuli acquire control of students' responding. Thus, the selection and use of reinforcers is a critical issue in designing instruction for the acquisition of skills.

Three facts about reinforcers highlight the need to identify them individually for each student: (a) A reinforcer for one student may not be a reinforcer for another; (b) the reinforcing value of stimuli change from time to time (Mason et al., 1989); and (c) the use of individually determined reinforcers may reduce problem behaviors (Dyer, 1987; Mason et al., 1989).

When identifying and selecting reinforcers, instructors find four strategies useful. First, an instructor should attempt to use those reinforcers that are effective with other students. Second, the teacher should ask students' families specific questions about what students like, what objects they prefer, and what activities they do readily. Third, the instructor should observe students to identify any behaviors they do frequently and any objects they manipulate frequently. Being allowed to do those behaviors or have access to those objects may serve reinforcing functions. Fourth, the teacher should perform a reinforcer preference test. This involves providing students with an array of choices of different stimuli that may be reinforcing. The stimuli that are frequently selected may then be used as reinforcers. Because the power of reinforcers changes with use and the passage of time, frequent identification of reinforcers is appropriate (Mason et al., 1989). Common reinforcers for many students include access to toys and leisure materials (games and radios), free time, interaction with peers, attention from adults, physical contact, and certain smells.

There are several general guidelines for using reinforcers. The responses for which the reinforcers are to be given should be specified clearly. If they are not, reinforcement may be delivered for inferior behaviors rather than for the desired behaviors. Reinforcers should be administered immediately after the behaviors are done, since reinforcers increase the behaviors they follow. Therefore, provide reinforcers immediately after the target behaviors occur. Third, tangible reinforcers (food, drink, materials, and so on) should be paired with more natural stimuli, such as praise, pats on the back, and calling attention to students' accomplishments. This will build the more naturally occurring stimuli as reinforcers. Also, a variety of reinforcers should be used. Increasing the variety of reinforcers appears to produce greater learning (Egel, 1981). This can be done by providing students with choices at the beginning of the day, at the beginning of the session, or after each trial. When possible, naturally occurring reinforcers should be used. These are the events that would usually follow the particular behavior students just performed. In addition, continuous reinforcement (reinforcement for each target behavior) during initial instruction should be used, followed by intermittent reinforcement. Intermittent reinforcement means that students are reinforced not for every correct response but only for some correct responses. For more detailed discussions of the identification and use of reinforcement, consult Cooper et al. (1987), Baer (1978), Vargas (1977), Bailey and Wolery (in press), and Wolery et al. (1988).

Feedback for incorrect responses can occur in two basic forms. The first type of feedback can simply communicate that the behavior was not correct. For example, if a student attempts to pour milk into a glass and instead pours it on the table, the lack of milk in the glass will communicate that the behavior was not correct. The second type of feedback for incorrect responses is called error correction. With error correction, the feedback communicates that the response was incorrect and also contains information on how to do the skill correctly. If when the student spilled the milk, the teacher then physically assisted the student in pouring the milk into the glass, this teacher assistance would communicate how to perform the behavior correctly.

Several general guidelines can be used to provide feedback to students when they perform incorrectly. First, the type of feedback to be used should be identified and provided consistently. In some cases, feedback for incorrect responses will simply be lack of reinforcement; in others, some error correction procedure will be used. Regardless of the type of feedback, it should be delivered consistently. If students receive feedback on some occasions but not on others, their learning may be slowed. Second, feedback for incorrect responses, as for correct responses, should be provided immediately. This helps students discriminate which responses were incorrect. Third, the feedback should be specific and salient. To be useful, feedback should be presented in a manner that communicates with students. If the feedback is not obvious, then its value will be reduced. Feedback can be made more obvious by verbally labeling incorrect responses, by providing assistance so that students will get information on how to perform the behaviors, and by having students participate in correcting their errors.

In addition to ensuring that students attend to the target stimulus and that they receive feedback for their correct and incorrect behaviors, providing students with information about how to perform target behaviors will promote acquisition. This information can be provided in at least three ways. Error correction as described above can be used. Although error correction is sometimes effective, it frequently results in a high proportion of errors during initial instruction and may result in slow learning (Ault et al., 1989). **Response prompting strategies** can also be used. These procedures provide extra teacher assistance (called prompts) to students and then remove (fade) that assistance as instruction progresses. The prompts are provided before students respond; thus, errors are frequently minimized. These strategies are described in Chapters 3–8. Also, **stimulus modification procedures** can be used (Cooper et al., 1987; Etzel & LeBlanc, 1979). These strategies involve gradual changes in the instructional stimuli from easy to more difficult levels (i.e., from currently controlling stimuli to target stimuli). Although these procedures are highly effective, they may require considerable material preparation time and are not easily used with some skills (Ault et al., 1989).

Identifying and Solving Acquisition Problems.   When attempting to teach the acquisition of a new skill, a teacher should carefully monitor and analyze students' responses. This monitoring allows the teacher to determine whether sufficient progress is being made and to identify possible changes that would solve the acquisition problems when progress is not being made (Haring et al., 1980; White & Haring, 1980; Wolery et al., 1988). To facilitate decision making, these data should be graphed. Fuchs and Fuchs (1986) present findings indicating that teachers who graph their data have students who make more progress than the students of teachers who simply collect data.

　　After graphing the data, a teacher should draw an aim line to determine whether adequate change is occurring. An **aim line** is a projection of the amount of learning that is needed each day to reach the criterion set in the objective by a previously identified date. It is calculated by the following steps:

1.   Graph the student's data.
2.   Identify the criterion statement in the objective.
3.   Estimate how long it will take the student to reach criterion under optimal conditions.
4.   Identify the criterion level and the date at which the student should reach criterion on the graph. Indicate this intersection by making an *A* (for aim) on the graph.
5.   Identify the mid-date and mid-rate for the last three data points. The mid-date is the second of the last three data points, and the mid-rate is the data point that is the middle value of the last three data points.
6.   Draw a straight line between the intersection of the mid-date and mid-rate (see step 5) and the *A* you marked on the graph. This is the aim line.

　　A completed aim line for some hypothetical data is illustrated in Figure 1.1. The aim line shows how much progress the student must make each day to reach the criterion by the target date. Generally, changes in the instructional procedures should occur if three consecutive data points fall below the aim line. Common data patterns, interpretation of those patterns, and suggested changes are shown in Table 1.2 and described below.

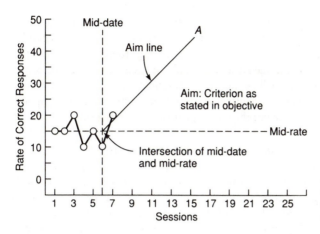

Figure 1.1. An example of the components of an aim line for determining the adequacy of daily progress.

TABLE 1.2. Summary of Data-Based Decisions

Data Pattern	Interpretation	Suggested Decision
Correct responses are improving; error responses are flat or decreasing.	Program is working.	Continue present instructional program; it is successful.
Correct responses are at or near zero percent; error responses are frequent and high.	Task is too difficult.	Step back to easier skill and/or teach prerequisite skill to target behavior; use response prompting strategies.
Progress is stalled; correct responses are between 20 and 50 percent.	Student can perform some but not all parts of the task.	Slice back to simpler variation of the target response; use more or different prompts; analyze errors to determine if systematic errors are occurring, and if so, add prompts to correct systematic error; highlight salient dimensions of stimulus.
Correct responses are highly variable, or correct responses have dropped sharply.	Compliance or attention problem.	Implement compliance management program; change reinforcer for correct responses and change consequences for errors.
Correct responses are about 80 percent and are not increasing.	Student is ready for fluency-building program.	Increase practice time and change consequences to increase participation in practice sessions.
Correct responses are at criterion.	Successful instructional program.	Implement procedures to teach fluency, maintain performance, and ensure application of behaviors.

[Adapted from Wolery, Bailey, and Sugai (1988, p. 137).]

If Correct Responses Are Improving.   If an instructional program is implemented and the collected data indicate that the percent, or rate, of correct responses is steadily improving while the errors are remaining constant or decreasing, then the instructional program is deemed successful. No change should be made in such a program. In some cases, the percent of correct responses will be increasing, but doing so too slowly. Changing the reinforcer, ensuring that students are attending to the instructional stimuli, and/or adding more information (teacher prompts) are appropriate modifications.

If Correct Responses Are at or Near Zero.   Sometimes no progress occurs on instructional programs. If no progress is apparent after three or four days of instruction, a change is needed. Frequently, it is appropriate to move back to an easier skill or a prerequisite skill for the original behavior. However, if the teacher is using only trial-and-error instruction, the use of one of the response prompting strategies (Chapters 3–8) may solve the acquisition problem. If no progress occurs after a few days of using a response prompting strategy, then stepping back to an easier skill is clearly warranted.

If Progress Is Stalled.   Sometimes students will initially make some progress and then their progress will appear to stop. Typically, the percent of correct responses will range between 20 and 50. This indicates that students can do part of the skill but not the entire skill. Several options exist at this point. Given adequate student attention and use of positive reinforcers, the teacher should analyze the error responses and attempt to determine if some systematic error is being made. Systematic errors occur because students are using inappropriate strategies or rules or because they have not identified the relevant dimension of the stimulus (Wolery et al., 1988). For example, Larry is learning to put on a pullover shirt; however, he consistently puts it on backwards. He is responding as though he believes that the tag should go in the front; the stimulus of the tag has not acquired stimulus control. In such a case, this inappropriate strategy (putting the tag in front) should be targeted for specific instruction. Assistance to help Larry get the tag in the back should be provided, and then that assistance should be faded.

If Correct Responses Are Highly Variable or Drop Sharply.   Sometimes students will have high percentages of correct responses on some days and low percentages on other days. In other cases, students will appear to be making steady progress and then the amount of correct responses will decrease quickly. Both of these patterns indicate that compliance problems may exist. Compliance problems are solved by increasing the amount of reinforcement for being correct, by changing reinforcers, and by changing the feedback for errors. For example, having students re-do the behavior correctly contingent upon each error may decrease the amount of errors. Also, the manner in which instruction is provided should be analyzed to ensure that subtle differences do not exist on days when performance is low as compared to days when it is high.

If Correct Responses Are at 80 Percent but Not Increasing.   This pattern indicates that students have acquired the basic requirements of the behavior. Adding new information or using teacher assistance probably will not increase the amount of correct responses. As a result, fluency-building procedures should be implemented. These are described in the next section of this chapter.

If Students Are at the Criterion for the Objective.   When students reach the criterion (the aim) specified in the instructional objective, then successful learning has been demonstrated and stimulus control has been established. Instruction, however, is not complete. Instruction should focus on teaching students to do the behavior proficiently, helping students maintain correct responding, and helping students apply the skill when and wherever it is needed.

Fluency

Defining Fluency.   **Fluency** is the "speed or ease with which a child performs a movement or series of movements" (White & Haring, 1980, p. 312). *Proficiency* is a synonym for *fluency*. In addition, the smoothness and naturalness of the behavior also are dimensions of fluency. Fluency is important for several reasons (Wolery et al., 1988). Students are more likely to use skills that they perform fluently than to use those they do not. Fluent responding on a given behavior is sometimes a prerequisite for more complex skills. Sometimes fluent responding will appear more "normal" or less deviant, and with some skills fluency is important for safety reasons. For example, accurate walking is not sufficient to get across the street; frequently walking must occur quickly.

Procedures for Facilitating Fluency.   Before a teacher attempts to enhance fluency, it is important for her to know how fluent students should be on the skill. In the curriculum area of academics, a number of rates for different types and levels of behaviors are known (Mercer & Mercer, 1985). However, for many important skills, fluency levels have not been established. Thus, there is little information about how quickly and smoothly the behavior should be performed for it to be considered fluent. As a result, individuals who already perform the behavior can be measured; their rates of performance can be used as the criterion statement for fluency-building objectives.

Fluency is promoted, as any accomplished musician will tell you, by practice. However, practice is frequently boring and unpleasant for students. Strategies exist for structuring practice: (a) Use relatively short practice sessions; (b) schedule several practice sessions each day; and (c) ensure that students have as many opportunities as possible to do the behavior during each practice session. Finally, during each practice session, reinforcers should be used to increase the speed, smoothness, and ease with which students perform. This is basically a refinement of the stimulus control that was established during acquisition training. During acquisition, the goal is to have the target stimulus cue students that if they perform the behavior, then reinforcement is likely. During fluency-building programs, the goal is to refine this control; that is, the target stimulus should cue students that reinforcement is probable *if* they perform the behavior rapidly and smoothly.

Data Patterns Indicating Problems with Fluency.   At least three data patterns indicate problems during fluency-building programs: (a) The data are stable and not increasing or decreasing, (b) the data are stable and followed by deteriorating performance, and (c) the data become variable. In each of these cases, the initial data are usually above 80 percent correct, indicating that students have acquired the behavior (Haring et al., 1980). Since students have learned how to do the behavior, providing them with assistance on how to do the skill correctly probably will not change their performance (Haring et al., 1980).

Potential Solutions for Fluency Problems.   At least four changes in how reinforcement is used will promote fluency (Wolery et al., 1988). First, reinforcement should be given based on students' overall performance rather than on when each response occurs. During initial acquisition, it is important for teachers to provide differential reinforcement for each correct response because this helps students learn how to do the skill. When promoting fluency, the reinforcement should be provided for the entire practice session rather than for each response. For example, if Heather is learning to wash dishes fluently, then reinforcement should be provided when she has washed all the dishes. Second, reinforcement can be made available only if students perform at some predetermined level. If students do not meet that level, the reinforcement will not be given. After a student consistently responds at the first level for three or four sessions, the level could be increased; this second level would be raised after the student was consistent in meeting it. If Heather was consistently washing two plates per minute, then the new criterion could be three plates per minute. Reinforcement would be given only if she washes three plates per minute; later, it would be increased to four and then to five plates per minute. By systematically increasing the level as students perform at each previous level, fluent responding can be established. A variation of this procedure is to provide reinforcement if performance in each practice session is higher than it was in the previous session. Third, reinforcement can be given only if students are on or above an aim line. As noted earlier, the aim line is a projection of how much change must occur during each session to move students from their current levels to the criterion level by a given date. In this case, an aim line would be drawn from Heather's current rate to the target rate at some date in the future. If she was at or above the aim line each day, she would be reinforced. Fourth, reinforcement can be given only if the correct performance is at a given level (e.g., a predetermined level, higher than in the previous session, or above the aim line) *and* errors are below a certain level. Sometimes in fluency-building programs, students focus on doing the behavior faster, and errors become more frequent. The fourth strategy will help address this issue. Thus, reinforcement is made available for Heather only if she meets the criterion for the number of plates being washed on a given day and only if none of the plates was still dirty after she washed it.

In addition to manipulating the reinforcement contingencies during practice sessions, making the sessions into a game format promotes fluency. Having students beat the clock and structuring races between students are means of making the practice sessions more "gamelike." Liberty and Michael (1985) suggest that using self-control procedures such as self-monitoring and self-reinforcement may increase the fluency of responding for students with moderate and severe disabilities. However, these procedures may not be useful if students do not understand how to use them.

Maintenance

Defining Maintenance.   **Maintenance** refers to continued performance of a target behavior after teaching has stopped. In terms of stimulus control, the goal of instruction designed to promote maintenance is to ensure that the target stimulus continues to cue students that reinforcement is likely (for at least some instances) if the behavior is performed. Maintenance of learned behaviors is important because many skills are incorporated into more complex skills. If students do not maintain the more basic skills, then they will not be able to learn the more complex skills. Also, before use of skills can occur in situations other than teaching, the behaviors must be maintained.

Procedures for Facilitating Maintenance.   Maintenance of skills appears to be promoted by several factors (Cooper et al., 1987; Wolery et al., 1988). Only useful or functional skills are likely to be maintained. Frequently people learn a skill but do not use it, and as a result they lose that skill. Examples would include playing musical instruments, speaking a non-native language, and remembering algebraic formulas. Thus, the skills that are taught to students must be useful to them. If they are not, they may not be maintained. However, this should be addressed during the curriculum-based assessment activities. Only those skills that will be needed and useful to students should be taught.

Overlearning a skill may facilitate maintenance. Sustained practice with a response will make it stronger for students and more likely for them to maintain it. However, because of the skill deficits of most students with moderate and severe disabilities, we have to balance overlearning with moving on to other skills. Frequently, we can promote overlearning by providing students with review sessions on previously learned behaviors.

Another set of strategies for promoting maintenance is to manipulate the reinforcement contingencies. At least three manipulations are possible: (a) thin the reinforcement schedule, (b) use natural reinforcers and natural schedules of reinforcement, and (c) delay the reinforcement. Thinning the reinforcement schedule means that the reinforcer is given only occasionally, not every time the correct response occurs. There are many different schedules for delivering reinforcers (Cooper et al., 1987; Vargas, 1977), and different schedules will produce different patterns of responding. However, in general, the goal of maintenance training is to provide systematically less reinforcement as instruction progresses. Frequently, this is accomplished by delivering reinforcers for every other correct response, then for every fourth correct response, and then for every eighth correct response. If correct responding begins to decrease, then the reinforcement has been thinned too quickly. In such cases, more frequent reinforcement should be provided, and then the thinning process should continue. At the end of instruction, the reinforcer should be delivered on a schedule consistent with the natural environment.

In addition to thinning the schedule of reinforcement, a teacher should use reinforcers that are available in the natural environment. This will vary from behavior to behavior, but a useful question is this: What is the usual result of doing this behavior in the natural environment? Whatever positive consequence occurs for the response naturally should be programmed into the instruction. For example, in self-feeding programs, the natural reinforcer may be the taste of the food; for communication behaviors, the natural reinforcer may be being understood; and for vocational skills, the natural reinforcer frequently is the money that is earned.

Maintenance also can be facilitated by delaying the reinforcer (Dunlap et al., 1987). This is done by delivering the reinforcer for a particular practice or instructional session later in the day. Token systems can be used to delay reinforcers. For example, rather than providing reinforcement after the correct responses or after a session, students are each given a token or ticket that they can exchange for reinforcers at a later point in the day.

Generalization

Defining Generalization.   **Generalization** refers to correct responding in situations other than the training situation. However, there are several different types of generalization, including generalization across persons, across materials, across natural consequences, across stimuli, across setting, and across time (Haring, 1988). In terms of stimulus control, the goal of generalization-promoting instruction is to extend the control to all relevant target stimuli *and* to only those stimuli. Generalization is important because it lies at the heart of education's goal: to improve students' lives in situations other than training. Thus, when students fail to apply their required skills in situations other than training, the educational program has not met its primary goal.

Procedures for Facilitating Generalization.   Teachers frequently do not write objectives that focus on generalization, although doing so probably increases the likelihood that generalization training will occur (Billingsley, 1984, 1988). Because generalization occurs outside the instructional context, generalization should be probed in the natural environment, at times when the behavior should occur, with individuals who are a part of the natural environment, with naturally occurring cues and assistance, and with naturally occurring consequences (White, 1988). In recent years several major documents have focused on issues related to generalization and produced several recommendations (see Haring, 1988; Horner, Dunlap, & Koegel, 1988; Stokes & Baer, 1977).

White et al. (1988) divide the strategies for promoting generalization into four groups: setting, consequent, antecedent, and other strategies. One *setting strategy* is conducting training in the natural environment, such as community-based teaching. By implementing training where the skills are needed, the probability of generalization is greater. Another setting strategy is sequential modification. This involves measuring students' performance for generalization in nontraining settings and implementing training in those settings if generalization does not occur. There are three *consequent strategies.* The first is to use natural reinforcers, as mentioned above, in maintenance training. The second is to make the contingencies between training and nontraining situations difficult to discriminate; this involves delaying the delivery of reinforcement and providing reinforcement for general improvement in performance rather than for specific improvement. The third consequent strategy is to train students to generalize; this involves reinforcing students for generalized performance rather than for acquisition performance. *Antecedent strategies* are commonly used when selecting examples for instruction. They include using materials that are likely to be found in the natural environment, using multiple examples of each stimulus, and using general case programming. There are two other strategies: (a) to "train loosely" or make the training as unstructured as possible while retaining sufficient acquisition and (b) to mediate generalization by using self-control procedures and providing students with instructions to generalize (White et al., 1988). These strategies can be used alone and in combination with other strategies. Liberty (1988) presents a data decision model for analyzing generalization data, including suggestions for changes when generalization is not occurring.

Summary of Phases of Performance

The performance of students can be conceptualized as occurring through four phases: acquisition, fluency, maintenance, and generalization. Each phase is facilitated by slightly different instructional strategies. Attention to instructional stimuli and motivation are necessary for acquisition, but providing additional information on how to perform correctly is the primary means of teaching students to do new behaviors. Fluency is promoted by adding structured practice times and manipulating the reinforcement contingencies to facilitate performance during practice. Maintenance is facilitated by teaching useful skills; ensuring that the skills are performed fluently; and manipulating the reinforcement contingencies by thinning the schedule of reinforcement, delaying reinforcement, and using naturally available reinforcers. Generalization is influenced by manipulating setting, consequent, and antecedent events.

SUMMARY COMMENTS

- Teaching is the process of causing students to perform target behaviors under new and/or different stimulus conditions.
- Stimulus control is the reliable, or predictable, responding in the presence of a particular stimulus and the absence of responding in the absence of that stimulus.
- Transfer of stimulus control involves shifting the control of behavior from one set of stimuli to another.
- Systematic instruction includes identifying the curriculum content, using curriculum-based assessment practices, involving interdisciplinary teams, planning instructional programs, implementing and monitoring progress, and evaluating progress at regular intervals.
- Effective teaching is characterized by management of instructional time, management of student behavior, clear presentation of instructional stimuli, frequent monitoring of student progress, and frequent use of instructional feedback.
- Acquisition is the learning of the basic requirements of a behavior.
- Acquisition requires attention to instructional stimuli, motivation to respond, and presentation of information on how to perform the behavior correctly.
- Fluency is the performance of target behaviors at rapid or natural rates.
- Fluency is facilitated by practice and manipulation of procedures to enhance engagement in practice.

- Maintenance is the continued performance of behavior after teaching has stopped.
- Maintenance is enhanced by fluent responding; teaching useful skills; and manipulating the reinforcing contingencies by thinning the schedule of reinforcement, delaying reinforcement, and using natural reinforcers and reinforcement schedules.
- Generalization is the performance of target behaviors in situations other than training.
- Generalization is enhanced by teaching useful behaviors and manipulating setting, antecedent, and consequent events.

The next chapter provides some general guidelines for organizing instruction and guidelines about how to provide instruction and describes different types of prompts (teacher assistance). The chapter also includes guidelines for using these prompts.

EXERCISES

1. Identify some behavior you do regularly and attempt to identify which stimuli in your environment control the occurrence of that behavior.
2. Describe to a friend how learning is different from teaching.
3. Identify some skill that you are learning and describe it in terms of (a) the process of establishing stimulus control and (b) the phase of performance that characterizes your current patterns of responding.
4. With different examples of graphed data, attempt to apply the data decision rules related to acquisition and fluency.
5. Make a list of instructional modifications that will promote (a) acquisition, (b) fluency, (c) maintenance, and (d) generalization.

REFERENCES

Ault, M. J., Wolery, M., Doyle, P. M., & Gast, D. L. (1989). Review of comparative studies in instruction of students with moderate and severe handicaps. *Exceptional Children, 55,* 346–356.

Baer, D. M. (1978). The behavioral analysis of trouble. In K. E. Allen, V. J. Holm, & R. L. Schiefelbusch (Eds.), *Early intervention—a team approach* (pp. 37–93). Baltimore: University Park Press.

Bailey, D. B., & Wolery, M. (in press). *Teaching infants and preschoolers with disabilities* (2nd ed.). Columbus, OH: Charles Merrill.

Bennett, W. J. (1986). *What works: Research about teaching and learning.* Washington, DC: U.S. Department of Education.

Bickel, W. E., & Bickel, D. D. (1986). Effective schools, classrooms, and instruction: Implications for special education. *Exceptional Children, 52,* 489–500.

Billingsley, F. F. (1984). Where are the generalized outcomes? (An examination of instructional objectives). *Journal of the Association for Persons with Severe Handicaps, 9,* 186–192.

———— (1988). Writing objectives for generalization. In N. G. Haring (Ed.), *Generalization for students with severe handicaps: Strategies and solutions* (pp. 123–128). Seattle: University of Washington Press.

Bishop, K. D., & Falvey, F. A. (1986). Motor skills. In M. A. Falvey (Ed.), *Community-based curriculum: Instructional strategies for students with severe handicaps* (pp. 139–161). Baltimore: Paul Brookes.

Browder, D. M. (1987). *Assessment of individuals with severe handicaps: An applied behavior approach to life skills assessment.* Baltimore: Paul Brookes.

Browder, D. M., & Snell, M. E. (1987). Functional academics. In M. E. Snell (Ed.), *Systematic instruction of persons with severe handicaps* (pp. 436–470). Columbus, OH: Charles Merrill.

Campbell, P. H. (1987a). Physical management and handling procedures with students with movement dysfunction. In M. E. Snell (Ed.), *Systematic instruction of persons with severe handicaps* (pp. 174–187). Columbus, OH: Charles Merrill.

———— (1987b). Programming for students with dysfunction in posture and movement. In M. E. Snell (Ed.), *Systematic instruction of persons with severe handicaps* (pp. 188–211). Columbus, OH: Charles Merrill.

Cooper, J. O., Heron, T. E., & Heward, W. L. (1987). *Applied behavior analysis.* Columbus, OH: Charles Merrill.

Dever, R. B. (1988). *Community living skills: A taxonomy.* Washington, DC: American Association on Mental Retardation.

Dunlap, G., Koegel, R. L., Johnson, J., & O'Neill, R. E. (1987). Maintaining performance of autistic clients in community settings with delayed contingencies. *Journal of Applied Behavior Analysis, 20,* 185–191.

Dyer, K. (1987). The competition of autistic stereotyped behavior with usual and specifically assessed reinforcers. *Research in Developmental Disabilities, 8,* 607–626.

Egel, A. L. (1981). Reinforcer variation: Implications for motivating developmentally disabled children. *Journal of Applied Behavior Analysis, 14,* 345–360.

Etzel, B. C., & LeBlanc, J. (1979). The simplest treatment alternative: Appropriate instructional control and errorless learning procedures for the difficult-to-teach child. *Journal of Autism and Developmental Disorders, 9,* 361–382.

Evans, I., Meyer, L., Derer, K. R., & Hanashiro, R. Y. (1985). An overview of the decision model. In I. Evans & L. Meyer (Eds.), *An educative approach to behavior problems: A practical decision model for interventions with severely handicapped learners* (pp. 43–61). Baltimore: Paul Brookes.

Falvey, M. A. (1986). *Community-based curriculum: Instructional strategies for students with severe handicaps.* Baltimore: Paul Brookes.

Fuchs, L. S., & Fuchs, D. (1986). Effects of systematic formative evaluation: A meta-analysis. *Exceptional Children, 53,* 199–208.

Gagne, R. M. (1985). *The conditions of learning and theory of instruction.* New York: Holt, Rinehart & Winston.

Gaylord-Ross, R. (1980). A decision model for the treatment of aberrant behavior in applied settings. In W. Sailor, B. Wilcox, & L. Brown (Eds.), *Methods of instruction for severely handicapped students* (pp. 135–158). Baltimore: Paul Brookes.

Grenot-Scheyer, M., & Falvey, M. A. (1986). Functional academic skills. In M. A. Falvey (Ed.), *Community-based curriculum: Instructional strategies for students with severe handicaps* (pp. 187–215). Baltimore: Paul Brookes.

Haring, N. G. (Ed.) (1988). *Generalization for students with severe handicaps: Strategies and solutions.* Seattle: University of Washington Press.

Haring, N. G., Liberty, K. A., & White, O. R. (1980). Rules for data-based strategy decision in instructional programs. In W. Sailor, B. Wilcox, & L. Brown (Eds.), *Methods of instruction for severely handicapped students* (pp. 159–192). Baltimore: Paul Brookes.

Haring, T. G., & Kennedy, C. H. (1988). Units of analysis in task-analytic research. *Journal of Applied Behavior Analysis, 21,* 207–215.

Helmstetter, E., & Guess, D. (1987). Application of the individualized curriculum sequencing model to learners with severe sensory impairments. In L. Goetz, D. Guess, & K. Stremel-Campbell (Eds.), *Innovative program design for individuals with dual sensory impairments* (pp. 255–282). Baltimore: Paul Brookes.

Horner, R. H., Dunlap, G., & Koegel, R. L. (1988). *Generalization and maintenance: Life-style changes in applied settings.* Baltimore: Paul Brookes.

Kaiser, A. P., Alpert, C. L., & Warren, S. F. (1987). Teaching functional language: Strategies for language intervention. In M. E. Snell (Ed.), *Systematic instruction of persons with severe handicaps* (pp. 247–272). Columbus, OH: Charles Merrill.

Liberty, K. A. (1988). Decision rules and procedures for generalization. In N. G. Haring (Ed.), *Generalization for students with severe handicaps: Strategies and solutions* (pp. 177–204). Seattle: University of Washington Press.

Liberty, K. A., & Haring, N. G. (1990). Introduction to decision rule systems. *Remedial and Special Education, 11,* 32–41.

Liberty, K. A., & Michael, L. J. (1985). Teaching retarded students to reinforce their own behavior: A review of process and operation in the current literature. In N. G. Haring, K. A. Liberty, F. F. Billingsley, V. Lynch, J. Kayser, & F. McCarty (Eds.), *Investigating the problem of skill generalization* (3rd ed.) (pp. 88–106). Seattle: Washington Research Organization.

Lyon, S., & Lyon, G. (1980). Team functioning and staff development: A role release approach to providing integrated educational services for severely handicapped students. *The Journal of the Association for the Severely Handicapped, 5,* 250–263.

Mason, S. A., McGee, G. G., Farmer-Dougan, V., & Risley, T. R. (1989). Practical strategy for ongoing reinforcer assessment. *Journal of Applied Behavior Analysis, 22,* 45–68.

McCollum, J. A., & Hughes, M. (1988). Staffing patterns and team models in infancy programs. In J. B. Jordan, J. J. Gallagher, P. L. Hutinger, & M. B. Karnes (Eds.), *Early childhood special education: Birth to three* (pp. 129–146). Reston, VA: The Council for Exceptional Children.

McCormick, L., & Goldman, R. (1979). The transdisciplinary model: Implications for service delivery and personnel preparation for the severely and profoundly handicapped. *AAESPH Review, 4,* 152–161.

Mercer, C. D., & Mercer, A. R. (1985). *Teaching students with learning problems* (2nd ed.). Columbus, OH: Charles Merrill.

Mercer, C. D., & Snell, M. E. (1977). *Learning theory research in mental retardation: Implications for teaching.* Columbus, OH: Charles Merrill.

Miller, J., & Allaire, J. (1987). Augmentative communication. In M. E. Snell (Ed.), *Systematic instruction of persons with severe handicaps* (pp. 273–297). Columbus, OH: Charles Merrill.

Nietupski, J. A., & Hamre-Nietupski, S. M. (1987). An ecological approach to curriculum development. In L. Goetz, D. Guess, & K. Stremel-Campbell (Eds.), *Innovative program design for individuals with dual sensory impairments* (pp. 225–253). Baltimore: Paul Brookes.

Orelove, F. P., & Sobsey, D. (1987). *Educating children with multiple disabilities: A transdisciplinary approach.* Baltimore: Paul Brookes.

Paine, S. C., Radicchi, J. Rosellini, L. C., Duetchman, L., & Darch, C. B. (1983). *Structuring your classroom for academic success.* Champaign, IL: Research Press.

Repp, A. C., & Singh, N. N. (Eds.) (1990). *Perspectives on the use of nonaversive and aversive interventions for persons with developmental disabilities.* Sycamore, IL: Sycamore Publishing.

Rowland, C., & Stremel-Campbell, K. (1987). Share and share alike: Conventional gestures to emergent language for learners with sensory impairments. In L. Goetz, D. Guess, & K. Stremel-Campbell (Eds.), *Innovative program design for individuals with dual sensory impairments* (pp. 49–75). Baltimore: Paul Brookes.

Rusch, F. R., Chadsey-Rusch, J., & Lagomarcino, T. (1987). Preparing students for employment. In M. E. Snell (Ed.), *Systematic instruction of persons with severe handicaps* (pp. 471–490). Columbus, OH: Charles Merrill.

Sailor, W., Gee, K., Goetz, L., & Graham, N. (1988). Progress in educating students with the most severe disabilities: Is there any? *Journal of the Association for Persons with Severe Handicaps, 13,* 87–99.

Snell, M. E. (1987a). *Systematic instruction of persons with severe handicaps* (3rd ed.). Columbus, OH: Charles Merrill.

——— (1987b). Basic self-care instruction for students without motor impairments. In M. E. Snell (Ed.), *Systematic instruction of persons with severe handicaps* (pp. 334–389). Columbus, OH: Charles Merrill.

Snell, M. E., & Browder, D. M. (1987). Domestic and community skills. In M. E. Snell (Ed.), *Systematic instruction of persons with severe handicaps* (pp. 390–434). Columbus, OH: Charles Merrill.

Stokes, T. F., & Baer, D. M. (1977). An implicit technology of generalization. *Journal of Applied Behavior Analysis, 10,* 349–367.

Vargas, J. S. (1977). *Behavioral psychology for teachers.* New York: Harper & Row.

White, K. P., Wyne, M. D., Stuck, G. B., & Coop, R. H. (1983). *Teaching effectiveness evaluation project* (Final report). Chapel Hill: School of Education, University of North Carolina at Chapel Hill.

White, O. R. (1988). Probing skill use. In N. G. Haring (Ed.), *Generalization for students with severe handicaps: Strategies and solutions* (pp. 131–141). Seattle: University of Washington Press.

White, O. R., & Haring, N. G. (1980). *Exceptional teaching* (2nd ed.). Columbus, OH: Charles Merrill.

White, O. R., Liberty, K. A., Haring, N. G., Billingsley, F. F., Boer, M., Burrage, A., Connors, R., Farman, R., Fedorchak, G., Leber, B. D., Liberty-Laylin, S., Miller, S., Opalski, C., Phifer, C., & Sessoms, I. (1988). Review and analysis of strategies for generalization. In N. G. Haring (Ed.), *Generalization for students with severe handicaps: Strategies and solutions* (pp. 15–51). Seattle: University of Washington Press.

Wilcox, B., & Bellamy, G. T. (1987). *The activities catalog: An alternative curriculum for youth and adults with severe disabilities.* Baltimore: Paul Brookes.

Winton, P. J. (1988). The family-focused interview: An assessment measure and goal-setting mechanism. In D. B. Bailey & R. J. Simeonsson (Eds.), *Family assessment in early intervention* (pp. 185–205). Columbus, OH: Charles Merrill.

Wolery, M. (1989a). Using assessment information to plan instructional programs. In D. B. Bailey & M. Wolery (Eds.), *Assessing infants and preschoolers with handicaps* (pp. 478–495). Columbus, OH: Charles Merrill.

——— (1989b). Using direct observation in assessment. In D. B. Bailey & M. Wolery (Eds.), *Assessing infants and preschoolers with handicaps* (pp. 64–96). Columbus, OH: Charles Merrill.

Wolery, M., Bailey, D. B., & Sugai, G. M. (1988). *Effective teaching: Principles and procedures of applied behavior analysis with exceptional students.* Boston: Allyn & Bacon.

CHAPTER 2

Principles of Programming and Prompting

Chapter Overview

Key Terms

Principle of Partial Participation

Form

Function

Community-Based Instruction

Effectiveness

Efficiency

Intrusiveness

Restrictiveness

Response Prompts

Controlling Prompts

Noncontrolling Prompts

Response Prompting Strategies

Stimulus Control

Gestural Prompts

Verbal Prompts

Pictorial Prompts

Two-Dimensional Prompts

Model Prompts

Partial Physical Prompts

Full Physical Prompts

Discriminative Stimulus Relationship

Questions to Be Answered by This Chapter

1. What are the goals of education for students with moderate to severe disabilities?
2. What guidelines can be used to make decisions about what should be taught?

3. What guidelines can be used to make decisions about how instruction should be provided?
4. What guidelines can be used to make decisions about which strategies to use?
5. What are prompts, different types of prompts, and general guidelines for the use of prompts?

As stated in Chapter 1, these are the goals of education for students who have moderate to severe disabilities: (a) increase their adaptive performance related to living and functioning in the community, (b) maximize their participation in community activities, (c) enhance the quality of their lives (as defined by their families and themselves), and (d) ease the care-giving responsibilities and stress of their families (Sailor et al., 1988; Snell, 1987). To meet these goals, teachers should use systematic instruction and effective teaching practices, and this book is devoted primarily to describing effective strategies. However, instructional activities with students who have moderate to severe disabilities require more than systematic and effective instructional strategies. General principles or guidelines are needed to organize instruction. This chapter first describes guidelines that teachers should use for making decisions about teaching, then describes prompts (teacher assistance or "help"). The chapter also illustrates various types of prompts and includes guidelines for using prompts. This information is provided because prompts are used extensively in the strategies described in Chapters 3–8.

The following section includes general guidelines for instruction that are taken from the literature and from current perspectives of what constitutes quality education for individuals with moderate and severe disabilities. They are a framework for making decisions related to providing instruction. Some of them focus on decisions concerning which skills should be taught, others address decisions related to the focus of instruction, and others deal with decisions related to the selection of instructional strategies. Chapter 9 presents a detailed discussion of the issue of selecting instructional strategies, so this chapter describes only a general framework.

GUIDELINES FOR SELECTING TARGET BEHAVIORS

A high-quality curriculum-based assessment of students with moderate to severe disabilities frequently will identify more skills than it is possible to teach. Therefore, the team (including families and students when possible) must identify those skills that are of the highest priority. There are three guidelines that the team should consider when determining which behaviors to teach:

Select Target Behaviors That Maximize Independence and Participation. Most students' performance on needed skills fall on a continuum from total independence (adaptation) to total dependence. Ideally, students would perform independently all of the skills they need to function and participate in the community. Unfortunately, current practice suggests that this is not a reality for all students on all skills. Thus, the team must select those behaviors that will maximize adaptive performance and participation in community activities. A general rule is to *select skills that are needed and can be performed independently; however, adapted or supported performance is better than dependence.*

This rule suggests two things. First, whenever possible, instruction should focus on maximizing students' independence on needed skills and activities. Thus, the team should review those skills that are needed, identify the high-priority skills, and determine which of them will likely result in independent student functioning after appropriate instruction is provided. Second, this rule suggests that if independent performance is unlikely, then adaptations and support should be provided to allow student participation in the activity or routine. Baumgart et al. (1982) state that students frequently are excluded from community activities because they are unable to perform all the steps of the activities independently. They contend that providing support or adaptations will allow students to participate in activities and thus be more viable members of the community. This is called the **principle of partial participation**. To implement this principle, Baumgart et al. (1982) delineate the eight-step process described in Table 2.1. Many different types of support and adaptations are possible—including using or creating materials and devices, using personal assistance, modifying skill sequences, adapting rules, and modifying attitudes (Baumgart et al., 1982).

Adaptations of materials and devices involves using common devices, such as wheelchairs and hearing aids, as well as microcomputer equipment and adaptive switches. Support with personal assistance involves using various prompts (teacher assistance), such as verbal or physical prompts that allow students to participate in particular activities or parts of activities. Adapting skill sequences requires modification in the order with which steps are performed or the elimination of some steps of chained responses. Adapting rules involves establishing changes in what is perceived as accepted behavior in a particular social setting. Adapting social attitudes frequently includes providing information to nondisabled persons in the community who, as a result of that information, change their views about individuals with moderate to severe disabilities. The underlying assumption of this principle and guideline is that it is beneficial for individuals with moderate to severe disabilities to live, function, and participate in the community. If students are unable to perform some activity, routine, or skill independently, then supported or adapted participation is better than no participation or total dependence.

Select Target Behaviors That Are Valued By Families.   The selection of target behaviors and skills is, of course, a team decision. That team should include representatives from relevant disciplines, students when appropriate, and students' families. Parents or guardians should play significant roles in determining which of the needed skills are high-priority objectives. Parents of students with moderate to severe disabilities have more opportunities for participation than do parents of nondisabled students, and they appear to be satisfied with that involvement (Salisbury & Evans, 1988). However, not all parents or guardians become involved, and of those who do, some do not take an active role in decisions about their students' IEPs. Parents who participate in the assessment activities prior to the actual IEP meeting tend to make more decisions in the meeting, generate more objectives for their children, and participate more in meetings than do parents who are not involved in the assessment

TABLE 2.1. Steps for Implementing the Principle of Partial Participation

Step	Description
1. Complete an inventory of a nondisabled person doing the skill.	Observe a nondisabled individual complete the target skill or activity in the designated environment and record the needed behaviors and their sequence.
2. Complete an inventory of the target student doing the skill.	Observe the student perform the target skill or activity in the designated environment and record all the behaviors that are performed independently and those that are not performed independently.
3. Identify the behaviors that the student can be expected to learn independently.	Meet with relevant persons, such as the student's family and therapists, to determine which skills the student can be expected to learn to do independently. Make a list of these skills.
4. Identify the behaviors that the student cannot be expected to learn independently.	Meet with relevant persons to determine which skills the student is unlikely to learn over a long period of time. Make a list of these skills.
5. Develop hypotheses about adaptations that would allow participation.	Identify adaptations that could be used to allow the student to participate in the activity.
6. Complete an inventory using the identified adaptation(s).	Attempt to use the adaptation of the skill or activity in the designated environment. Collect data on the extent to which the adaptation is successful in promoting participation.
7. Decide which adapation will be used.	Over several opportunities, use the adaptations and retain the most successful one.
8. Identify skills that will likely be acquired using individualized adaptations.	Identify the behaviors that are likely to be acquired if the adaptation is used. Employ systematic attempts to teach these skills.

[Adapted from Baumgart et al. (1982).]

activities (Brinckerhoff & Vincent, 1986). Thus, families should be involved in the assessment activities. Bailey (1987) suggests that teachers can increase family involvement in setting goals if they (a) view the family as a system within a society of systems, (b) assess family needs and plan interventions related to those needs, (c) interview and listen to families during the assessment, (d) negotiate goals and interventions when different values arise, and (e) assist families in securing the resources that they need.

When teams select skills for instruction, the notion of social validity is relevant. Wolf (1978) states that social validity is a construct that attempts to solicit the value of consumers and experts concerning educational practice. Specifically, he suggests that the value of the *goals* of instruction, the *procedures* used, and the *effects* of that use in meeting the goals are important variables to assess. The targeted skills should be ones that the families value, the procedures used should be ones that the families perceive as appropriate, and the extent to which the goals are achieved by the procedures should be evaluated (i.e., were these procedures worth their benefit?).

Analyze the Functions and Forms of High-Priority Objectives.   Each high-priority skill or activity should be analyzed in terms of its forms (topography) and functions. **Form** refers to the actual behaviors used to complete a skill or activity, and **function** refers to the effects of that behavior (Wolery, 1989a). Walking is a form (behavior), and getting from one place to another is the function (effect). Theoretically, every form, or behavior, has some function; that is, it causes some effect. Likewise, every function, or effect, is caused by some behavior. Some high-priority skills and activities are functions that can be performed by many different forms (behaviors). Examples are requesting, greeting others, protesting, initiating social interactions, terminating social interactions, and moving from one place to another. Several forms can be used to fulfill each of these functions; or, said another way, several behaviors can be used to cause these effects. If a student wants a drink of water, she can request it by pointing to the water fountain, moving next to and standing near the water fountain, asking for a drink of water with one word (e.g., "Water.") or a phrase or sentence, using a manual sign, or writing a note. All of these forms may result in the same effect: The student's request for a drink is honored, and her thirst is quenched. For other high-priority skills, a student's independent functioning requires the use of specific behaviors or perhaps only two or three behaviors are perceived as appropriate. For example, when a student wishes to eat a particular food that requires the use of utensils, acceptable forms would be his grasping a spoon or fork, getting the food on the utensil, moving the food to his mouth, and taking the food from the utensil. Another acceptable form would be to have him ask someone else to do the feeding. However, eating such food with his fingers or putting his face in the plate and eating the food are considered unacceptable forms.

When planning an instructional program, the team should answer the following questions about each skill: (a) What is the function of the given skill or activity, or what effect will be produced by this skill? (b) What forms are acceptable means of expressing this function? (c) Is form or function more important for this student in this activity? (d) What forms exist in the student's repertoire that could be used to teach this function? (e) What functions exist that could be used to teach any new forms? The answers to these questions both will assist the team in developing a program that maximizes independence and are necessary to focus attention on the effects of behavior. A form for recording the answers to these questions, which will help organize what is taught, is shown in Figure 2.1. Neel et al. (1983) suggest that each objective can be analyzed in terms of whether the forms are adequate or limited and whether the functions are limited or multiple. Each combination of these factors results in a different description of what should be taught. These combinations and their potential impact on educational focus are shown in Table 2.2.

Three principles related to forms, functions, and teaching are described below. The first principle is this: *Old forms should be used to teach new functions.* When the team determines that a new function (e.g., requesting and initiating social interactions) should be taught, then it should identify the forms or behaviors the student already does that could be used to teach that function. The underlying assumption of this principle is that learning both a new form and a new function is more difficult than using an existing form to learn a new function. For example, LaShonda uses single-word labels for objects and actions and never uses two-word phrases. If she needs to learn the function of requesting, then one-word requests are more appropriate

Student _____   Date ____/____/____

Curricular domain _____   Instructor _____

Identify Function of the Skill or Activity.	Identify Acceptable Forms for this Skill or Activity.	Is Form or Function More Important?	Does Student Display the Function and Acceptable Forms?	What Forms Are in Student's Repertoire to Teach this Function?	What New Forms Are Needed for this Function?

Figure 2.1. A planning sheet that can be used to analyze assessment data to determine which forms and functions should be targeted for instruction.

forms for her than are two-word requests. A teacher will be more successful in teaching LaShonda to request using one-word rather than two-word statements because it will be considerably easier. With one-word statements, LaShonda needs to learn only one thing ("One word will get what I want."); with two-word statements, LaShonda would need to learn, "I can express what I want with two words."

The second principle is this: *Old functions should be used to teach new forms.* The assumption underlying this principle is similar to that described above—i.e., it is easier to learn one new thing rather than two new things at once (Carr, 1988). For example, if after instruction LaShonda learns to request food, drink, snacks, affection, and assistance with one-word statements, then she will have the function of requesting. The teacher can then use this old function, one that is acquired, to teach a new form, e.g., two-word statements. Since LaShonda has learned to request, the new thing that she learns would be to use two words for requesting objects and activities for which she previously used one word. Since she already performs the function of requesting with one-word statements, she needs only to learn that two-word statements can be used to get objects.

The third principle related to forms, functions, and teaching is this: *Replace old forms with new, more normalized and adaptive forms.* A large part of education focuses on teaching students to perform specific skills and activities in more advanced ways. In such cases, existing functions that are performed with specific forms are used to teach students more advanced and adaptive forms for doing the same function. There are several reasons for teaching more advanced forms for existing function. The more

TABLE 2.2. Potential Combinations of Form and Function and Resulting Intervention Focus

Form	Function	Potential Intervention Forms
Adequate	Multiple	Continue monitoring child's performance.
Adequate	Limited	Teach new functions using existing forms; promote maintenance of existing functions.
Limited	Multiple	Teach new forms for existing functions; promote maintenance of existing forms.
Limited	Limited	Teach new functions with existing forms; teach new forms with existing functions.
No identifiable form	No identifiable function	Teach new forms and new functions.

[From Wolery (1989a, p. 485). Used with permission.]

advanced forms help students to (a) appear less disabled and more "normal," (b) display the function in more varied settings, and (c) have more control over their environment. For example, Chow-Ling is a 3-year-old with severe disabilities who currently fulfills the locomotion function (i.e., getting from one place to another) by crawling. The function is locomotion, and the form is crawling. A form that is more advanced, more normalized, and more adaptive is walking. Thus, if Chow-Ling learns to walk, the new form (walking) can result in him appearing less disabled; allow him to locomote in situations where crawling may be inappropriate (e.g., at a shopping mall and in a gravel driveway); and allow him to locomote in more environments, thus increasing his control of those environments.

Use of these three principles will help the team teach functional behaviors. In the literature, the term *functional behavior* has two definitions. Sometimes it is a synonym for *useful, practical,* or *desirable.* In other cases, it is used to describe any response that produces an effect or performs a function. The latter definition is used here. Teams should identify forms that fulfill functions (produce effects) needed by students. When a form does this, it is called a functional behavior. Carr (1988) states the following: "The ultimate task of an intervention agent is to assess what functions are currently in a child's repertoire and then to teach the child appropriate forms that serve those functions. Grafting arbitrarily selected forms . . . onto nonexistent functions is a prescription for failure, because the motivation necessary for maintenance is absent" (p.237).

GUIDELINES FOR ORGANIZING INSTRUCTION

The following are the guidelines for organizing how instruction is presented. The guidelines described above also influence how instruction is presented, and the following guidelines also influence, in part, what is taught. Their focus, however, is on how instruction is presented rather than on what is taught.

Ensure Generalization and Skill Application.   The purpose of public instruction is to teach students skills and knowledge that they can use in situations other than schools.

As a result, generalized skill use of what students have learned is the ultimate criteria by which the effectiveness of instruction should be judged. No objective should be considered mastered until students have demonstrated the use or application of that skill in situations where it is needed outside of school. To facilitate generalization of skills, teachers (a) teach relevant behaviors (Stokes & Osnes, 1988), (b) carefully select examples to be used during teaching (Albin & Horner, 1988), (c) use self-control and peer-mediated strategies (Fowler, 1988; Guevremont, Osnes, & Stokes, 1988), (d) manipulate the antecedent events involved in instruction (e.g., vary stimuli, use multiple stimuli, and use multiple trainers and settings) (White et al., 1988), (e) manipulate consequent events (Dunlap & Plienis, 1988), (f) make instructional settings similar to generalization settings (Stokes & Osnes, 1988), and (g) move instruction into the natural environment (White et al., 1988).

Moving instruction into generalization settings means that the instruction is frequently applied in settings other than school. This, known as **community-based instruction** (Snell & Browder, 1986; Snell & Grigg, 1987), is used frequently in educating students with moderate and severe disabilities because it does not assume that generalization will occur. By teaching students in settings where the behaviors are needed, teachers solve the problem of generalization. For example, an important skill for Maria is to shop for her groceries independently. To teach her shopping, her teacher takes her to the local supermarket and provides the instruction in that setting. As a result, the generalization setting becomes the training setting, and the problem of setting generalization is avoided. When it is not practical to teach in the generalization setting, teachers frequently use simulations. Nietupski et al. (1986) suggest five guidelines for using simulations: (a) Analyze the community setting to identify the range of stimulus and response variations that exist; (b) vary the simulated training systematically to provide a sufficient range of training examples; (c) collect data on community performance to plan and implement modifications in the simulated training; (d) use simulated training to provide intense or repeated practice in problem areas; and (e) schedule simulations so that sufficient training in the natural environment can occur and so that simulated training occurs in close temporal proximity to training in the natural environment.

In short, there are many strategies for ensuring the generalization of skills. Instruction should be provided only for skills that will be useful to the students in their meeting the individualized goals related to community living and participation, quality of life, and ease of care giving. Further, for every high-priority skill, there should be a generalization plan.

Ensure That Fluent Performance Is Maintained By Natural Contingencies.   As noted in Chapter 1, many behaviors must be performed fluently if they are to be useful to students. Likewise, that level of performance should be maintained by natural contingencies and effects if the responses are to be used regularly. Natural contingencies are those that occur without special programming when the behavior is performed in the natural environment. The teacher must identify both the appropriate rates of the high-priority skills and the natural effects and contingencies for students performing those behaviors (Wolery, Bailey, & Sugai, 1988). The procedures described in Chapter 1 for increasing fluency and ensuring maintenance should be used. As with generalization of high-priority skills, every behavior that is taught should include a plan for ensuring that it is performed fluently and that it comes under the control of naturally occurring contingencies (Billingsley, 1984, 1988).

Ensure That Performance Is Monitored Regularly.   Teams may develop sophisticated plans to ensure acquisition, fluency, maintenance, and generalization of high-priority skills; however, few teams will always develop plans that are successful from the beginning. Many times, teams will develop plans that need modification. There are at least three reasons for this. First, instructional technology is still being developed; thus, it is neither a complete science nor a complete practice. Second, students may present unique learning histories, disordered learning styles, and multiple sensory impairments. Third, the demands of the environments into which students are expected to generalize their target behaviors are unique and highly varied. It is unreasonable to expect a team to develop for each behavior and student plans that do not need further modification as instruction progresses.

   To determine when changes are needed, teachers must collect data on students' performance. Frequently, this is done through direct observation with event-based recording, time-based recording, category sampling, levels of assistance recording, and task-analytic recording (Wolery, 1989b). Collection of data and analysis of that information allows teachers to form hypotheses about what changes they need to make when instruction is not progressing as desired (Wolery, Bailey, & Sugai, 1988). The data decisions rules, described in Chapter 1 and discussed in the literature (Liberty, 1988a, 1988b), should be used by teachers in implementing and evaluating their instruction.

Ensure That Instruction Is Integrated Across Curricular Domains and Activities.   In the past, the instructional schedule was organized so that individual skills were taught in individual instructional sessions. Currently, the literature suggests that instruction should be provided on skills as they are needed and integrated into ongoing routines and activities (Helmstetter & Guess, 1987). To integrate skills from different domains, the teacher should embed the instruction from different areas in (a) the same activity or routine, (b) naturally occurring routines and activities, (c) student-directed activities, and (d) different activities throughout the day (Wolery, 1989a). Integrating instruction in this manner will undoubtedly increase the likelihood that the skills will be used when needed. For example, teaching self-feeding and communication skills during meal and snack times will increase the probability that students will engage in appropriate self-feeding and will communicate during meals.

Guidelines for Selecting Instructional Strategies

Although specific guidelines and issues related to selecting instructional strategies are described in Chapter 9, three organizational guidelines are presented here. These should be considered when deciding how to teach.

Use Effective and Efficient Instructional Strategies.   Because of the skill deficits of students with moderate and severe disabilities, ineffective or inefficient instruction cannot be tolerated. **Effectiveness** refers to whether students learn from a procedure, and **efficiency** refers to the relative amount of time and effort students require to learn the skill (Wolery, Bailey, & Sugai, 1988). Two procedures may be effective; if they are used, students will eventually learn the target behaviors. However, one procedure may be more efficient than the other because it requires fewer instructional sessions, produces fewer errors, requires less teacher involvement, and results in fewer minutes of direct instruction. When all things are equal, the procedure that has been shown to be the most efficient should be used. Effectiveness and efficiency are the two most important dimensions on which instructional strategies are evaluated and selected. While other variables—such as naturalness, intrusiveness, and restrictiveness—are important, a strategy should never be used if it is ineffective or results in tremendously slow learning simply because the procedure is rated by others as "natural."

Use Natural, Less Restrictive, Less Intrusive Procedures If Learning Is Equal.   If the benefit that accrues to students in terms of generalized learning is equal, then the more natural, less intrusive, and less restrictive procedures should be used. **Intrusiveness** refers to the extent to which an instructional procedures impinges or intrudes upon the student's body. **Restrictiveness** is a similar notion, but it refers to the extent to which an instructional procedure inhibits or restrains a student's freedom (Wolery, Bailey, & Sugai, 1988, p. 369). If two procedures are effective and both have demonstrated efficiency, then each's naturalness, intrusiveness, and restrictiveness are legitimate dimensions on which to make choices about the use of either procedure. Ideally, the instructional strategies should appear normal and natural and be non-intrusive and nonrestrictive; however, if strategies are selected on only these dimensions, ineffective strategies might be used.

Use Student-Directed Teaching Procedures Rather Than Adult-Directed Teaching If Learning Is Equal.   If generalized learning is equal, then the instruction should be organized so that students, rather than teachers, make choices about how time is spent. Many educators believe that students learn only from activities in which their attention is focused and in which they participate in performing the activity (Mahoney & Powell, 1986); students are more likely to attend and participate in activities that are a result of their own choices and over which they have some control. Thus, student-directed learning is desirable (Brinker, 1985). However, some students with moderate to severe disabilities make relatively few choices, tend not to be engaged in meaningful activities for long periods of time, and may not be highly motivated learners. For such students, teacher-directed learning activities and instructional sessions appear necessary. In most cases, there should be a balance between teacher- and student-directed learning (Bailey & Wolery, 1984).

   In summary, although effective instructional strategies and practices are important parts of quality education for students with moderate to severe disabilities, that instruction should be implemented in concordance with general organizing principles. When selecting target behaviors, teachers should identify those that maximize student independence and participation, value family input concerning what should be taught, and analyze each high-priority objective for relevant forms and functions. When implementing the instruction, teachers should ensure that acquired behaviors are generalized and applied where needed, that fluent performance is maintained by natural contingencies, that performance is monitored regularly, and that instruction is integrated across curricular domains. Teachers, when selecting among instructional strategies, should use only effective and efficient strategies; but if the degree of generalized performance is equal, then the less intrusive, less restrictive, and most natural strategies should be used; likewise, if the amount of generalized learning is equal, then student- rather than teacher-directed learning should be employed.

USING TEACHER PROMPTS

The following chapters describe several different strategies for providing and removing teacher assistance. The following section defines that assistance, describes various forms, and suggests some guidelines for using those forms.

Defining Prompts and the Rationale for Using Them

In a broad sense, prompts are any teacher behaviors that cause students to know how to do a behavior correctly. In a more precise sense, **response prompts** are teacher behaviors presented to increase the probability of correct responding (Wolery, Bailey, & Sugai, 1988). They may be presented prior to the occurrence of a behavior or after a student responds. Prompts are also known as assistance, support, help, hints, and cues. There are two types of prompts: controlling prompts and noncontrolling prompts. **Controlling prompts** are teacher behaviors that ensure that students will respond correctly when asked to do the behavior. These prompts already have stimulus control of the students' behavior. **Noncontrolling prompts** are teacher behaviors that increase the probability of students responding correctly but do not ensure that correct responses will occur.

Prompts can be classified by the behaviors teachers do in providing assistance, or they can be classified by the sensory modality through which students receive that assistance. For example, Teresa is learning to put dishes in the dishwasher, and her teacher points to the location in the dishwasher where each dish should be placed. The pointing is the prompt. If it is classified by teacher behavior, then it is a gestural prompt; if it is classified by sensory modality, then it is a visual prompt, because Teresa sees the point and makes use of it. Similarly, if Teresa's teacher tells her where the dishes should be placed, then the prompt would be verbal if classified by teacher behavior but would be auditory if classified by sensory modality. In this book, we have chosen to classify prompts by the type of teacher behavior used. This classification provides a more precise description of what the teacher is to do when using various prompts.

Teaching strategies that use prompts are called **response prompting strategies**. The purpose of response prompting strategies is to transfer stimulus control from the prompts to the target stimuli. As defined in Chapter 1, **stimulus control** is reliable or predictable responding in the presence of one stimulus and the absence of the response when the stimulus is not present. Stimulus control is established when a student is reinforced for doing the target behavior when the stimulus is present and when reinforcement is withheld if the behavior occurs and the stimulus is not present. Response prompts are used to increase the chances that the behavior will occur when the stimulus is present. Ideally, the prompts will already have stimulus control of the student's behavior, so the teacher's task is to transfer the stimulus control from the prompt to the naturally occurring or target stimulus. If the student performs the behavior when the target stimulus is present, the student can be reinforced. The reinforcement increases the probability that the target stimulus will acquire control of the behavior; that is, when the stimulus is present, it is likely that the response will occur because the stimulus communicates that reinforcement will probably follow. We then say that learning has happened.

The primary rationale for using response prompts is that they are effective in getting students to perform the target behaviors when the target stimuli are present. Thus, response prompts allow for more efficient establishment of stimulus control, helping students to learn more quickly. Another rationale for using response prompts is that they reduce teacher material preparation time. If teachers did not use response prompts, they would need to modify their materials considerably to promote learning. With response prompts, teachers usually do not need to do any modification.

Various Types of Prompts

At least six types of response prompts have been described and used in the literature (Wolery, Bailey, & Sugai, 1988), including gestural prompts; verbal prompts; pictorial, or two-dimensional, prompts; model prompts; partial physical prompts; and full physical prompts.

Gestural Prompts. **Gestural prompts** are nonverbal behaviors—such as hand movements and facial expressions—that "tell" students what to do. In the example of Teresa putting dishes in the dishwasher, the teacher's point indicating where each dish should be placed is a gestural prompt. Rae and Roll (1985) used a gestural pointing prompt when teaching adults who were classified as having profound mental retardation to leave their apartments during fire drills. A staff member said, "Fire drill," when the fire drill began; if the residents did not begin to leave the apartment, the staff member frequently pointed (gestural prompt) toward the exit. After several fire drills, the students learned to leave their apartments when a staff member said, "Fire drill."

Gestural prompts are nonintrusive, natural prompts. When they control students' responses, they have several advantages. They are easy to use, can be used with a group of students at once, do not involve touching students, and can be delivered when the teacher is not near the students. However, the primary disadvantage of gestural prompts is that students must understand the content of the gesture.

Verbal Prompts. **Verbal prompts** are teachers' vocal statements that help students perform the correct response. Verbal prompts are not task directions or statements that communicate to students that they are to respond but are statements that tell them *how* to respond. For example, Wendy is learning to set the table. When it is time to set the table, her teacher says, "Wendy, time to set the table." This statement is a task direction rather than a verbal prompt: It tells Wendy *to* perform, but it does not tell her *how to do the correct response.* If her teacher gives Wendy a task direction (e.g., "Time to set the table.") and, after a short opportunity for Wendy to respond, the teacher says, "Get the plates out of the cabinet," this is a verbal prompt. The former tells her to respond; the latter tells her how to respond. William is learning to read words commonly found in recipes; his teacher holds up a flashcard with a word on it and asks, "What's this?" This is a task direction rather than a verbal prompt because it tells him to respond but does not tell him how to perform the correct response. If the word was *mix* and the teacher said, "It means 'put things together'," this would be a verbal prompt because it gives William information about how to respond correctly.

There are at least five types of verbal prompts: (a) tell students how to do the behavior, (b) tell them how to do part of the behavior, (c) give them a rule to use, (d) provide them with hints or indirect verbal information, and (e) provide them with verbal options. When telling students how to do a behavior, a teacher should provide a description of the responses students are to perform. For example, when Wendy's teacher tells her, "Get the plates out of the cabinet," his statement describes exactly what she is to do. If he uses a partial verbal prompt, he might say, "Get the plates." If he gives her a rule, he might say, "Have one plate for every person." If he uses an indirect verbal prompt, he might say, "What do you put your food on?" If he provides her with options, he might say, "You could get the plates, glasses, cups, or silverware."

The type of verbal prompt used for a particular student should depend upon his ability to understand the meaning of the statement. Also, the type used will vary by the behaviors being taught. For example, if a response is not rule governed, then using a rule statement would not be appropriate. When using verbal prompts, many researchers and teachers use more than one type at a time. For example, a teacher might begin with an indirect verbal prompt. If the student behavior is not correct, she could provide a rule statement; if the student behavior still is not correct, she could give a direct verbal prompt describing how to do the behavior. Alper (1985) used four different levels of questions that each provided slightly more direct information to teach students with mild and moderate mental retardation to solve problems. Similarly, many researchers combine verbal prompts with other, more intrusive prompts. For example, Cronin and Cuvo (1979) used verbal prompts alone and then paired them with models and physical prompts when teaching sewing skills to students with moderate mental retardation.

The advantages of verbal prompts are that they do not involve physical contact with students, can be provided while students attend to the relevant materials, can be given to groups of students at once, and can be provided from a distance. The disadvantage of verbal prompts is that they rely on students' understanding of the message and on their compliance with that message.

Pictorial, or Two-Dimensional, Prompts.   **Pictorial prompts**, also called **two-dimensional prompts**, refer to pictures or written messages that tell students how to do a behavior. In some cases, these will be pictures of the completed response. For example, when Wendy is being trained to set the table, her teacher could use a pictorial prompt such as a picture of one place setting. This would give Wendy a model of where the napkin, utensils, and drinking glass should be placed in relation to the plate.

Frequently, teachers use picture prompts to provide students with information about the steps for completing a long task. For example, Wilson, Schepis, and

Mason-Main (1987) used picture prompts to teach a student with severe mental retardation to complete work at a restaurant. For teaching washing dishes, they used a series of pictures with separate ones for (a) the sink without water, (b) the sink with the drain plug placed in the drain, (c) the water being put in the sink, (d) the full sink, (e) the soap in a measuring cup, (f) the soap being put in the water, (g) dishes being put in the water, (h) someone washing the dishes, (i) someone rinsing the dishes, and (j) someone placing the dishes to dry. Such pictures prompt students to do the next step of a complex chain of responses. These pictures are frequently put into a "book," and students can flip a page each time they complete a step. Picture recipe books are examples of the use of pictorial prompts.

In addition to these types of two-dimensional prompts, written messages can be used. Many people use lists of tasks to do to prompt completion of daily activities or provide written instructions to fellow workers about how particular tasks should be completed. The requirement for such prompts, of course, is that students can read the messages. However, pictures are sometimes used in lists. For example, Jennifer is a student with moderate mental retardation who is learning to shop for groceries. She can read some words, and these words are placed on her list of items to buy. For those words she cannot read, a picture from newspaper advertisements is taped to her list.

The advantage of pictorial prompts is that they can be relatively permanent, so it is not necessary for the teacher to present the prompts each time they are used. Thus, students can learn to do new responses in a relatively independent manner. One disadvantage of picture prompts is that students must understand what is depicted and identify the relevant characteristics of the pictures. Another disadvantage is the difficulty of depicting some important components of a behavior with pictorial prompts. For example, Tyrone is learning to tie his shoes. Although he can use a pictorial prompt to know which step to complete, he might not know to pull the strings tightly because it is difficult to depict that action. Thus, on those steps his teacher should use a verbal prompt in addition to the pictures.

Model Prompts.   **Model prompts** are demonstrations of the correct behavior; the teacher does the behavior that students are learning, and students are expected to imitate the teacher's model. When the target behavior is verbal, the model should be verbal. When the target behavior is a motor response, the model should be that motor response.

Model prompts can be used in at least two ways: complete models and partial models. For example, when teaching Juan to describe events that he observes, his teacher uses a partial model. If Juan's friend throws a ball to another student, the teacher might say, "What did Mike do?" If Juan does not respond, the teacher might say, "Mike threw . . . " and then wait expectantly for Juan to repeat that part of the sentence and complete it (e.g., "Mike threw the ball to Lisa."). If his teacher was using a complete model, she would say, "Mike threw the ball to Lisa." Models have been used to teach students with moderate mental retardation many different tasks: They have been used to teach students with moderate mental retardation to read community sign words (Ault, Gast, & Wolery, 1988), students with moderate and severe mental retardation to use manual signs (Bennett et al., 1986), students with moderate retardation to cook (Schuster et al., 1988), students with autism to label pictures (Wolery, Gast, Kirk, & Schuster, 1988), and preschoolers with delays to read words (Doyle et al., 1990).

The advantages of model prompts are that they do not require physical contact with students, can be given to a group of students at once, can be provided from a distance, and can be used with nearly all behaviors. The primary disadvantage of model prompts is that students must be imitative; if they do not imitate, then the models will most likely be ineffective. However, because of the potential for observational learning (i.e., learning from watching others) and the frequency with which models are used, in most cases students should be taught to imitate others (see Bailey & Wolery, 1984, Chapter 4).

Partial Physical Prompts.   **Partial physical prompts** are teacher behaviors that involve touching students but not controlling their movements. Examples are nudging, tapping, and light pulling and pushing. Partial physical prompts are used frequently to assist students in starting a sequence of responses, but also are used to help students do particular behaviors. For example, Heather is learning to use a vacuum cleaner, with her teacher providing partial physical prompts. When she has completed a given area of the carpet, her teacher will nudge her to move to the next part of the carpet. This nudge, given at her elbow, causes her to change the direction of the vacuum cleaner. Partial physical prompts have been used extensively in teaching a variety of skills. Sometimes they are used in conjunction with other prompts, such as full physical prompts (Kayser, Billingsley, & Neel, 1986) or verbal and model prompts (Cuvo, Jacobi, & Sipko, 1981).

The advantage of partial physical prompts is that they can provide control over the student's behavior without extensive physical contact. Also, since partial physical prompts are brief, the teacher can use them with more than one student. The disadvantage of partial physical prompts is that they require contact with the student so they cannot be used from a distance. When using partial physical prompts, teachers must take considerable care not to injure students, push them off balance, or appear to harm them.

Full Physical Prompts.   Teachers use **full physical prompts** when they place their hands on top of students' hands and move them through the target behavior. Thus, the teacher not the student exerts the effort. Frequently, the teacher stands behind the student so that the arm movements will be smooth and natural. For example, Phil is learning to fold towels from the laundry. His teacher stands behind him, grasps his hands, and helps him to grasp the towel and make the movements to fold it. Full physical prompts have been used in combination with many other prompts and are frequently the most intrusive prompt in a prompt sequence (Doyle et al., 1988).

The advantage of full physical prompts is that teachers can completely control students' responses, so errors can be minimized. The disadvantage, of course, is the extensive physical contact teachers have with students. When using full physical prompts, teachers must be careful not to harm students by holding them too tightly and forcing movements that are not possible.

Guidelines for Using Prompts

There are at least six guidelines for using prompts (Wolery, Bailey, & Sugai, 1988):

Select the Least Intrusive but Effective Prompt.   When determining which prompt to use, a teacher should evaluate the effects of different types of prompts. After that assessment, she can choose only those prompts that assist students in responding correctly. Some of the instructional procedures that are described in the following chapters (e.g., constant and progressive time delay) require a controlling prompt. For these procedures, only those prompts that ensure that students will be correct should be considered. Other procedures (e.g., system of least prompts) allow the use of non-controlling prompts. Therefore, prompts that provide assistance but do not necessarily ensure the correct response could be used. In either case, the teacher should identify those prompts that have sufficient effectiveness and from those she should choose the least intrusive prompt. Intrusiveness, as defined earlier, refers to the extent to which a prompt impinges or intrudes on a student's body. A model or verbal prompt is less intrusive than a partial physical prompt, and a partial physical prompt is less intrusive than a full physical prompt.

Combine Prompts If Necessary.   The literature includes many studies using hierarchies of prompts and many using two or more prompts at the same time (e.g., see Wolery et al., 1986). It is common to use verbal prompts with models or partial physical prompts and also to use partial physical and full physical prompts in a sequence. The use of combinations may facilitate learning and may allow students to become independent more quickly. Thus, when it appears appropriate, teachers should combine their prompts.

Select Natural Prompts and Those That Are Related to the Behavior.   Natural prompts are those that are likely to be used by someone who is not trained in special education. For example, many conventional gestural prompts are used by individuals in the community. When a teacher uses such prompts, students may learn to benefit from the prompts that occur naturally. Also, the teacher should use prompts that are related to the target behavior. For example, if the response is verbal, then a verbal cue may be more appropriate than a picture prompt, but if the target behavior is written, then a picture prompt may be more appropriate.

Provide Prompts Only When Students Are Attending.   Prompts, like other instructional stimuli, should be provided only when students are attending. If students are not attending to the teacher or materials, whichever is appropriate, then the teacher should not provide the prompt and should attempt to secure student's attention. Common indications that students are attending include eye contact, orientation of their faces toward materials or their teacher, and discontinuations of inappropriate or competing behaviors.

Provide Prompts in a Supportive, Instructive Manner.   The purpose of response prompts is to cause students to perform the target behavior when the target stimulus is present. The purpose of prompts is not to punish errors, although they are sometimes provided after incorrect responses occur. Thus, response prompts should be used in supportive and instructive ways rather than in corrective ways. Some of the response prompting strategies described in the following chapters employ prompts before students are expected to respond.

Fade Prompts as Soon as Possible.   As noted above, the purpose of the prompts is to cause students to perform a behavior so that it can be reinforced when the target stimulus is present. This reinforcement causes a relationship, called a **discriminative stimulus relationship**, between the target stimulus and the behavior to be established; that is, the stimulus cues students that reinforcement is probable if they perform the target behavior. Originally the response prompt controls students' behavior; when the prompt is provided, the target behavior occurs and reinforcement is given. As the response prompt and the target stimulus are paired over time, the stimulus control can be shifted (transferred) from the response to the target stimulus. To shift the stimulus control from the prompt to the target stimulus, the teacher must remove the prompt. The procedures described in the following chapters are systematic means of removing prompts. It is important to note that these procedures for fading prompts should be planned before the prompts are first used. Failure to plan carefully how prompts will be provided and removed will produce ineffective and/or inefficient learning.

SUMMARY COMMENTS

- Teachers need guidelines for organizing their instruction and practice.
- Guidelines related to selecting target behaviors include these: (a) identify behaviors that maximize independence and participation, (b) place value on the input from families concerning what should be taught, and (c) analyze each high-priority objective for relevant forms and functions.
- Guidelines related to implementing instruction include the following: (a) ensure that acquired behaviors are generalized and applied where needed, (b) ensure that fluent performance is maintained by natural contingencies, (c) ensure that performance is monitored regularly, and (d) integrate instruction across domains.
- Guidelines related to selecting instructional strategies include these: (a) use only effective and efficient strategies; (b) use less intrusive, less restrictive, more natural procedures if the degree of generalized performance is equal; and (c) use student- rather than teacher-directed learning if the degree of generalized performance is equal.
- Prompts are teacher behaviors designed to increase the probability that students will respond correctly.
- There are several types of response prompts including gestural prompts, verbal prompts, pictorial prompts, models, partial physical prompts, and full physical prompts.
- There are several guidelines for using prompts, including (a) select the least restrictive but most effective prompt, (b) combine prompts when appropriate and needed, (c) select natural prompts and those related to the target behavior, (d) provide prompts only when students are attending, (e) provide prompts in a supportive and instructive manner, and (f) fade prompts as soon as possible.

The first two chapters described issues about teaching students with disabilities. These issues are the context in which instructional strategies are used, thus these chapters addressed foundational notions about teaching. Chapters 3-8 describe many instructional strategies. Each chapter is devoted to a single instructional strategy or a group of similar strategies and describes guidelines for using those strategies. Chapter 3 addresses a response prompting strategy called constant time delay. This procedure fades the prompt by inserting time between the target stimulus and the controlling prompt.

EXERCISES

1. For a given student, design a partial participation program.
2. Observe a student with moderate or severe disabilities and for any behavior (form) he or she exhibits, identify the function that it serves.
3. How would you develop a simulated program for teaching students to make a deposit at the bank?
4. Observe a teacher instructing a student with moderate or severe disabilities and identify the prompts that the teacher uses.

REFERENCES

Albin, R. W., & Horner, R. H. (1988). Generalization with precision. In R. H. Horner, G. Dunlap, & R. L. Koegel (Eds.), *Generalization and maintenance: Life-style changes in applied settings* (pp. 99–120). Baltimore: Paul Brookes.

Alper, S. (1985). The use of teacher questioning to increase independent problem solving in mentally retarded adolescents. *Education and Training of the Mentally Retarded, 20,* 83–88.

Ault, M. J., Gast, D. L., & Wolery, M. (1988). Comparison of progressive and constant time delay procedures in teaching community-sign word reading. *American Journal of Mental Retardation, 93,* 44–56.

Bailey, D. B. (1987). Collaborative goal-setting with families: Resolving differences in values and priorities for service. *Topics in Early Childhood Special Education, 7*(2), 59–71.

Bailey, D. B., & Wolery, M. (1984). *Teaching infants and preschoolers with handicaps.* Columbus, OH: Charles Merrill.

Baumgart, D., Brown, L., Pumpian, I., Nisbet, J., Ford, A., Sweet, M., Messina, R., & Schroeder, J. (1982). Principle of partial participation and individualized adaptations in educational programs for severely handicapped students. *Journal of the Association for the Severely Handicapped, 7*(2), 17–22.

Bennett, D., Gast, D. L., Wolery, M., & Schuster, J. (1986). Time delay and system of least prompts: A comparison in teaching manual sign production. *Education and Training of the Mentally Retarded, 21,* 117–129.

Billingsley, F. F. (1984). Where are the generalized outcomes? (An examination of instructional objectives). *Journal of the Association for Persons with Severe Handicaps, 9,* 186–192.

———— (1988). Writing objectives for generalization. In N. G. Haring (Ed.), *Generalization for students with severe handicaps: Strategies and solutions* (pp.123–128). Seattle: University of Washington Press.

Brinckerhoff, J. L., & Vincent, L. J. (1986). Increasing parental decision making at the individualized educational program meeting. *Journal of the Division for Early Childhood, 11*(1), 46–58.

Brinker, R. P. (1985). Curricula without recipes: A challenge to teachers and a promise to severely mentally retarded students. In D. Brinker & J. Filler (Eds.), *Severe mental retardation: From theory to practice* (pp.208–229). Reston, VA: Division on Mental Retardation of the Council for Exceptional Children.

Carr, E. G. (1988). Functional equivalence as a mechanism of response generalization. In R. H. Horner, G. Dunlap, & R. L. Koegel (Eds.), *Generalization and maintenance: Lifestyle changes in applied settings* (pp. 221–241). Baltimore: Paul Brookes.

Cronin, K. A., & Cuvo, A. J. (1979). Teaching mending skills to mentally retarded adolescents. *Journal of Applied Behavior Analysis, 12,* 401–406.

Cuvo, A. J., Jacobi, L., & Sipko, R. (1981). Teaching laundry skills to mentally retarded students. *Education and Training of the Mentally Retarded, 16,* 54–64.

Doyle, P. M., Wolery, M., Ault, M. J., & Gast, D. L. (1988). System of least prompts: A review of procedural parameters. *Journal of the Association for Persons with Severe Handicaps, 13,* 28–40.

Doyle, P. M., Wolery, M., Gast, D. L., Ault, M. J., & Wiley, K. (1990). Comparison of constant time delay and the system of least prompts in teaching preschoolers with developmental delays. *Research in Developmental Disabilities, 11,* 1–22.

Dunlap, G., & Plienis, A. J., (1988). Generalization and maintenance of unsupervised responding via remote contingencies. In R. H. Horner, G. Dunlap, & R. L. Koegel (Eds.), *Generalization and maintenance: Life-style changes in applied settings* (pp. 121–142). Baltimore: Paul Brookes.

Fowler, S. A. (1988). The effects of peer-mediated interventions on establishing, maintaining, and generalizing children's behavior changes. In R. H. Horner, G. Dunlap, & R. L. Koegel (Eds.), *Generalization and maintenance: Life-style changes in applied settings* (pp. 142–170). Baltimore: Paul Brookes.

Guevremont, D. C., Osnes, P. G., & Stokes, T. F. (1988). The functional role of preschoolers' verbalizations in the generalization of self-instructional training. *Journal of Applied Behavior Analysis, 11,* 225–241.

Helmstetter, E., & Guess, D. (1987). Application of the individualized curriculum sequencing model to learners with severe sensory impairments. In L. Goetz, D. Guess, & K. Stremel-Campbell (Eds.), *Innovative program design for individuals with dual sensory impairments* (pp. 255–282). Baltimore: Paul Brookes.

Kayser, J. E., Billingsley, F. F., & Neel, R. S. (1986). A comparison of in-context and traditional instructional approaches: Total task, single trial versus backward chaining, multiple trials. *Journal of the Association for Persons with Severe Handicaps, 11*(1), 28–38.

Liberty, K. A. (1988a). Characteristics and foundations of decision rules. In N. G. Haring (Ed.), *Generalization for students with severe handicaps: Strategies and solutions* (pp. 55–72). Seattle: University of Washington Press.

——— (1988b). Decision rules and procedures for generalization. In N. G. Haring (Ed.), *Generalization for students with severe handicaps: Strategies and solutions* (pp. 177–204). Seattle: University of Washington Press.

Mahoney, G., & Powell, A. (1986). *The transactional intervention program: A child centered approach to developmental intervention with young handicapped children.* Unpublished document. Farmington: University of Connecticut School of Medicine, Pediatric Research and Training Center.

Neel, R. S., Billingsley, F. F., McCarty, F., Symonds, D., Lambert, C., Lewis-Smith, N., & Hanashiro, R. (1983). *Impact curriculum.* U.S. Department of Education (Contract No. 300-80-0842). Seattle: University of Washington, College of Education.

Nietupski, J., Hamre-Nietupski, S., Clancy, P., & Veerhusen, K. (1986). Guidelines for making simulation an effective adjunct to *in vivo* community instruction. *Journal of the Association for Persons with Severe Handicaps, 11,* 12–18.

Rae, R., & Roll, D. (1985). Fire safety training with adults who are profoundly mentally retarded. *Mental Retardation, 23,* 26–30.

Sailor, W., Gee, K., Goetz, L., & Graham, N. (1988). Progress in educating students with the most severe disabilities: Is there any? *Journal of the Association for Persons with Severe Handicaps, 13,* 87–99.

Salisbury, C., & Evans, I.M. (1988). Comparison of parental involvement in regular and special education. *Journal of the Association for Persons with Severe Handicaps, 13*(4), 268–272.

Schuster, J. W., Gast, D. L., Wolery, M., & Guiltinan, S. (1988). The effectiveness of a constant time-delay procedure to teach chained responses to adolescents with mental retardation. *Journal of Applied Behavior Analysis, 21,* 169–178.

Snell, M. E. (1987). *Systematic instruction of persons with severe handicaps* (3rd ed.). Columbus, OH: Charles Merrill.

Snell, M. E., & Browder, D. M. (1986). Community-referenced instruction: Research and issues. *Journal of the Association for Persons with Severe Handicaps, 11,* 1–11.

Snell, M. E., & Grigg, N. C. (1987). Instructional assessment and curriculum development. In M. E. Snell (Ed.), *Systematic instruction of persons with severe handicaps* (3rd ed.) (pp. 64–109). Columbus, OH: Charles Merrill.

Stokes, T. F., & Osnes, P. G. (1988). The developing applied technology of generalization and maintenance. In R. H. Horner, G. Dunlap, & R. L. Koegel (Eds.), *Generalization and maintenance: Life-style changes in applied settings* (pp. 5–19). Baltimore: Paul Brookes.

White, O. R., Liberty, K. A., Haring, N. G., Billingsley, F. F., Boer, M., Burrage, A., Connors, R., Farman, R., Fedorchak, G., Leber, B. D., Liberty-Laylin, S., Miller, S., Opalski, C., Phifer, C., & Sessoms, I. (1988). Review and analysis of strategies for generalization. In N. G. Haring (Ed.), *Generalization for students with severe handicaps: Strategies and solutions* (pp. 15–51). Seattle: University of Washington Press.

Wilson, P. G., Schepis, M. M., & Mason-Main, M. (1987). In vivo use of picture prompt training to increase independent work at a restaurant. *Journal of the Association for Persons with Severe Handicaps, 12,* 145–150.

Wolery, M. (1989a). Using assessment information to plan instructional programs. In D. B. Bailey & M. Wolery (Eds.), *Assessing infants and preschoolers with handicaps* (pp. 478–495). Columbus, OH: Charles Merrill.

——— (1989b). Using direct observation in assessment. In D. B. Bailey & M. Wolery (Eds.), *Assessing infants and preschoolers with handicaps* (pp. 64–96). Columbus, OH: Charles Merrill.

Wolery, M., Ault, M. J., Doyle, P. M., & Gast, D. L. (1986). *Comparison of instructional strategies: A literature review.* U.S. Department of Education, Grant No. G008530197. Lexington, KY: Department of Special Education.

Wolery, M., Bailey, D. B., & Sugai, G. M. (1988). *Effective teaching: Principles and procedures of applied behavior analysis with exceptional students.* Boston: Allyn & Bacon.

Wolery, M., Gast, D. L., Kirk, K., & Schuster, J. (1988). Fading extra-stimulus prompts with autistic children using time delay. *Education and Treatment of Children, 11,* 29–44.

Wolf, M. M. (1978). Social validity: The case for subjective measurement or how applied behavior analysis is finding its heart. *Journal of Applied Behavior Analysis, 11,* 203–214.

CHAPTER 3

Constant Time Delay Procedure

Chapter Overview

Describing the Constant Time Delay Procedure
Effects of Using the Constant Time Delay Procedure
Steps for Using the Constant Time Delay Procedure
Sample Constant Time Delay Program
Summary Comments
Exercises
References

Key Terms

Constant Time Delay	Task Direction
Task Direction	Naturally Occurring Events
Controlling Prompt	Wait Training
Zero-Second Delay Trials	Unprompted Corrects
Constant Delay Trials	Prompted Corrects
Prompt Delay Interval	Unprompted Errors
Discrete Responses	Prompted Errors
Chained Responses	No Response Errors
Parsimonious	Consequent Events

Questions to Be Answered by This Chapter

1. What is constant about the constant time delay procedure?
2. How are prompts faded when the constant time delay procedure is used?
3. What are zero-second delay trials?

4. What populations and behaviors have been taught using the constant time delay procedure?
5. Why is it desirable for students to be signaled to respond with a naturally occurring event?
6. Why is the prompt used in constant time delay called the controlling prompt?
7. Why is a waiting response a prerequisite skill for the constant time delay procedure, and when should wait training be implemented?
8. Why should the same consequences be provided for correct responses before and after the prompt?

The **constant time delay** procedure is an instructional strategy that has been used successfully in teaching students with moderate and severe disabilities. This chapter describes the procedure, reviews the research that has been conducted, and defines and illustrates the steps in implementing an instructional program using this procedure.

DESCRIBING THE CONSTANT TIME DELAY PROCEDURE

With constant time delay, a target stimulus is presented a task and then a prompt is provided that ensures the student will perform the task correctly. The prompt is faded by systematically inserting a fixed amount of time between presenting the target stimulus and providing the prompt that will ensure the student does the task correctly (Snell & Gast, 1981). One way to present the target stimulus is known as the **task direction** (i.e., a question or command that cues the student to respond), and the prompt that ensures that the student will do the task correctly is called the **controlling prompt**. A visual representation of this aspect of the constant time delay procedure might look like Figure 3.1.

During initial time delay trials, the task direction and the controlling prompt are presented simultaneously. These trials are called **zero-second delay trials** (0-second) because no amount of time is inserted between the task direction and the controlling prompt. For example, Joshua is learning to name objects when his teacher, Ms. Lopez, holds up an object and asks, "What is this?" (i.e. task direction). Ms. Lopez knows that if she says the object's name, Joshua will repeat the name after her (i.e., controlling

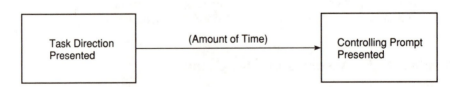

Figure 3.1. Depiction of the placement of the task direction and controlling prompt in a constant time delay trial.

prompt). Therefore, during 0-second delay trials, Ms. Lopez asks, "Joshua, what is this?," then immediately names the object. After a specified number of 0-second delay trials, the time between the task direction and the controlling prompt is systematically increased to a certain number of seconds, and **constant delay trials** are begun. The amount of time that is inserted between the task direction and the prompt is called the **prompt delay interval**. For all remaining trials until criterion is met, this delay interval stays the same (i.e., remains constant), thus the name constant time delay. For example, Ms. Lopez holds up an object and asks, "Joshua, what is this?" but she waits 4 seconds (i.e., counts silently to herself—"1001, 1002, . . ."), before naming the object. The goal of this time delay procedure is for Joshua to respond correctly during the delay interval or to wait for the prompt if he is unsure of the answer. Ms. Lopez should continue to use the 4-second delay interval until Joshua consistently names the object before she provides the prompt.

There are five types of student responses to the constant time delay prodedure: A student can respond correctly before or after the prompt, can respond incorrectly before or after the prompt, or may not respond at all. The goal is for students to respond consistently and correctly before the prompt. A flow chart for using the constant time delay procedure is shown in Figure 3.2.

EFFECTS OF USING THE CONSTANT TIME DELAY PROCEDURE

Students and Behaviors Taught

The constant time delay procedure has been used successfully to teach students with a wide range of disabilities, including learning disabilities (Stevens & Schuster, 1987), developmental disabilities (Schoen & Sivil, 1989), moderate mental retardation (Ault, Gast, & Wolery, 1988), severe and profound mental retardation (Browder, Morris, & Snell, 1981; McIlvane, Withstandley, & Stoddard, 1984), autism (Ault, Wolery, Gast, Doyle, & Eizenstat, 1988), and multiple handicaps (Johnson, 1977; Kleinert & Gast, 1982). Also, the ages of participants have ranged widely from preschool children (Doyle et al., 1990; Schoen & Sivil, 1989) to adults (Kleinert & Gast, 1982) but have predominately been conducted with elementary- (Gast et al., 1988; McIlvane et al., 1984) and secondary-aged students (Browder et al., 1981; Schuster et al., 1988). In most of these studies, a controlling prompt was identified for the subjects, reinforcers were identified, and many of the subjects were imitative.

A variety of both discrete and chained behaviors have been taught with the constant time delay procedure. **Discrete responses**, those that require a single response, that have been taught with the procedure include matching (McIlvane et al., 1984), sight word reading (Doyle et al., 1990; Gast et al., 1988), manual signing (Browder et al., 1981; Kleinert & Gast, 1982), spelling (Stevens & Schuster, 1987), identifying symbols (Johnson, 1977), and identifying numerals (Ault et al., 1988). **Chained responses**, those that involve a number of behaviors sequenced together to form a complex skill, also have been taught with the procedure and include cooking (Schuster et al., 1988), purchasing (McDonnell, 1987), banking (McDonnell & Ferguson, 1989),

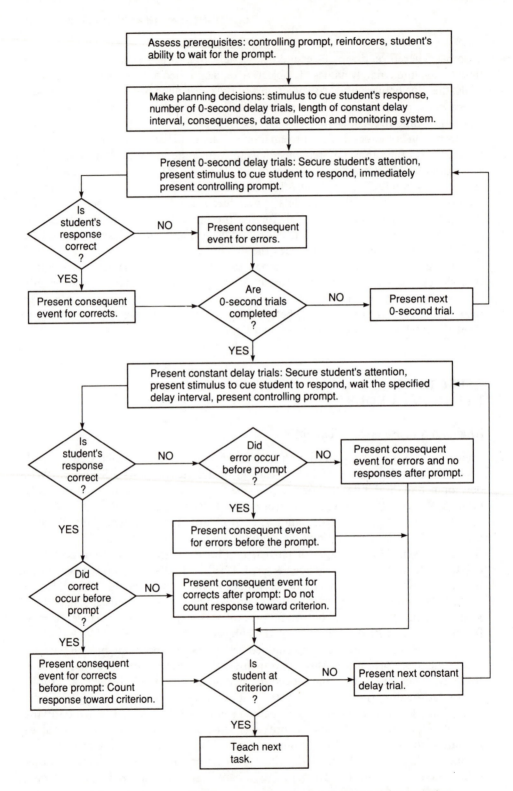

Figure 3.2. A flow chart representing the sequence of the constant time delay procedure.

doing laundry (Miller & Test, 1989), and performing the self-help skills of making a snack and getting a drink of water (Schoen & Sivil, 1989).

Results of Using Constant Time Delay

The constant time delay procedure has been shown to be an effective procedure in teaching a variety of skills to students with varying degrees of functioning levels; however, it has not been studied as extensively as some other instructional strategies. The bulk of the research done with the procedure has been in teaching students discrete tasks in one-to-one instructional arrangements. Recently, though, several investigations have shown the effectiveness of the procedure in small-group instruction (Gast et al., 1991; Wolery et al., 1991) and in teaching chained tasks. Investigations using the procedure have reported that it was effective in teaching students with a wide range of ability levels. The procedure also has been shown to be an efficient procedure since students learn tasks quickly, with an error rate that is generally less than 10 percent, although some individual students had higher error percentages (Handen & Zane, 1987).

Only a few research studies have compared the constant time delay procedure to other instructional strategies (Ault et al., 1989; Billingsley & Romer, 1983; Schoen, 1986). Constant time delay has been compared to progressive time delay in teaching community-sign word reading to students with moderate retardation (Ault, Gast, & Wolery, 1988). In this investigation, both procedures were effective, and no substantial differences between the two procedures were found on efficiency measures such as trials to criterion, percent of errors to criterion, and direct instructional time to criterion. Constant time delay also has been compared to the most-to-least prompting strategy (see Chapter 6) in teaching banking skills (McDonnell & Ferguson, 1989) and laundry skills (Miller & Test, 1989) to students with moderate mental retardation. Both investigations found the two procedures to be effective—but McDonnell and Ferguson (1989) found most-to-least prompting to be more efficient, while Miller and Test (1989) found constant time delay to be more efficient. The constant time delay procedure has most often been compared to the system of least prompts procedure (see Chapter 5), and investigations have taught sight word reading to elementary students with moderate retardation (Gast et al., 1988), numeral identification to elementary students with autism (Ault, Gast, & Wolery, 1988), self-help skills to preschool children with autism (Schoen & Sivil, 1989), and purchasing skills to adolescents with severe mental retardation (McDonnell, 1987). Across this range of ages, ability levels, and tasks, both instructional strategies were effective, but the constant time delay procedure was more efficient in terms of the number of sessions, errors, and minutes of direct instructional time to criterion.

Recommendations for Practice

The constant time delay procedure is useful because of its relative simplicity, high level of effectiveness, and demonstrated efficiency. The practice of delaying a prompt on a time dimension has probably been used by teachers for years without being called constant time delay. Using the procedure, teachers will experience success because students learn quickly, with few errors. Also, students may enjoy the procedure because they engage in positive interactions with their teachers and learn successfully. When learning to use the procedure, a teacher may first want to attempt one-on-one instruction with discrete tasks since the majority of the work with the procedure has been done in this way. However, chained tasks also have been successfully taught, and the procedure can be used easily in teaching tasks in a small-group format.

Several aspects of the constant time delay procedure make it **parsimonious**—that is, relatively simple to use (Etzel & LeBlanc, 1979). First, only one prompt is identified and delivered, since the controlling prompt is faded on a time dimension. Second, once the delay interval is inserted, the same interval is used for all remaining trials. Third, decision rules for modifying procedures based on student responses are well defined and can be easily implemented.

STEPS FOR USING THE CONSTANT TIME DELAY PROCEDURE

This section describes eight steps a teacher needs to follow when developing an effective constant time delay program:

- Identify the stimulus that cues the student to respond.
- Identify the controlling prompt.
- Determine the student's ability to wait for the prompt.
- Identify the number of 0-second delay trials needed.
- Determine the length of the prompt delay interval.
- Determine the consequences based on the student's responses.
- Select a data collection system.
- Implement, monitor, and adjust the program based on the student's data patterns.

Prior to using these steps, a teacher should conduct an appropriate, interdisciplinary curriculum-based assessment to identify useful behaviors for instruction.

Identify the Stimulus That Cues the Student to Respond

The first step in any instructional program is to identify a stimulus that cues a student that it is time for him to respond. The stimulus can be (a) something the teacher says or does or (b) something in the natural environment that signals the student to perform a certain task.

Task Directions.   To signal the student that it is time to respond, a **task direction** is given. Task directions are questions directed to the student (such as "What's this word?," "What is the time?," and "What is your address?") or commands (such as "Set the table," "Sweep the floor," and "Tie your shoes.").

Environmental Manipulations.   Rather than directly presenting a verbal task direction, a teacher can manipulate the environment so that it signals the student to respond. These manipulations include showing the student a flashcard, putting work materials on a table, and pointing to a numeral to be identified on a piece of paper. For some students with more severe disabilities, a verbal direction and an environmental manipulation may be combined. For example, a teacher might stand a student in front of a sink; provide all the necessary materials; and say, "Wash the sink."

Naturally Occurring Events.   Although task directions are one way to cue students to respond, stimuli that naturally occur in everyday life should also be considered. For example, if a student is learning to brush her teeth, then awaking in the morning and finishing meals are events that should signal her to do the task. A student who is learning to hang up clothes should be signaled to respond upon taking off his clothes or seeing clean clothing in a laundry basket. Stimuli that occur in the environment are called **naturally occurring events**. Ideally, a teacher should identify naturally occurring events so that students will learn to respond appropriately during their everyday lives when the behavior is needed, without help from another person. However, natural stimuli are more easily identified for some tasks than for others, and task directions are appropriate for skills that may not occur naturally, such as preacademic or academic types of tasks.

In addition, some students with moderate and severe disabilities may not be able to discriminate the naturally occurring events in their environment. In such cases, a teacher needs to pair a task direction with the natural event, then systematically fade the task direction until the student responds to the natural stimulus alone. For example, Mr. Jackson is teaching JoAnne to wash her hands. He wants her to wash her hands in response to the naturally occurring event of preparing for lunch. JoAnne, however, does not respond to this natural stimulus, so Mr. Jackson pairs his task direction ("It's lunch time. Wash your hands."), with the natural stimulus of lunch preparation by the class. Once JoAnne is able to wash her hands in response to the task direction plus the naturally occurring event, Mr. Jackson can fade the verbal direction until JoAnne responds to lunch preparation alone. The verbal direction can be faded first by using an indirect verbal direction (e.g., "It's lunch time. What are you supposed to do?"), second by omitting the indirect verbal cue (e.g., "It's lunch time."), and finally by saying nothing as JoAnne begins to respond to each of these stimuli.

Prior to instruction on a task and based on the individual characteristics of the student and the task, a teacher must define the stimulus that will be used throughout instruction to signal the student that it is time for a response.

Identify the Controlling Prompt

After defining the stimulus that will cue the student to respond, the teacher then identifies the controlling prompt. As noted previously, the controlling prompt is some form of teacher assistance that, when given, results in the student making the correct response. Since constant time delay uses only one prompt, the teacher must be sure that when the prompt is delivered, the student will be able to make the correct response. For example, Shea does not touch an adapted switch to activate a toy when Mr. Bowers places the toy before her and says, "Play with the toy." However, when Mr. Bowers delivers a partial physical prompt by lifting Shea's hand and pushing it toward the switch, Shea is able to touch the switch and activate the toy. The partial physical prompt is the controlling prompt because every time Mr. Bowers does this, Shea is able to activate the switch.

When identifying a controlling prompt, a teacher should identify the least amount of assistance that will consistently result in the student making the correct response. This should be done before instruction occurs by presenting the task to the student, then delivering a series of prompts that are ordered by intrusiveness (see Chapter 2 for examples). The prompt that consistently controls the student's response but uses the least amount of assistance is a good choice as the controlling prompt. Examples of controlling prompts include physically guiding a student to stand up when asked, verbally directing a student to put clothes in a washer, writing the letter *S* and having the student imitate the letter, and showing a quarter and having the student select a quarter from the change in his pocket.

Determine the Student's Ability to Wait for the Prompt

A necessary prerequisite skill with the constant time delay procedure is the ability to wait for a prompt. As noted earlier, following 0-second delay trials, the prompt is delayed for a few seconds. During this delay, the student should (a) wait for the prompt if she is unsure of the correct response or (b) perform the target skill if she is sure of the response. This ability to wait for the prompt is vital to the success of the procedure because, by waiting for the prompt if she is not sure or by responding before the prompt if she *does* know the correct response, a student learns more quickly and makes fewer errors.

Assessing the Wait Response.   Because the ability to wait is such an important part of the constant time delay procedure, a teacher needs to assess the student before instruction occurs to ensure that he is able to wait for a prompt. To do this, the teacher presents a real or nonsense task that she knows the student is unable to perform correctly, then gives a task direction and waits the same number of seconds the student will wait during training before she provides the prompt. By using this procedure, the teacher can assess if the student waits for the prompt or attempts to make a response. Any assessment of a waiting response should be conducted using the same type of task that the student will be asked to learn during instruction. For example, Ms. Wong wants to teach William how to touch line drawings of objects on his communication board. Therefore, to assess a wait response, she chooses a receptive task and prepares several line drawings of nonsense symbols. She places a choice of four symbols in front of William and delivers the task direction, "William, touch (nonsense word) ." She waits 5 seconds (i.e., prompt delay interval), then arbitrarily touches one of the symbols (i.e., controlling prompt). She does this for several trials and records his response on each trial. After collecting this data, she analyzes it. If William waits for the prompt consistently, then he is ready for instruction. If he does not wait consistently for the prompt, then Ms. Wong probably should not use the constant time delay procedure with William until he learns how to wait for the prompt.

Teaching Students to Wait.   For a student who does not wait but has good receptive language skills, the teacher may go ahead and use the delay procedure and simply instruct the student to wait during training. For example, before each instructional session, the teacher would say, "If you know the answer, tell me, but if you don't know, wait and let me help you."

For other students, such verbal directions may not be effective, so **wait training** should be used. The goal of wait training is not to teach a skill but to teach a student to wait for a prompt from his teacher. This is done by presenting the student with a task that is impossible for him to perform correctly unless he waits for a prompt. The prompt is first presented at a 0-second delay interval so the student does not have to wait. The delay interval is then gradually increased so that the student is required to wait longer amounts of time before the prompt is given. As with the waiting assessment, the task to be used during wait training should be similar to what will be taught during instruction. That is, if the student will be taught to read words expressively, an expressive task should be used; likewise, a receptive task or chained task should be used during wait training if this is the type of task to be taught. For example, Mr. Jones wants to teach Kashana to read food words found in grocery store aisles for her community-based shopping trips. He uses a constant time delay procedure with a 3-second prompt delay interval. During his assessment procedure, he discovers that Kashana does not wait 3 seconds for a prompt when he shows her words that he knows she is unable to read. Each time Mr. Jones presents a flashcard during the assessment, Kashana guesses an incorrect word even after he instructs her to wait. He decides to instigate a wait training program with Kashana using the following steps:

1. Mr. Jones makes a collection of flashcards containing very difficult words that Kashana is not able to read.
2. Mr. Jones presents a flashcard; gives the task direction, "Kashana, what word?"; and immediately states the word. This is the same as a 0-second delay trial.
3. When Kashana repeats the word after him, he provides descriptive verbal praise and a tangible reinforcer.
4. Mr. Jones continues to present different flashcards and provide prompts until Kashana correctly repeats after him for three consecutive trials at this 0-second delay interval.
5. Mr. Jones presents another flashcard, gives the task direction, and waits 1 second before saying the word. Kashana is then required to wait a very small amount of time before she receives the prompt.
6. When Kashana repeats the word after him, he again praises her for waiting for him to tell her the answer and provides a reinforcer.
7. Mr. Jones continues to present flashcards and provide prompts until Kashana waits for the prompt for three consecutive trials at this 1-second delay interval.
8. This process continues, with Mr. Jones increasing the prompt delay interval by one second until Kashana consistently waits for the prompt for 3 seconds. Mr. Jones selected this number of seconds because it is the prompt delay interval that he will use in Kashana's instructional program.

At any time during this procedure when Kashana does not wait for the prompt, Mr. Jones says, "No, wait for me to tell you"; withholds the reinforcer; and presents the next trial at the delay interval that he used immediately before the error occurred. The delay schedule Mr. Jones used during wait training, with Kashana's responses, is shown in Table 3.1.

Kashana's wait training example is for an expressive task, but the same sequence of delaying the prompt would be used for a receptive or a chained task. A receptive task would be conducted like the expressive example, except the student would make a receptive response. If a chained task was to be taught, then wait training would consist of identifying a series of motor responses that the student is able to perform. During wait training, the teacher would give the task direction but would always change the sequence of skills so that the student could not predict what to do without waiting for the prompt. The behaviors could be kept unpredictable by changing the sequence of the steps in a chain or by changing the response that is usually made with an item (e.g., placing a dish under a dish drainer).

TABLE 3.1. Sequence of Prompt Delay Interval and Student Responses During a Wait Training Procedure

Trial	Prompt Delay Interval (seconds)	Kashana's Wait Responses
1	0	Correct
2	0	Correct
3	0	Correct
4	1	Correct
5	1	Correct
6	1	Correct
7	2	Incorrect
8	1	Correct
9	1	Correct
10	1	Correct
11	2	Correct
12	2	Correct
13	2	Incorrect
14	1	Correct
15	1	Correct
16	1	Correct
17	2	Correct
18	2	Correct
19	2	Correct
20	3	Correct
21	3	Correct
22	3	Correct
23	3	Correct
24	3	Correct
25	3	Correct
26	3	Correct
27	3	Correct
28	3	Correct
29	3	Correct

In some cases, even after wait training procedures have been implemented, a student may still not wait for a prompt. If this occurs, the teacher should gesturally prompt a waiting response by gently placing a hand near the student's mouth and asking the student to be quiet for an expressive response or should hold the student's hands or gesture for the student to keep her hands down for a motor response during the delay interval. Students can then be reinforced for waiting because the teacher is ensuring that a wait response will occur by using prompts. The physical or gestural prompt is then gradually faded over trials until students will wait without the use of prompts.

Identify the Number of 0-Second Delay Trials Needed

Once a teacher determines that a student is able to wait for a prompt, she needs to determine the number of 0-second delay trials that she will use before the prompt is delayed. No set rules have been established for the number of 0-second delay trials to be used. The number ranges from two trials per stimulus (Stevens & Schuster, 1987) to ten trials per stimulus (Gast et al., 1988). Some teachers find it easier to conduct an entire session or two using a 0-second delay interval before delaying the prompt, while others provide a certain number of trials before the prompt is delayed. There are some general rules that should be followed, however: (a) More 0-second trials should occur when multiple behaviors are being taught at one time; (b) fewer 0-second trials are needed when a student is being taught as part of a group and each student is learning the same stimuli; (c) a student with a severe disability may need more 0-second trials than a student with a mild or moderate disability; (d) a student who has past successful learning experiences with the procedure or the content being taught should require fewer 0-second trials; (e) a young student who has little experience with direct instruction may need more 0-second trials than an older student; (f) as task difficulty increases, so should the number of 0-second trials; and (g) ideally, the fewest number of 0-second trials needed should be used. Of course, the student's response during intervention is the most important consideration. A student should consistently respond correctly on 0-second delay trials before the prompt is delayed. In addition, if the student makes many errors when the prompt is delayed, more 0-second trials should be used in future programs; if the student makes all correct responses before the prompt during the first delayed session, then fewer 0-second trials should be used. Generally, if the student begins to make some correct responses before the prompt in the first couple of sessions after the prompt has been delayed, then the teacher is probably using an adequate number of 0-second trials.

Determine the Length of the Prompt Delay Interval

The unique characteristic of the constant time delay procedure as compared to other response prompting strategies is that the controlling prompt is faded on a time dimension. The teacher must determine before instruction begins how long the delay between the task direction and the prompt will be. The most common prompt delay interval, 4 seconds, has been used to teach such discrete skills as sight word reading (Gast et al., 1988; Doyle et al., 1990), manual signing (Browder et al., 1981; Kleinert & Gast,

1982), and numeral identifying (Ault et al., 1988). Other delay intervals have ranged from 2 seconds to teach purchasing skills (McDonnell, 1987) to 5 seconds to teach cooking (Schuster et al., 1988) and spelling (Stevens & Schuster, 1987). In addition, the teacher must use the same interval following the prompt to give the student the opportunity to respond correctly or incorrectly or to not respond. Determing the length of the delay interval is ultimately an arbitrary decision, but both task and student characteristics should be considered.

Considering Task Characteristics.   The first question a teacher should ask when considering task characteristics is, "What is a reasonable amount of time for the student to initiate and complete a target response?" If sight word reading is the target task, then the student should probably read the word within a few seconds of seeing it. However, if the target task is choosing an activity during break time, a longer amount of time may be reasonable. When a discrete task is to be taught, the teacher will need to identify the interval that a student will need to complete the response. However, for responses of longer duration, the teacher must define a delay interval for the student to begin the response and then identify the amount of time that the student will be given to complete the response (e.g., 2 seconds to initiate combing hair and 30 seconds to complete the response). One way for a teacher to determine interval size is observing how long it takes a fluent student or worker who knows the task to respond correctly.

Considering Student Characteristics.   The student's characteristics also need to be considered when a teacher defines the delay interval. If the student will be using the skill in another setting, such as a mainstreamed classroom or job site, then the delay interval used during instruction should reflect that used by the students or workers in those environments. The delay interval also may need to be adapted for a student with a physical disability who does not have the motor skills to respond within a certain number of seconds. Before instruction begins with such a student, the teacher must assess how long it takes the student to initiate a response on a similar task and then begin timing the delay interval after this amount of time has elapsed.

Determine the Consequences for Each Student Response

There are five types of student responses to the constant time delay procedure. The two kinds of correct responses are (a) **unprompted corrects**, also known as anticipations, in which students make correct responses *before* the controlling prompt; and (b) **prompted corrects**, also known as correct waits, in which students make correct responses *after* the controlling prompt. The three kinds of incorrect responses are (a) **unprompted errors**, also known as nonwait errors, in which students respond incorrectly *before* the controlling prompt; (b) **prompted errors**, also known as wait errors, in which students make incorrect responses *after* the controlling prompt; and (c) **no response errors**, in which students do not respond *after* the controlling prompt. Prior to instruction, the teacher should be prepared by knowing what her response will be when a student makes any of the possible responses. These teacher responses are referred to as **consequent events**.

Responding to Correct Responses.   Both prompted and unprompted correct responses should be reinforced. Most researchers have reinforced both types of correct responses in the same way to reduce the complexity of the procedure. Since both types of responses receive the same reinforcement, a student will learn that if he knows the answer, he will be reinforced, but if he waits for the prompt, he also will be reinforced. This characteristic of the constant time delay procedure enables the student to learn without making a large number of errors. A slightly more complicated, but still effective, way to reinforce correct responses and still maintain low numbers of errors is for a teacher to assign more reinforcement value to unprompted corrects than to prompted corrects or to reinforce unprompted corrects more often than prompted corrects. This type of reinforcement schedule was used successfully by Touchette and Howard (1984) when they reinforced unprompted corrects each time those corrects occurred and reinforced prompted corrects every third time those corrects occurred. Browder et al. (1981) provided edible reinforcers only if a student's correct unprompted responses improved. McDonnell (1987) provided descriptive verbal praise for unprompted corrects and merely confirmed a correct response following prompted corrects. Whichever reinforcement schedule a teacher uses, unprompted corrects are the only responses that count toward criterion because they are the only responses that indicate independent performance.

Responding to Incorrect Responses.   A variety of consequences have been used in studies when students made errors: removing the stimulus and providing the next trial (Doyle et al., 1990), prompting a correct response (Browder et al., 1981), using an instruction to wait for the prompt (Ault, Gast, & Wolery, 1988; Gast et al., 1988), using an instruction to wait plus a model (Schuster et al., 1988), using a mild reprimand plus a short in-seat timeout procedure (Ault, Gast, & Wolery, 1988; Kleinert & Gast, 1982; Stevens & Schuster, 1987), and providing full physical assistance (McDonnell, 1987; Schoen & Sivil, 1989).

Research has not compared these different types of consequent events for errors; thus, a teacher must rely on his best judgment concerning what type to use with an individual student. When selecting an error consequence, he must assess the student's reaction to the event and ensure that incorrect responses receive less reinforcement than correct responses. On the other hand, consequent events for errors should not result in the student becoming upset in any way or otherwise interfere with the pace of instruction. As a general rule, the teacher needs to select the consequence for incorrect responses that is the least aversive but still effective event that he can find.

Select a Data Collection System

To monitor the effectiveness of a constant time delay program, a teacher should collect data each time he teaches a task. A data collection sheet should contain situational information—such as the student's name, the date, the session number, the instructor, the task or objective, the time of day, and the delay interval. In addition, the teacher needs to include on the data sheet, performance information about the student's responses on each trial as well as summary information, such at the total time of the session and the number and percent of each type of student response (Tawney & Gast,

1984). It is important for the teacher to record data on each of the five possible types of responses so he can monitor progress and make changes in the program if needed. Several sample data collection sheets are included in Figures 3.3 and 3.4.

Student ____Joe____   Instructor ____S. L.____   Date __6/1__ Session __3__

Start time __2:00__   Stop time ___2:10___   Total time ___10'___

Task _____Counting dollar bills_____

Trial/ Step	Stimulus/Task Analysis	Delay	Student Responding				
			Unprompted Correct	Prompted Correct	Unprompted Error	Prompted Error	No Response
1	$5	4"		✓			
2	$3	4"		✓			
3	$4	4"		✓			
4	$1	4"	✓				
5	$2	4"	✓				
Number of Each Response Type			2	3	0	0	0
Percent of Each Response Type			40	60	0	0	0

Key: ✓ = occurrence

Student ____Pam____   Instructor ____M. R.____   Date __7/4__ Session __1__

Start time __10:05__   Stop time ___10:10___   Total time ___5'___

Task _____Naming numerals_____

Trial/ Step	Stimulus/Task Analysis	Delay	Student Responding	
			Before	After
1	3	0"		+
2	3	0"		+
3	3	0"		+
4	3	0"		+
5	3	0"		+
Number Corrects			0	5
Percent Corrects			0	100
Number Incorrects			0	0
Percent Incorrects			0	0
Number No Response			XXXXXX	0
Percent No Response			XXXXXX	0

Key: + = correct, − = incorrect, 0 = no response

Figure 3.3. On the top data collection form, a check mark is placed in the appropriate column to indicate the student's response on the trial or step of the task analysis. On the bottom form, a "+" is placed for a correct response, a "−" is placed for an incorrect response, and a "0" is placed for no response in the before or after column. The before column indicates that the response occurred before the prompt, and the after column indicates that the response occurred after the prompt.

Date __8/3__   Session __6__   Instructor ____J. T._____

Start time ___11:07___   Stop time ___11:19___   Total time ___12'___

Task _____Reading Words_____

			Gail		Howard		Bob	
Trial/ Step	Stimulus/Task Analysis	Delay	Student #1 Responding		Student #2 Responding		Student #3 Responding	
			Before	After	Before	After	Before	After
1	stop	4"	+					
2	exit	4"				+		
3	enter	4"					+	
4	exit	4"		+				
5	enter	4"			+			
6	stop	4"					−	
7	enter	4"	+					
8	stop	4"			+			
9	exit	4"					+	
Number/Percent Corrects			2/67	1/33	2/67	1/33	2/67	0/0
Number/Percent Incorrects			0/0	0/0	0/0	0/0	1/33	0/0
Number/Percent No Response			XXXXXX	0/0	XXXXXX	0/0	XXXXXX	0/0

Student _____Al_____   Instructor _____T. P._____

Start time ___8:50___   Stop time ___9:00___   Total time ___10'___

Task _____Making toast_____

Step	Task Analysis	Student Responding									
1	Plug in toaster.	+/−	+/	−							
2	Put in bread.	+/	+/	+/							
3	Push handle down.	+/	+/	/+							
4	Remove cooked toast.	+/	+/	/+							
Delay Interval		0"	4"	4"							
Date		1/3	1/4	1/5							
Session/Trial		1	2	3							
Number Corrects		4	4	3							
Percent Corrects		100	100	75							
Number Incorrects		0	0	1							
Percent Incorrects		0	0	25							
Number No Response		0	0	0							
Percent No Response		0	0	0							

Key: + = correct, − = incorrect, 0 = no response

Figure 3.4. The top data collection form is used when teaching a small group of students. The bottom form is designed to be used when teaching a chained task and enables a teacher to monitor a student's progress on each step of a task analysis. A " + " for a correct, a " − " for an incorrect, or a "0" for a no response is placed above the diagonal line to indicate if a response occurred before the prompt and below the diagonal line to indicate if a response occurred after the prompt. Unprompted corrects are completely darkened, prompted corrects are partially darkened, and errors are not darkened.

Implement, Monitor, and Adjust the Program Based on the Student's Data Patterns

Daily data collection enables a teacher to ensure that the student is progressing adequately and frequently helps the teacher decide when and what changes are needed. By graphing these data on a line graph, the teacher can determine if sufficient progress is being made or if changes in the instructional procedures are necessary. The information in this section, which presents data patterns that may occur when using the delay procedure, is taken in part from Wolery, Bailey, and Sugai (1988). With time delay programs, correct responses are usually graphed—that is, the percentages of unprompted and prompted correct responses are graphed and analyzed. A sample line graph with time delay data is shown in Figure 3.5a; the percentage of unprompted correct responses is shown with triangles, and the percentage of prompted correct responses is shown with circles. This graph, used with chained tasks, includes the data collection sheet shown in Figure 3.4 to help monitor performance on the individual steps of a task analysis (Ault et al., in press; Haring & Kennedy, 1988). The baseline data show that unprompted corrects were at the 0 percent level, indicating that the student was unable to perform the response. When the constant time delay procedure was introduced in the fourth session, unprompted corrects remained low and prompted corrects were high because all trials were presented using a 0-second delay in this session. During the fifth session, when a 4-second delay was implemented, some unprompted corrects occurred because the student was given the opportunity to respond before the prompt. As instruction continued, the percentage of unprompted corrects continued to increase until the student responded on all trials before the prompt and the task was learned. This is a typical data pattern that shows a student progressing quickly and requiring no changes or modifications in the program.

However, some students do require modifications in the constant time delay program. A data pattern indicating that a change in programming is needed is shown in Figure 3.5b. In this data pattern, the student did not respond correctly during baseline, indicating that he did not know the correct response. Following intervention, the student did not make errors, but the percentage of unprompted corrects remained low while the percentage of prompted correct responses stayed the same or increased. This data pattern indicates that the student was waiting for the prompt and was not attempting to respond before the prompt—that is, the student may have learned that "If I wait, the teacher will give me a prompt and I won't have to take a chance on making an error." To encourage students to respond before the prompt, a teacher should differentially reinforce unprompted correct and prompted correct responses after a specified number of sessions (e.g., three consecutive sessions) in which unprompted corrects do not increase. The teacher, when using differential reinforcement, should in some way provide more reinforcement when the student responds correctly before the prompt than when the student responds correctly after the prompt. The student should receive acknowledgment that she is correct after the prompt but should receive more attention for corrects before the prompt. For example, Ms. Claunch is teaching Jeremiah how to identify coins. Following several time delay sessions, Jeremiah seldom responds correctly before the prompt but always responds correctly after the prompt. Ms. Claunch decides that she will differentially reinforce correct

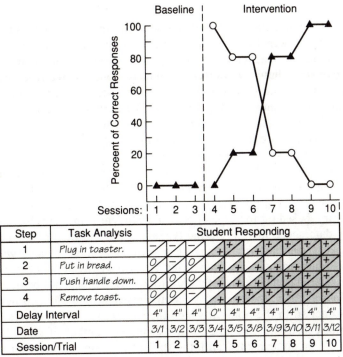

Step	Task Analysis	Student Responding									
1	Plug in toaster.	−	−	−	+		+	+	+	+	+
2	Put in bread.	0	−	0	+	+	+	+	+	+	+
3	Push handle down.	0	0	0	+	+	+	+	+	+	+
4	Remove toast.	0	0	−	+	+	+	+	+	+	+
Delay Interval		4"	4"	4"	0"	4"	4"	4"	4"	4"	4"
Date		3/1	3/2	3/3	3/4	3/5	3/8	3/9	3/10	3/11	3/12
Session/Trial		1	2	3	4	5	6	7	8	9	10

Key: + = correct response, − = incorrect response, 0 = no response

(a)

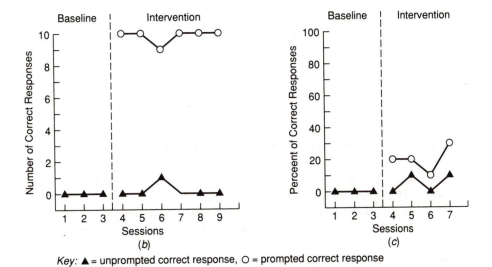

Key: ▲ = unprompted correct response, ○ = prompted correct response

Figure 3.5. The sample data pattern in graph (*a*) indicates a typical data pattern in which no changes in programming are required. Graph (*b*) shows data in which unprompted correct responses are not occurring but errors are low. Graph (*c*) shows data in which an excessive number of errors are occurring.

responses, so she tells Jeremiah that if he knows the answer he should tell her before she tells him the answer. From this point on, each time Jeremiah responds correctly *before* the prompt, his teacher says, "Good, that is a penny," and delivers a preferred small edible or sip of liquid. However, when he responds correctly *after* the prompt, she simply says, "Good, that is a penny," without delivering the edible.

The data pattern shown in Figure 3.5c indicates that the student is not learning because he made an excessive number of errors. By using a line graph and plotting both unprompted and prompted correct responses, a teacher can add the two percentages on any given session or day, then subtract that sum from 100 to obtain the percentage of errors for that session. In addition, the teacher can analyze the data collection forms and calculate the percent of errors. If the data indicate that the student is making 25 percent or more errors of any one type, the teacher needs to make changes in the program (based on the type of error the student is making) by referring back to the daily data sheet, identifying the type of error, and then making appropriate modifications. If the student is making a high percentage of *unprompted errors,* the teacher should (a) use a shorter delay interval or (b) implement wait training procedures. If the student consistently waits for a period of seconds before responding, but not as long as the specified delay interval, the teacher should consider decreasing the prompt interval to the point at which the student is waiting successfully. If the student is not consistently waiting for a reasonable number of seconds, then wait training should be implemented until the student consistently waits for the prompt. If *prompted errors* are occurring, the teacher needs to (a) examine the controlling prompt, since it is in fact not controlling the student's behavior when it is delivered; (b) examine the reinforcers to make sure that they are powerful; or (c) decrease the session length if errors are occurring at the end of the session. Finally, if *no response errors* are occurring, the teacher should (a) examine the controlling prompt to make sure that it does control the student's behavior, (b) change the reinforcer to a more powerful one that will encourage the student to respond, (c) make sure the task is not too difficult, or (d) shorten the session length if errors occur at the end of the session.

SAMPLE CONSTANT TIME DELAY PROGRAM

As noted above, preparing to use constant time delay requires a teacher to consider eight steps. The following example illustrates these steps:

Chrystal is a 13-year-old girl with severe mental retardation. She travels to her home on a daily basis with her special-education teacher, Mr. Randolph, to receive instruction in daily living skills. Chrystal is learning to set the table in her home in one-on-one sessions. She sets the table in her home during the school day and then leaves it set for her family to use during supper that evening. Mr. Randolph developed the task analysis for setting the table that is shown in Table 3.2. Chrystal is able to imitate her teacher's model and follow one-step verbal directions, and Mr. Randolph has identified praise and tokens as reinforcers for Chrystal.

TABLE 3.2. Task Analysis for Setting a Table

1. Remove four plates from cabinet.
2. Place one plate in front of each of four chairs around the table.
3. Remove four napkins from the drawer.
4. Place one napkin to the left of each of the four plates.
5. Remove four forks from the drawer.
6. Place one fork on top of each napkin.
7. Remove four knives from the drawer.
8. Place one knife to the right of each plate.
9. Remove four spoons from the drawer.
10. Place one spoon to the right of each knife.
11. Remove two glasses from the cabinet.
12. Place one glass at the tip of each of two knives.
13. Remove two more glasses from the cabinet.
14. Place one glass at the tip of each of the two other knives.

Identify the Stimulus That Cues the Student to Respond

Since Chrystal sets the table for supper during the school day, Mr. Randolph decides that the natural stimulus of preparing for supper is not possible to use at this time. Therefore, Mr. Randolph decides to use a verbal task direction, "Set the table," as a stimulus to cue Chrystal to respond initially. Once Chrystal meets criterion during the day following this task direction, Chrystal's father will have her set the table for supper during the evening. Mr. Randolph will instruct Chrystal's father to pair the natural stimulus of preparing for supper with the task direction, "Set the table," until Chrystal sets the table without her father telling her to do so.

Identify the Controlling Prompt

Mr. Randolph knows that Chrystal responds correctly to some verbal prompts, model prompts, and physical prompts. He wants to use a controlling prompt that provides the least amount of assistance necessary but still results in Chrystal consistently performing the correct response. Mr. Randolph first decides against verbal prompts because he knows that setting the table would require Chrystal to respond correctly to verbal directions such as "in front of," "to the left of," and "at the tip of," which Chrystal is unable to do. He next considers model prompts but wants to assess her to make sure that she can imitate a model prompt on tasks where objects must be placed in correct positions on a table in arbitrary relation to one another. Mr. Randolph chooses several unrelated objects, places them on the table in relation to one another, and then asks Chrystal to imitate the model. Mr. Randolph finds that Chrystal is able to imitate this type of prompt successfully, so he decides that a model will control Chrystal's response. Mr. Randolph also decides that Chrystal might learn to follow some verbal directions if they are used consistently during instruction, so he chooses a model prompt plus a verbal description of the step as the controlling prompt (e.g., putting plates in front of each chair while simultaneously saying, "Put a plate in front of each chair.").

Determine the Student's Ability to Wait for the Prompt

Since Chrystal will be learning a chained task in a total task format, Mr. Randolph chooses a dish drainer and dishes to assess waiting. Mr. Randolph knows that Chrystal is able to place dishes in a dish drainer, but he wants to assess if she will wait for the prompt from him. Mr. Randolph delivers the task direction, "Put the dishes where they go," and waits 4 seconds. At the end of each 4-second interval, Mr. Randolph provides a model prompt and arbitrarily decides to place a dish in, beside, or under the drainer. During the first two trials of the assessment, Chrystal does not wait for the prompt. Mr. Randolph places Chrystal's hands to her side and says, "Wait, let me show you." On the next ten trials, Chrystal successfully waits for Mr. Randolph to prompt her after each task direction and thus he concludes that Chrystal has the prerequisite skill of waiting.

Identify the Number of 0-Second Delay Trials Needed

Mr. Randolph thinks that this task may be difficult for Chrystal, especially since she will have only one trial a day on setting the table. Therefore, he decides that he will conduct two sessions using 0-second delay trials and will require that Chrystal receive 100 percent unprompted responses for at least one session on all steps of the task analysis before delaying the prompt.

Determine the Length of the Prompt Delay Interval

Because this is a task that needs to be done on a daily basis and could possibly be used in a vocational setting, Mr. Randolph wants Chrystal to be able to set the table in a reasonable amount of time. He observes his son setting the table at home and decides that for each step in the task analysis, Chrystal will be given 4 seconds to initiate the step and 10 seconds to complete the step.

Determine the Consequences for Each Student Response

For each type of correct response, both prompted and unprompted, Mr. Randolph will praise Chrystal. For unprompted errors, Mr. Randolph will say, "Wait, let me show you if you don't know," then physically guide her to complete the step correctly. For prompted errors or no responses, Mr. Randolph will physically guide Chrystal in making the correct response. At the end of the session, if Chrystal has 80 percent or greater correct responses, she will receive a token to exchange for a backup reinforcer.

Select a Data Collection System

For each step in the task analysis, Mr. Randolph will record the five types of responses on the data collection sheet shown in Figure 3.6.

Student ___Chrystal___ Instructor ___Randolph___

Start time ___11:00___ Stop time ___11:15___ Total time ___15'___

Task ___Setting table___

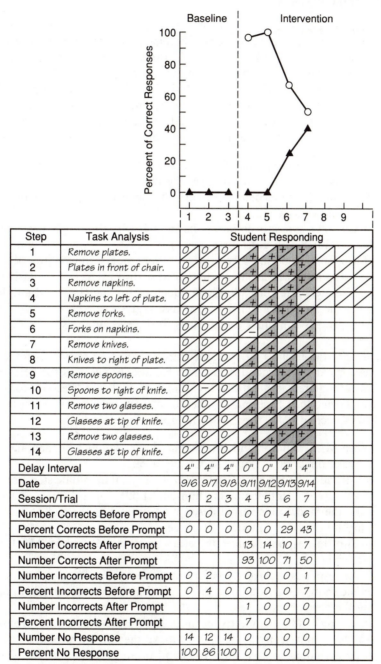

Step	Task Analysis	Student Responding									
		1	2	3	4	5	6	7	8	9	
1	Remove plates.	O	O	O	+	+	+	+			
2	Plates in front of chair.	O	O	O	+	+	+	+			
3	Remove napkins.	O	–	O	+	+	+	+			
4	Napkins to left of plate.	O	O	O	+	+	+	–			
5	Remove forks.	O	O	O	+	+	+	+			
6	Forks on napkins.	O	O	O	–	+	+	+			
7	Remove knives.	O	O	O	+	+	+	+			
8	Knives to right of plate.	O	O	O	+	+	+	+			
9	Remove spoons.	O	O	O	+	+	+	+			
10	Spoons to right of knife.	O	–	O	+	+	+	+			
11	Remove two glasses.	O	O	O	+	+	+	+			
12	Glasses at tip of knife.	O	O	O	+	+	+	+			
13	Remove two glasses.	O	O	O	+	+	+	+			
14	Glasses at tip of knife.	O	O	O	+	+	+	+			
Delay Interval		4"	4"	4"	0"	0"	4"	4"			
Date		9/6	9/7	9/8	9/11	9/12	9/13	9/14			
Session/Trial		1	2	3	4	5	6	7			
Number Corrects Before Prompt		O	O	O	O	O	4	6			
Percent Corrects Before Prompt		O	O	O	O	O	29	43			
Number Corrects After Prompt					13	14	10	7			
Number Corrects After Prompt					93	100	71	50			
Number Incorrects Before Prompt		O	2	O	O	O	O	1			
Percent Incorrects Before Prompt		O	4	O	O	O	O	7			
Number Incorrects After Prompt					1	O	O	O			
Percent Incorrects After Prompt					7	O	O	O			
Number No Response		14	12	14	O	O	O	O			
Percent No Response		100	86	100	O	O	O	O			

Key: ▲ = unprompted correct response, O = prompted correct response

Figure 3.6. A data collection sheet and line graph for sample constant time delay program.

Implement, Monitor, and Adjust the Program Based on the Student's Data Patterns

Mr. Randolph will graph Chrystal's prompted and unprompted correct responses on the line graph shown in Figure 3.6. If errors become evident, Mr.Randolph will analyze the errors and make changes accordingly. He also will analyze the data to determine if errors are occurring on the same steps in the task analysis. If Chrystal consistently makes errors on one step of the task analysis, he will adapt that step by changing the controlling prompt, breaking the task down into smaller steps, decreasing the prompt delay interval, or doing massed trials on the step.

Mr. Randolph conducts the first two sessions using the following procedures:

1. When Mr. Randolph and Chrystal are in her family's kitchen, he provides the task direction, "Chrystal, set the table."
2. Mr. Randolph immediately provides the model for step 1 of the task analysis (0-second delay trial).
3. If Chrystal correctly imitates the model, Mr. Randolph provides praise (e.g., "Good, you got four plates.").
4. If Chrystal responds incorrectly or does not respond after the model, Mr. Randolph physically guides her to perform step 1 of the task analysis.
5. Immediately after providing consequences for step 1, Mr. Randolph provides the model for step 2 of the task analysis.
6. This process continues for all steps in the task analysis.

When Chrystal displays 100 percent correct prompted responses for two consecutive sessions at the 0-second delay, Mr. Randolph increases the delay interval to 4 seconds. For all remaining trials, Mr. Randolph will wait 4 seconds for Chrystal to initiate a step and then 10 seconds for her to complete each step in the task analysis. He conducts 4-second delay sessions in the following way:

1. When Mr. Randolph and Chrystal are in her family's kitchen, he provides the task direction, "Chrystal, set the table."
2. Mr. Randolph then waits 4 seconds for Chrystal to initiate step 1 of the task analysis (i.e., silently counts to himself, "1,001; 1,002; 1,003; . . .") and provides the model plus verbal description prompt at the end of 4 seconds if Chrystal does not initiate a response.
3. If Chrystal responds correctly before or after the prompt, Mr. Randolph praises her.
4. If she responds incorrectly before the prompt, Mr. Randolph says, "Wait, let me show you if you don't know," and physically guides her in performing the correct response.
5. If she responds incorrectly or does not respond after the prompt, Mr. Randolph physically guides her to make the correct response.
6. After providing consequences for step 1 of the task analysis, Mr. Randolph waits 4 seconds for Chrystal to respond on step 2 of the task analysis and provides a prompt at the end of 4 seconds if she does not respond. The completion of step 1 signals Chrystal to start step 2.
7. This process continues for all steps in the task analysis.

Mr. Randolph continues to deliver 4-second delay trials until Chrystal consistently responds with 100 percent unprompted correct responses (i.e., independently sets the table).

SUMMARY COMMENTS

- The constant time delay procedure is an instructional strategy that fades a controlling prompt by inserting a fixed amount of time between the task direction and the prompt.
- Initial trials of the procedure are conducted using a 0-second prompt delay interval.
- Following 0-second delay trials, a fixed amount of time is inserted between the task direction and the controlling prompt; all remaining trials are conducted using this delay interval.
- Students with a wide range of disabilities have been taught chained and discrete tasks using the constant time delay procedure—including students with developmental disabilities; learning disabilities; autism; and moderate, severe, and profound mental retardation.
- Most constant time delay research has been conducted with elementary- and secondary-aged students, but preschoolers and adults have been taught as well.
- The constant time delay and the progressive time delay procedures are essentially equal in terms of their efficiency, with some individual preferences across students. When compared to the system of least prompts procedure, constant time delay has been found to be more efficient on measures such as sessions, errors, and direct instructional time to criterion.
- Five types of student responses are possible: unprompted corrects, prompted corrects, unprompted errors, prompted errors, and no response errors.
- The steps for implementing a constant time delay program are (a) identify the stimulus that cues the student to respond; (b) identify a controlling prompt; (c) assess the student's ability to wait for the prompt; (d) identify the number of 0-second delay trials; (e) identify the length of the prompt delay interval; (f) determine the consequences based on student responding; (g) select a data collection system; and (h) implement, monitor, and adjust the program based on data patterns.

This chapter described the constant time delay procedure, reviewed the research, and illustrated the steps used in designing an instructional program. The next chapter discusses the progressive time delay procedure. This procedure is very similar to the constant time delay procedure—the major difference between the two is the increment of time used in delaying the prompt.

EXERCISES

1. Design a data collection sheet for assessing wait training.
2. Given student participation in a constant time delay program whose data for several days show a high level of prompted correct responses and low errors but

no unprompted correct responses, explain how you would attempt to increase correct unprompted responding.

3. Choose one of the sample data sheets and fill it out properly for a hypothetical student and skill.
4. If the student you used for question 3 has a high percentage of prompted incorrect responses, explain what modifications you would make in the program and why.
5. Practice using this procedure with a friend: Choose ten stimuli that your friend does not know (e.g., foreign words, Greek letters, and nonsense words) and teach them using the constant time delay procedure.

REFERENCES

Ault, M. J., Gast, D. L., & Wolery, M. (1988). Comparison of progressive and constant time-delay procedures in teaching community-sign word reading. *American Journal of Mental Retardation, 93,* 44–56.

Ault, M. J., Gast, D. L., Wolery, M., & Doyle, P. M. (in press). A data collection and graphing method for use in teaching chained tasks with the constant time delay procedure. *Teaching Exceptional Children.*

Ault, M. J., Wolery, M., Doyle, P. M., & Gast, D. L. (1989). Review of comparative studies in the instruction of students with moderate and severe handicaps. *Exceptional Children, 55,* 346–356.

Ault, M. J., Wolery, M., Gast, D. L., Doyle, P. M., & Eizenstat, V. (1988). Comparison of response prompting procedures in teaching numeral identification to autistic subjects. *Journal of Autism and Developmental Disorders, 18,* 627–636.

Billingsley, F. F., & Romer, L. T. (1983). Response prompting and the transfer of stimulus control: Methods, research, and a conceptual framework. *Journal of the Association for the Severely Handicapped, 8,* 3–12.

Browder, D. M., Morris, W. W., & Snell, M. E. (1981). Using time delay to teach manual signs to a severely retarded student. *Education and Training of the Mentally Retarded, 16,* 252–258.

Doyle, P. M., Wolery, M., Gast, D. L., Ault, M. J., & Wiley, K. (1990). Comparison of constant time delay and the system of least prompts in teaching preschoolers with developmental delays. *Research in Developmental Disabilities, 11,* 1–22.

Etzel, B. C., & LeBlanc, J. M. (1979). The simplest treatment alternative: Appropriate instructional control and errorless learning procedures for the difficult-to-teach child. *Journal of Autism and Developmental Disorders, 9,* 361–382.

Gast, D. L., Ault, M. J., Wolery, M., Doyle, P. M., & Belanger, S. (1988). Comparison of constant time delay and the system of least prompts in teaching sight word reading to students with moderate retardation. *Education and Training in Mental Retardation, 23,* 117–128.

Gast, D. L., Doyle, P. M., Wolery, M., Ault, M.J ., & Baklarz, J. L. (1991). Acquisition of incidental information during small group instruction. *Education and Treatment of Children, 14,* 1–18.

Handen, B. L., & Zane, T. (1987). Delayed prompting: A review of procedural variations and results. *Research in Developmental Disabilities, 8,* 307–330.

Haring, T. G., & Kennedy, C. H. (1988). Units of task-analytic research. *Journal of Applied Behavior Analysis, 21,* 207–215.

Johnson, C. M. (1977). Errorless learning in a multihandicapped adolescent. *Education and Treatment of Children, 1,* 25–33.

Kleinert, H. L., & Gast, D. L. (1982). Teaching a multiply handicapped adult manual signs using a constant time delay procedure. *Journal of the Association for the Severely Handicapped, 6,* 25–32.

McDonnell, J. (1987). The effects of time delay and increasing prompt hierarchy strategies on the acquisition of purchasing skills by students with severe handicaps. *Journal of the Association for Persons with Severe Handicaps, 12,* 227–236.

McDonnell, J., & Ferguson, B. (1989). A comparison of time delay and decreasing prompt hierarchy strategies in teaching banking skills to students with moderate handicaps. *Journal of Applied Behavior Analysis, 22,* 85–91.

McIlvane, W. J., Withstandley, J. K., & Stoddard, L. T. (1984). Positive and negative stimulus relations in severely retarded individuals' conditional discrimination. *Analysis and Intervention in Developmental Disabilities, 4,* 235–251.

Miller, U. C., & Test, D. W. (1989). A comparison of constant time delay and most-to-least prompting in teaching laundry skills to students with moderate retardation. *Education and Training in Mental Retardation, 24,* 363–370.

Schoen, S. F. (1986). Assistance procedures to facilitate the transfer of stimulus control: Review and analysis. *Education and Training of the Mentally Retarded, 21,* 62–74.

Schoen, S. F., & Sivil, E. O. (1989). A comparison of procedures in teaching self-help skills: Increasing assistance, time delay, and observational learning. *Journal of Autism and Developmental Disorders, 19,* 57–72.

Schuster, J. W., Gast, D. L., Wolery, M., & Guiltinan, S. (1988). The effectiveness of a constant time-delay procedure to teach chained responses to adolescents with mental retardation. *Journal of Applied Behavior Analysis, 21,* 169–178.

Snell, M. E., & Gast, D. L. (1981). Applying delay procedure to the instruction of the severely handicapped. *Journal of the Association for the Severely Handicapped, 6,* 3–14.

Stevens, K., & Schuster, J. W. (1987). Effects of a constant time delay procedure on the written spelling performance of a learning disabled student. *Learning Disability Quarterly, 10,* 9–16.

Tawney, J. W., & Gast, D. L. (1984). *Single subject research in special education.* Columbus, OH: Charles Merrill.

Touchette, P. E., & Howard, J. S. (1984). Errorless learning: Reinforcement contingencies and stimulus control transfer in delayed prompting. *Journal of Applied Behavior Analysis, 17,* 175–188.

Wolery, M., Ault, M. J., Gast, D. L., Doyle, P. M., & Griffen, A. K. (1991). Teaching chained tasks in dyads: Acquisition of target and observational behaviors. *Journal of Special Education, 25,* 198–220.

Wolery, M., Bailey, D. B., Jr., & Sugai, G. M. (1988). *Effective teaching: Principles and procedures of applied behavior analysis with exceptional students.* Boston: Allyn & Bacon.

CHAPTER 4

Progressive Time Delay Procedure

Chapter Overview

Describing the Progressive Time Delay Procedure

Effects of Using the Progressive Time Delay Procedure

Steps for Using the Progressive Time Delay Procedure

Sample Progressive Time Delay Program

Summary Comments

Exercises

References

Key Terms

Progressive Time Delay

Constant Time Delay

Task Direction

Controlling Prompt

Prompt Delay Interval

Zero-Second Delay

Progressive Delay Trials

Unprompted Corrects

Prompted Corrects

Unprompted Errors

Prompted Errors

No Response Errors

Discrete Tasks

Chained Tasks

Parsimonious

Naturally Occurring Event

Near Errorless

Wait Training

Maximum Prompt Delay Interval

Questions to Be Answered by This Chapter

1. What is the primary difference between the progressive time delay procedure and the constant time delay procedure?
2. What populations have been taught using this procedure?

3. What were the results when progressive time delay was compared to other instructional strategies?

4. What three decisions should a teacher make when determining the length of the prompt delay interval?

5. How can a teacher manipulate the delay interval in progressive time delay?

6. How are the progressive and constant time delay procedures similar and different concerning the consequences to be delivered for responding?

The **progressive time delay** procedure is an instructional strategy that is similar to the **constant time delay** procedure described in the preceding chapter. Progressive time delay was developed before constant time delay and has been used extensively to teach students who have moderate and severe handicaps. In this chapter, progressive time delay is described, the results from the research on progressive time delay are summarized, and the steps for implementing a program using the procedure are listed and illustrated.

DESCRIBING THE PROGRESSIVE TIME DELAY PROCEDURE

Like constant time delay, progressive time delay is characterized by the delivery of a prompt followed by the fading of the prompt by systematically increasing the time between the stimulus that cues the student to perform a task (e.g., **task direction**) and the **controlling prompt** (i.e., the prompt that ensures the student will perform the correct response) (Snell & Gast, 1981). Unlike with constant delay, the time between the task direction and the controlling prompt (called the **prompt delay interval**) gradually increases over trials or blocks of trials rather than remaining constant across trials (Touchette, 1971). The initial trials of the progressive time delay procedure are conducted using a **zero-second delay** (0-second) exactly as if a constant time delay procedure were being used; that is, the task direction is followed immediately by the controlling prompt. For example, Mrs. Blankenship is teaching Junior to identify objects using manual signs. She holds up an object; asks, "Junior, what is this?"; and immediately models the correct manual sign. Following the 0-second trials, however, the difference between progressive and constant time delay becomes evident. After the specified number of 0-second delay trials have been delivered, the time between the task direction and the prompt is increased to a certain prompt delay interval. Following a specified number of trials at this delay interval, the time between the task direction and the prompt is increased again. This sequence continues until the student meets criterion or until a specified prompt delay interval is reached. These trials are known as **progressive delay trials.** For example, after Mrs. Blankenship has delivered 5 trials at the 0-second delay, she then holds up an object; delivers the task direction, "Junior, what is this?"; and waits 1-second before she models the manual sign. Following five trials at the 1-second delay, she holds up an object; asks, "Junior, what is this?"; and waits 2 seconds before modeling the manual sign. Following five trials at the 2-second delay, she delivers the task direction and waits 3 seconds before providing the prompt. Mrs. Blankenship continues to increase the delay interval progressively in 1-second increments until Junior meets criterion.

As noted with constant delay, five types of student responses are recorded using the progressive time delay procedure: **unprompted corrects** occur when the student responds correctly before the prompt, **prompted corrects** occur when the student responds correctly after the prompt, **unprompted errors** occur when the student responds incorrectly before the prompt, **prompted errors** occur when the student responds incorrectly after the prompt, and **no response errors** occur when the student does not respond at all. A flow chart for using the progressive time delay procedure is shown in Figure 4.1.

EFFECTS OF USING THE PROGRESSIVE TIME DELAY PROCEDURE

Students and Behaviors Taught

The progressive time delay procedure—studied more extensively than constant time delay—has been used successfully with students with profound mental retardation (Striefel, Bryan, & Aikins, 1974; Smeets & Striefel, 1980), severe mental retardation (McDonagh, McIlvane, & Stoddard, 1984; Touchette, 1971), moderate mental retardation (Braam & Poling, 1983; Browder et al., 1984), mild mental retardation (Walls et al., 1984), autism (Wolery et al., 1988), multiple disabilities (Goetz, Gee, & Sailor, 1983), and developmental disabilities (Luciano, 1986). The ages of participants in progressive time delay investigations have ranged widely. A few investigations have used preschool participants (Aeschleman & Higgins, 1982; Charlop, Schreibman, & Thibodeau, 1985), but more have been conducted with elementary-aged (Barrera & Sulzer-Azaroff, 1983), secondary-aged (Bennett et al., 1986), and adult participants (Zane et al., 1984). Most progressive time delay investigations have included elementary- and secondary-aged students.

More **discrete tasks** (i.e., tasks that involve one response) than **chained tasks** (i.e., tasks that involve several responses) have been taught with the progressive time delay procedure. These discrete tasks include identifying objects (Barrera & Sulzer-Azaroff, 1983; Godby, Gast, & Wolery, 1987), identifying pictures (Barrera & Sulzer-Azaroff, 1983; Wolery et al., 1988), reading words (Ault, Gast, & Wolery, 1988; Browder et al., 1984), signing manually (Bennett et al., 1986; McIlvane et al., 1984), identifying symbols (Touchette, 1971; Zane et al., 1984), following instructions (Striefel et al., 1974; Smeets & Striefel, 1980), and localizing toward sound (Goetz et al., 1983). Chained tasks that have been taught include assembling apparatus (Walls, Haught, & Dowler, 1982; Walls et al., 1984), making beds (Snell, 1982), and using vending machines (Browder, Snell, & Wildonger, 1988).

Results of Using Progressive Time Delay

The progressive time delay procedure has been shown to be effective in teaching skills to students with various disabilities. Few chained tasks have been taught using progressive time delay, but of those that have, students have successfully learned them. The majority of investigations reporting error rates during instructional conditions indicated that students learned skills with mean error rates of 10 percent or less to criterion (Snell, 1982; Touchette & Howard, 1984). However, a few studies reported higher error rates, with individual subject's data including 28 percent errors (Striefel et al., 1974) and 38 percent errors (Browder et al., 1988).

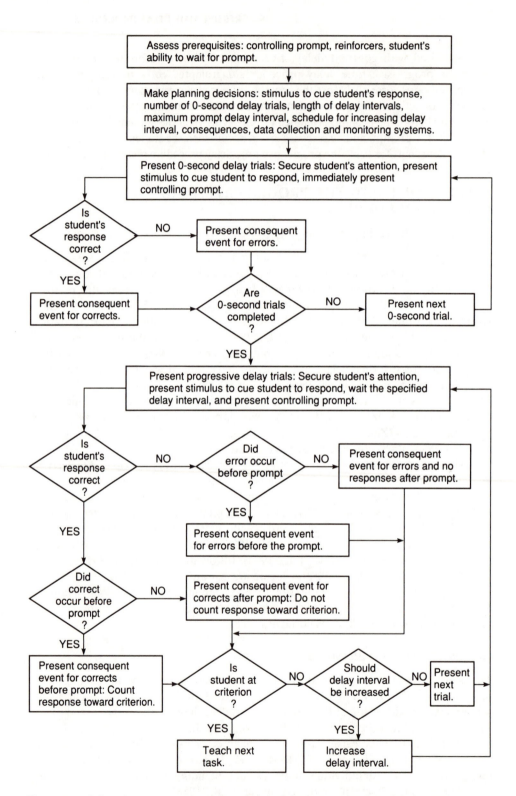

Figure 4.1. A flow chart representing the sequence of the progressive time delay procedure.

Some comparisons between progressive time delay and other instructional strategies have been made (Ault et al., 1989; Billingsley & Romer, 1983; Schoen, 1986). In terms of effectiveness, a stimulus-fading procedure was found to be more effective than progressive time delay when teaching concepts to developmentally delayed preschoolers (Aeschleman & Higgins, 1982). McGee and McCoy (1981) found mixed results when they compared progressive time delay to stimulus fading. The subject's history with either stimulus fading or time delay appeared to increase the effectiveness of each procedure, but they also found that progressive time delay was more effective than error correction. In terms of efficiency, when progressive time delay was compared to the system of least prompts, progressive time delay was found to be more efficient on measures such as sessions, errors, and minutes of instructional time to criterion in teaching manual signs (Bennett et al. 1986) and identifying receptive objects (Godby et al., 1987). In addition, when progressive time delay was compared to error correction, it was found that fewer errors resulted when the progressive time delay procedure was used (Aeschleman & Higgins, 1982; Walls et al., 1984). Progressive time delay also has been compared to the constant delay procedure in teaching word reading to students with moderate retardation (Ault et al., 1988). Results indicated that the two procedures were essentially equal on the efficiency measures of sessions, errors, and minutes of time to criterion.

Recommendations for Practice

The progressive time delay procedure has been shown to be an effective and efficient procedure in teaching different tasks to a variety of students. When using the procedure in the classroom, a teacher should expect most students to learn quickly, with few errors. Much of the research with the procedure has been conducted with discrete tasks in one-on-one instructional arrangements; a teacher may want to use the procedure in this way when becoming familiar with it. It has also been shown to be effective, however, in teaching chained tasks. The progressive time delay procedure is **parsimonious** because only one prompt needs to be identified and delivered. It is not as parsimonious as the constant delay procedure, however, since the delay interval must be gradually increased over trials or blocks of trials; the prompt delay interval is not increased to a fixed interval. Although research has not compared the progressive to the constant delay procedure using students with a variety of disabilities and ages, it would be logical to assume that students with more severe disabilities would be more successful with progressive time delay because it allows for a more gradual fading of prompts. After students have a history with the procedure and have learned appropriate waiting skills, constant time delay may be as efficient as progressive time delay.

STEPS FOR USING THE PROGRESSIVE TIME DELAY PROCEDURE

This section describes the nine steps involved in an effective progressive time delay program:

- Identify the stimulus that cues the student to respond.
- Identify the controlling prompt.

- Determine the student's ability to wait for the prompt.
- Identify the number of 0-second delay trials needed.
- Determine the length of the prompt delay interval.
- Determine the schedule for increasing the prompt delay interval.
- Determine the consequences for each student response.
- Select a data collection system.
- Implement, monitor, and adjust the program based on the student's data patterns.

Most of these steps are similar or identical to those used in constant time delay. All of these redundant steps will be described here, but in less detail than in the preceding chapter. Refer to the constant time delay chapter for a more thorough description of these. One step, however, is exclusive to the progressive time delay procedure, and it is discussed in detail.

Identify the Stimulus That Cues the Student to Respond

As in the constant time delay procedure, the first step in developing a time delay program is for the teacher to identify the stimulus that will cue the student that it is time to respond. This stimulus may be a task direction, the presentation of a stimulus not involving a question or command, a combination of the stimulus and a task direction, or a **naturally occurring event** (i.e., an event in the environment that naturally cues the student to perform a behavior).

Identify the Controlling Prompt

After determining what stimulus will be used to cue the student's response, the teacher needs to identify the controlling prompt. Since only one prompt is necessary with the progressive time delay procedure, the teacher must ensure that when this prompt is delivered, the student can make a correct response. The identified prompt should be one that uses the least amount of assistance necessary to control the student's response.

Determine the Student's Ability to Wait for the Prompt

As in constant time delay, a prerequisite skill for a student who will be learning with the progressive time delay procedure is the ability to wait a specified number of seconds for a prompt. Because both prompted and unprompted responses are considered correct, the procedure is **near errorless** when a student has this skill. The student learns that if she knows the answer, she can respond, but if she does not know it, she can wait until her teacher provides the prompt. Before instructing, a teacher must assess the student's ability to wait using the same type of task that he will teach during instruction. Although initial trials of the progressive time delay procedure require the student to wait only a short amount of time, the teacher should assess the student on her ability to wait the prompt delay interval that will be used during the final training sessions. For example, Mr. Magee is teaching Julia to point to coins when he names them. He begins with 0-second trials and increases the prompt delay interval in 1-second intervals after every 10 trials, until the prompt delay interval reaches

8 seconds. At this point, he continues to use an 8-second delay and does not increase the delay interval further. Therefore, when he assesses Julia on her ability to wait for a prompt, he ensures that she is able to wait for 8 seconds. Mr. Magee can help prevent errors by ensuring that Julia can successfully wait the maximum prompt delay interval that he will use during instruction. During the assessment procedure, Mr. Magee chooses an unknown or nonsense discrete task that requires Julia to point to the correct answer. He presents a task direction and then waits 8 seconds before giving a prompt to assess her ability to wait for 8 seconds. If he finds that Julia is not able to wait for the specified number of seconds, then he should implement **wait training** until Julia learns to wait the appropriate number of seconds. Wait training procedures for progressive time delay are conducted exactly as those described in the constant time delay chapter, and in fact, a progressive delay is used to teach a waiting response.

Identify the Number of 0-Second Delay Trials Needed

After the teacher is sure that a student is able to wait a specified number of seconds, he should determine the number of trials that he will deliver using a 0-second delay. The number of 0-second trials that have been delivered have ranged from 1 for each step of a task analysis (Walls et al., 1982) to 10 per stimulus taught (Wolery et al., 1988). With young students, students with severe disabilities, and difficult tasks, more 0-second trials may need to be used. As with constant time delay, the decision is really an arbitrary one, but the teacher needs to monitor the student's responding during intervention to determine if an appropriate number of 0-second trials are being delivered.

Determine the Length of the Prompt Delay Interval

When using the progressive time delay procedure, a teacher needs to make at least three decisions concerning the prompt delay interval. First, he must identify the time increments that he will use to delay the prompt gradually. Usually the time increments that are inserted between the task direction and the controlling prompt are of a small duration, since this allows for the gradual delay of the prompt. Time increments that have been used to delay the prompt in progressive time delay investigations have ranged from .5 seconds (Touchette, 1971) to 5 seconds (Walls et al., 1982). Walls et al. (1982) compared increasing the prompt delay interval in increments of 1, 3, and 5 seconds. Their results indicated that the 1-second increments produced fewer errors, required the shortest training time, and had the earliest acquisition of the three delay intervals. Therefore, when using progressive time delay in the classroom, a teacher should choose small increments of time to delay the prompt.

Second, the teacher must decide if the time used to delay the prompt will progressively increase in equal or unequal increments. Some researchers have increased the delay interval by inserting equal intervals of time between the task direction and the prompt (Bennett et al., 1986; Striefel et al., 1974; Zane et al., 1974). For example, each time the prompt was delayed, Striefel et al. (1974) inserted 1 second, so that the delay intervals used were 0, 1, 2, 3, 4 seconds and so on. Other researchers have delayed the prompt by inserting unequal increments of time between the task direction and the prompt each time the prompt was scheduled to be delayed (Goetz et al., 1983; Snell, 1982; Striefel et al., 1974). For example, Goetz et al. (1983) first inserted a 1-second increment of time, then a 2-second increment, and then 1-second increments thereafter; the delay schedule was 0, 1, 3, 4, 5, 6 seconds and so on. No research has compared inserting equal or varying increments of time in the prompt delay interval; however, equal time increments are probably the most parsimonious since the teacher has to remember only one increment of time that she will use to delay the prompt.

Third, the teacher must decide at what point in instruction he will no longer increase the delay. It is possible with the progressive time delay procedure that if the student does not meet criterion, the prompt delay interval could become quite long since the interval is always gradually increasing. Therefore, some teachers decide that when the delay interval reaches a certain number of seconds, it should not increase anymore. This **maximum prompt delay interval** should allow a reasonable amount of time for the student to respond, considering the task and student to be taught. When the student reaches this delay interval during instruction, all subsequent sessions would be conducted using this delay interval, which would no longer increase. Braam and Poling (1983) set a 2-second maximum delay interval and Browder et al. (1984) had an 8-second upper limit; McDonagh et al. (1984) and Touchette (1971) did not have a maximum delay interval. When considering the prompt delay intervals, the teacher needs to choose intervals that can be accurately timed and easily remembered.

Determine the Schedule for Increasing Prompt Delay Interval

Because the prompt is systematically and progressively delayed, the teacher should determine at what times during instruction the prompt will be delayed. Several schedules of increasing the prompt delay can be considered:

- Increase the delay interval each session of instruction (Ault et al., 1988; Browder et al., 1984; Godby et al., 1987).
- Increase the delay interval following a certain number of trials (Snell, 1982; Touchette & Howard, 1980).
- Increase the delay interval following a certain number of trials during which correct responses occurred (Braam & Poling, 1983; Charlop et al., 1985; Walls et al., 1984).

For example, Browder et al. (1984) increased the prompt delay interval by 2 seconds each session of instruction, Snell (1982) increased the delay interval by 1 or 2 seconds after four consecutive trials, and Charlop et al. (1985) increased the delay interval by 2 seconds after three consecutive correct responses. No research has compared the different ways to schedule the delay intervals, so the schedule to be used is an arbitrary decision. When a teacher is just beginning to teach with this procedure, increasing the delay interval every session is probably the easiest way for him to begin.

Determine the Consequences for Each Student Response

As in constant time delay, the teacher plans prior to instruction what his response will be when a student makes any of the following five possible responses.

Responding to Correct Responses. In order to keep errors low and the procedure simple to implement, the teacher should reinforce both prompted and unprompted correct responses in the same way. Again, unprompted corrects are the only responses that count toward criterion, since they represent independent responding. As with all procedures, reinforcers should be identified individually for each student, and those that occur naturally in the student's environment should be used whenever possible. In many progressive time delay studies, the consequence for a correct response also includes lengthening the prompt delay interval. Charlop et al. (1985) increased the delay interval by 2 seconds after three consecutive correct responses, and Smeets and Striefel (1976) increased the delay interval by 1 second after each correct response. Obviously, this method of increasing the delay interval adds to the complexity of the procedure, whereas increasing the delay interval after each session reduces the complexity.

Responding to Incorrect Responses. Consequences that have been used following incorrect responses in progressive time delay investigations include a verbal reprimand (e.g., "No.") plus removing the stimulus (Charlop et al., 1985); a model (Walls et al., 1982); a verbal reprimand, model, and full physical guidance (Smeets & Striefel, 1976; Snell, 1982); a short in-seat timeout (e.g., looking away from the student for 10 seconds) (Barrera & Sulzer-Azaroff, 1983; Luciano, 1986; Snell, 1982; Zane et al., 1984); and a reminder to wait (e.g., "Wait for me to tell you if you don't know.") (Ault et al., 1988). In addition to these consequences, some researchers manipulated the length of the prompt delay interval when an error occurred by (a) returning to 0-second delay trials and progressively increasing the delay again (Browder et al., 1988); (b) presenting one 0-second delay trial and then returning to the prompt delay interval used before the error (Striefel et al., 1974); and (c) reducing the delay interval to what was used immediately prior to the error (Smeets & Striefel, 1980; Touchette, 1984). Ault, Gast, and Wolery (1988) and Snell (1982) continued at the same delay interval following an error. Since these manipulations of the delay interval following error responses have not been investigated and also increase the complexity of the procedure, a teacher may not want to manipulate the delay interval following an error when learning to use the procedure.

Select a Data Collection System

As with other instructional procedures, it is important for the teacher to monitor performance on a daily basis when using a progressive time delay procedure. All of the data sheets included in the constant time delay chapter can be used with progressive time delay programs. As with constant time delay, all five responses should be included on the data collection sheet. Another sample data sheet designed to be used exclusively with the progressive time delay procedure when the delay interval is manipulated following correct and/or incorrect responses is included in Figure 4.2. For example, this data sheet would be appropriate for Mr. Dubois in teaching Jackie to identify two different food items. Mr. Dubois has designed his program so that for each item, following two consecutive correct responses, he increases the delay interval by 1 second. In addition, for each item, following two consecutive incorrect

Student _____Jackie_____ Instructor _____DuBois_____ Date __5/5__ Session __1__

Start time ___1:20___   Stop time ___1:27___   Total time ___7'___

Task _____Identifying food items_____

Trial/ Step	Stimulus One	Delay	Student Responding		Stimulus Two	Delay	Student Responding	
			Before	After			Before	After
1	egg	0"		+				
2					banana	0"		+
3					banana	0"		+
4	egg	0"		+				
5	egg	1"		−				
6					banana	1"		+
7	egg	1"		−				
8					banana	1"		+
9	egg	0"		+				
10					banana	2"	+	
Number/Percent Corrects			0/0	3/60	N/% Corrects		1/20	4/80
Number/Percent Incorrects			1/20	1/20	N/% Incorrects		0/0	0/0
Number/Percent No Response			XXXXXX	0/0	N/% No Response		XXXXXX	0/0
Total Number/Percent Corrects for Both Stimuli							1/10	7/70
Total Number/Percent Incorrects for Both Stimuli							1/10	1/10
Total Number/Percent No Response for Both Stimuli							XXXXXX	0/0

Key: + = correct, − = incorrect, 0 = no response

Figure 4.2. This data collection sheet is designed to be used with progressive time delay programs that manipulate the delay interval for each stimulus following correct responses, incorrect responses, or both.

responses, he decreases the delay interval by 1 second. Mr. Dubois decides to present five trials on each food item and randomly intermix the presentation of each food across ten trials. He decides that if he uses his typical time delay data sheet, he may become confused—during instruction he will have to locate the last trials he delivered on each item and check to see if two correct or incorrect responses occurred consecutively before he can determine the next delay interval. Therefore, he decides to use the data sheet shown in Figure 4.2. He can still randomly intermix the two food items across ten trials, but by placing one stimulus on one side of the data sheet and the other stimulus on the other side, he can quickly determine the responses Jackie had for each stimulus and record the delay interval used.

Implement, Monitor, and Adjust the Program Based on the Student's Data Patterns

Graphing correct unprompted and prompted responses is also an essential part of the progressive time delay procedure. All of the data patterns presented in the constant time delay chapter may also occur during the progressive time delay procedure, and

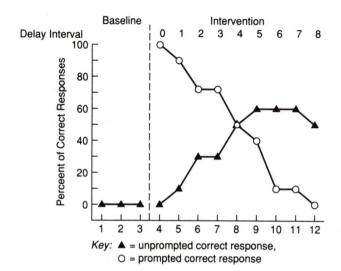

Figure 4.3. This graph shows a sample data pattern for a progressive time delay program. The delay interval used for each session is indicated at the top of the graph. The data show adequate progress being made until the student receives a session using a 6-second delay and greater, indicating that excessive errors are being made and an adjustment is necessary.

the same types of data-based decision rules are used. Because several prompt delay intervals are used in progressive time delay, the teacher must specify the delay interval on the graph so that he can make appropriate adjustments if the student does not progress as expected. For example, Mrs. Epstein is teaching her daughter, Joy, to respond to the naturally occurring event of getting out of bed each morning by going immediately into the bathroom. The sample graph presented in Figure 4.3 shows a data pattern for Joy's progressive time delay program, in which Mrs. Epstein recorded the delay interval she used during each session at the top of the graph. Joy's data indicate that she made adequate progress until the tenth session, when she made an excessive number of errors. Mrs. Epstein checks the data collection sheet and finds that the majority of the errors Joy makes are unprompted incorrect responses. By examining this data pattern and because the delay intervals were inserted directly on the graph, Mrs. Epstein can easily see that Joy began making unprompted incorrect responses when the delay interval reached 6 seconds or more. She can then make adjustments by decreasing the delay interval to the point where Joy was responding correctly and hold the delay interval at that point.

SAMPLE PROGRESSIVE TIME DELAY PROGRAM

As noted above, there are nine steps a teacher needs to follow to implement a progressive time delay program. The following example illustrates these steps:

Ramon is a 16-year-old with moderate mental retardation. His teacher, Ms. Coovert, is working with him on securing employment in the community. She wants to teach him how to fill out an application form appropriately, so she decides to teach Ramon to read words found on application forms. Ramon is already able to read some community-sign and grocery words, and he can imitate a verbal model.

Ms. Coovert has identified praise and money as reinforcers for Ramon. She decides to teach Ramon two words at a time and begins with the words *name* and *address.*

Identify the Stimulus That Cues the Student to Respond

Since Ms. Coovert wants Ramon to be able to read the words when he sees them on job applications, she will use a variety of different job applications as stimuli. She also knows that when Ramon is filling out job applications, the natural stimulus will be only the presence of the form. Therefore, she decides that placing a job application in front of Ramon and pointing to the word that she wants him to read is the stimulus that will cue him to respond.

Identify the Controlling Prompt

Ms. Coovert knows that Ramon can imitate words, so she chooses a verbal model as the controlling prompt. For an expressive word reading task, this is the prompt that provides the least amount of assistance but also controls correct responses.

Determine the Student's Ability to Wait for the Prompt

Because Ramon will be learning an expressive word reading task, Ms. Coovert assesses a wait response by using a task that requires Ramon to respond as he will need to when the program is implemented. She also knows that Ramon may have to wait for at least 6 seconds during his instructional program, so she wants to assess whether he can wait 6 seconds for a prompt. To assess waiting, Ms. Coovert presents nonsense words for Ramon to read. She uses the same stimulus to cue Ramon to respond that she will use during instruction; that is, she places in front of Ramon a card that contains a nonsense word and points to it, then waits 6 seconds and provides a verbal model prompt by saying any arbitrary real or nonsense word. On the first trial, Ramon responds incorrectly during the 6-second delay interval. Ms. Coovert says, "Wrong, this word is (arbitrary word). Wait for me to tell you." After several trials, Ramon continues to respond incorrectly before the prompt. Ms. Coovert encourages Ramon to wait by placing her hand near his mouth and telling him to wait. Again, after several trials, this procedure is not successful in getting Ramon to wait for the prompt; Ms. Coovert decides that she will need to teach a waiting response before she begins the progressive time delay program.

Wait Training.   To teach Ramon to wait, Ms. Coovert uses the same materials (nonsense words), the same stimulus to cue Ramon to respond (pointing to the word), and the same expressive response requirement that she used during the wait assessment (imitation of a verbal model) because these closely approximate what she will use during training. Ms. Coovert first reminds Ramon, using gestures and verbal directions, that he should wait for her to tell him before he responds. She then begins the session using a 0-second delay interval. When Ramon responds correctly (imitates her verbal model) after the prompt for three consecutive trials, she increases the delay interval by 1 second. When Ramon responds correctly after the prompt for three consecutive trials at the 1-second delay, she increases the delay interval by 1 second again, continuing this sequence until Ramon responds correctly at the 6-second delay interval for ten consecutive trials. Any time Ramon correctly waits for the prompt, Ms. Coovert praises him for saying the word *after* her and provides him with a penny. Any time Ramon responds incorrectly before the prompt, Ms. Coovert says, "Wrong. Wait for me to tell you," and decreases the delay interval on the next trial by 1 second. Thus, Ramon successfully learns to wait for 6 seconds for a prompt, and Ms. Coovert continues to design the program.

Identify the Number of 0-Second Delay Trials Needed

Ms. Coovert knows that Ramon is able to attend to a task for at least 15–20 minutes, so she decides to present 10 trials on each word, for a total of 20 trials each session. Thinking that 10 trials on each word will be an adequate number at the 0-second delay, she decides to conduct one session at the 0-second delay.

Determine the Length of the Prompt Delay Interval

Ms. Coovert wants to increase the delay interval in small increments, especially since she had to teach Ramon a correct waiting response. She decides to increase the delay interval in 1-second increments, particularly because it is easy for her to remember and she can consistently count in 1-second increments. In addition, she decides that 6 seconds is an adequate period of time for Ramon to be able to read the word correctly, so she decides that when the delay interval reaches 6 seconds, she will not increase it further.

Determine the Schedule for Increasing the Prompt Delay Interval

Because this is the first time that Ms. Coovert has used the progressive time delay procedure and the paraprofessional working in the classroom also will be implementing the procedure, she decides to increase the delay interval each session, lessening the complexity of implementation.

Determine the Consequences for Each Student Response

For all correct responses, both prompted and unprompted, Ms. Coovert will praise Ramon and deliver one penny. For unprompted incorrect responses, Ms. Coovert will say, "Wrong, this is (correct word). If you don't know, wait and let me tell you." For prompted errors or no responces, Ms. Coovert will repeat the model by saying, "Ramon, say (correct word)." At the end of each session, Ramon will deposit his earned money in his classroom bank. Later, he will be able to exchange the pennies for free time or snacks.

Select a Data Collection System

For each trial in the session, Ms. Coovert will record the five types of possible responses, using the data collection sheet shown in Figure 4.4. Ms. Coovert selects this data sheet because the summary data allows her to total Ramon's responses on each individual word as well as both words combined. In this way, she can easily determine if she needs to modify the program in case Ramon has more difficulty learning one word than another.

Student ___Ramon___ Instructor ___Coovert___

Task ___Reading words___

Date	2/14			2/15			2/16		
Session	1			2			3		
Session time	9:30			9:30			9:30		
Delay interval	0"			1"			2"		
Trial	Stimulus	B	A	Stimulus	B	A	Stimulus	B	A
1	name		+	address		+	address		+
2	address		+	address		+	name		+
3	address		+	name		+	address		+
4	name		+	name		+	name		+
5	address		+	name		+	name		+
6	name		+	address		+	address		+
7	name		+	address		+	name		+
8	address		+	address	+		name		+
9	address		+	name		+	address	+	
10	address		+	name		+	name		+
11	name		+	address	+		address	+	
12	address		+	name		+	name		+
13	name		+	address		+	address	+	
14	name		+	name		+	name		+
15	address		+	name		+	address	+	
16	address		+	address	+		address	+	
17	address		+	address		+	name	+	
18	name		+	name		+	address	+	
18	name		+	name		+	name	+	
20	name		+	address	+		address	+	
Stimulus 1 *(name)*									
Number/Percent Corrects		0/0	10/100		0/0	10/100		2/20	8/80
Number/Percent Incorrects		0/0	0/0		0/0	0/0		0/0	0/0
Number/Percent No Response		XXX	0/0		XXX	0/0		XXX	0/0
Stimulus 2 *(address)*									
Number/Percent Corrects		0/0	10/100		4/40	6/60		7/70	3/30
Number/Percent Incorrects		0/0	0/0		0/0	0/0		0/0	0/0
Number/Percent No Response		XXX	0/0		XXX	0/0		XXX	0/0
Total Stimuli									
Number/Percent Corrects		0/0	20/100		4/20	16/80		9/45	11/55
Number/Percent Incorrects		0/0	0/0		0/0	0/0		0/0	0/0
Number/Percent No Response		XXX	0/0		XXX	0/0		XXX	0/0

Key: + = correct, − = incorrect, 0 = no response, B = before, A = after

Figure 4.4. This sample data collection sheet allows three sessions of data to be shown on one form.

Implement, Monitor, and Adjust the Program Based on the Student's Data Patterns

Ms. Coovert will graph prompted and unprompted correct responses on a line graph like the one shown in Figure 4.3. She will closely monitor the graph and if Ramon makes errors, Ms. Coovert will analyze the errors and make changes as needed.

Ms. Coovert conducts the first two sessions of the progressive time delay program using the following procedures:

1. Ms. Coovert sits across a table from Ramon in the classroom, places a job application on the table in front of him, and points to one of the two words to be taught. She immediately provides the verbal model (i.e., 0-second delay trial).
2. If Ramon correctly imitates the model, Ms. Coovert praises him (e.g., "Great, that says *address.*") and gives Ramon one penny.
3. If Ramon responds incorrectly or does not respond after the model, Ms. Coovert says, "Ramon, say (correct word)."
4. Ms. Coovert waits a couple of seconds after delivering consequences on trial 1, then repeats the same sequence for trial 2.
5. This sequence continues until all 0-second delay trials have been delivered and the first session is completed.

Ms. Coovert conducts the next instructional sesion using a 1-second delay interval in the following sequence:

1. Ms. Coovert sits across a table from Ramon in the classroom, places a job application on the table in front of him, and points to one of the two words to be taught. She waits 1 second by silently counting to herself ("1,001") before she provides the verbal model (i.e., 1-second delay trial).
2. If Ramon responds correctly before or after the model, Ms. Coovert praises him and gives him one penny.
3. If Ramon responds incorrectly before the prompt, Ms. Coovert says, "Wrong, this is (correct word). If you don't know, wait and let me tell you."
4. If Ramon responds incorrectly or does not respond after the prompt, Ms. Coovert says, "Ramon, say (correct word)."
5. Ms. Coovert waits a couple of seconds after delivering consequences on trial 1 and then repeats the same sequence for trial 2.
6. This sequence continues until all 1-second delay trials have been delivered and the second session is completed.

Ms. Coovert continues to deliver trials to Ramon, increasing the delay interval by 1 second each session, until a 6-second delay is reached or until he meets the criterion. If the 6-second delay is reached, all other sessions will be conducted using this delay interval.

Ms. Coovert continues the procedure until Ramon receives 100 percent correct responses for two consecutive sessions. A high criterion is necessary when using progressive time delay, since students may have a high percent of correct unprompted responses but still wait for the prompt on the first trial. Therefore, a criterion of 100 percent is necessary; if it is less than 100 percent, the teacher must ensure that the first trial of each stimulus is a correct unprompted response. By using the progressive time delay procedure, Ms. Coovert can save valuable instruction time and can teach Ramon many behaviors with few errors.

SUMMARY COMMENTS

- The progressive time delay procedure is an instructional strategy that gradually fades a controlling prompt by inserting progressively longer amounts of time between the task direction and the controlling prompt.
- Initial trials of the procedure are conducted using a 0-second prompt delay interval.
- Progressive time delay is very similar to constant delay but differs in that the delay interval gradually increases across trials rather than remains at a fixed interval.
- Students with a wide range of disabilities have been taught using the progressive time delay procedure—including students with mild to profound retardation, autism, and developmental disabilities. The majority of studies have used elementary- and secondary-aged subjects.
- Very few investigations have been conducted using chained tasks; the majority of research has been conducted with discrete skills.
- Mixed results have been found when progressive time delay was compared to stimulus manipulation procedures. Progressive time delay has been shown to be more efficient than system of least prompts and essentially equal in efficiency when compared to constant time delay.
- The steps for implementing a progressive time delay procedure include (a) identify the stimulus that cues the student to respond, (b) identify a controlling prompt, (c) determine the student's ability to wait for the prompt, (d) identify the number of 0-second delay trials to be used, (e) determine the length of the prompt delay intervals, (f) determine the schedule for increasing the delay interval, (g) determine the consequences to be used for each response type, (h) select a data collection system for monitoring student performance, and (i) implement, monitor, and adjust the program based on the student's data patterns.

This chapter described the progressive time delay procedure, in which only one prompt is presented and then faded on a time dimension. The next chapter defines and describes the system of least prompts instructional strategy, in which the controlling prompt is faded by presenting a hierarchy of prompts to the student.

EXERCISES

1. For a classic article on time delay, read P. E. Touchette, "Transfer of Stimulus Control: Measuring the Moment of Transfer," *Journal of the Experimental Analysis of Behavior, 15* (1971): 347–354.

2. Describe the different schedules for increasing prompt delay intervals. Choose one of these or create one of your own for teaching a hypothetical or real student. Justify your decision.
3. Mr. Cowen wants to teach Emma to put on her coat before going outside. She can put on her coat independently when given the task direction, "Put coat on," but she does not do so unless specifically told. Explain how Mr. Cowen, using a progressive time delay procedure, should teach Emma to put on her coat in response to the naturally occurring event of preparing to go outside.

REFERENCES

Aeschleman, S. R., & Higgins, A.F. (1982). Concept learning by retarded children: A comparison of three discrimination learning procedures. *Journal of Mental Deficiency Research, 26,* 229–238.

Ault, M. J., Gast, D. L., & Wolery, M. (1988). Comparison of progressive and constant time-delay procedures in teaching community-sign word reading. *American Journal of Mental Retardation, 93,* 44–56.

Ault, M. J., Wolery, M., Doyle, P. M., & Gast, D. L. (1989). Review of comparative studies in the instruction of students with moderate and severe handicaps. *Exceptional Children, 55,* 346–356.

Barrera, R., & Sulzer-Azaroff, B. (1983). An alternating treatment comparison of oral and total communication training programs with echolalic autistic children. *Journal of Applied Behavior Analysis, 16,* 379–394.

Bennett, D. L., Gast, D. L., Wolery, M., & Schuster, J. (1986). Time delay and system of least prompts: A comparison in teaching manual sign production. *Education and Training of the Mentally Retarded, 21,* 117–129.

Billingsley, F. F., & Romer, L. T. (1983). Response prompting and the transfer of stimulus control: Methods, research, and a conceptual framework. *Journal of the Association for the Severely Handicapped, 8,* 3–12.

Braam, S. J., & Poling, A. (1983). Development of intraverbal behavior in mentally retarded individuals through transfer of stimulus control procedures: Classification of verbal responses. *Applied Research in Mental Retardation, 4,* 279–302.

Browder, D. M., Hines, C., McCarthy, L. J., & Fees, J. (1984). A treatment package for increasing sight word recognition for use in daily living skills. *Education and Training of the Mentally Retarded, 19,* 191–200.

Browder, D. M., Snell, M. E., Wildonger, B. A. (1988). Simulation and community-based instruction of vending machines with time delay. *Education and Training of the Mentally Retarded, 23,* 175–185.

Charlop, M. H., Schreibman, L., & Thibodeau, M. G. (1985). Increasing spontaneous verbal responding in autistic children using a time delay procedure. *Journal of Applied Behavior Analysis, 18,* 155–166.

Godby, S., Gast, D. L., & Wolery, M. (1987). A comparison of time delay and the system of least prompts in teaching object identification. *Research in Developmental Disabilities, 8,* 283–306.

Goetz, L., Gee, K., & Sailor, W. (1983). Crossmodal transfer of stimulus control: Preparing students with severe multiple disabilities for audiological assessment. *Journal of the Association for Persons with Severe Handicaps, 8,* 3–13.

Luciano, M. C. (1986). Acquisition, maintenance, and generalization of productive intraverbal behavior through transfer of stimulus control procedures. *Applied Research in Mental Retardation, 7,* 1–20.

McDonagh, E. C., McIlvane, W. J., & Stoddard, L. T. (1984). Teaching coin equivalences via matching to sample. *Applied Research in Mental Retardation, 5,* 177–197.

McGee, G. G., & McCoy, J. F. (1981). Training procedures for acquisition and retention of reading in retarded youth. *Applied Research in Mental Retardation, 2,* 263–276.

McIlvane, W. J., Bass, R. W., O'Brien, J. M., Gerovac, B. J., & Stoddard, L. T. (1984). Spoken and signed naming of foods after receptive exclusion training in severe retardation. *Applied Research in Mental Retardation, 5,* 1–27.

Schoen, S. F. (1986). Assistance procedures to facilitate the transfer of stimulus control: Review and analysis. *Education and Training of the Mentally Retarded, 21,* 62–74.

Smeets, P. M., & Striefel, S. (1976). Acquisition and cross-modal generalization of receptive and expressive signing skills in a retarded deaf girl. *Journal of Mental Deficiency Research, 20,* 251–260.

——— (1980). Transfer of instructional control from loud tone to normal tone in profoundly retarded adolescents. *Behavior Research of Severe Developmental Disabilities, 1*(2), 105–121.

Snell, M. S. (1982). Analysis of time delay procedures in teaching daily living skills to retarded adults. *Analysis and Intervention in Developmental Disabilities, 2,* 139–155.

Snell, M. E., & Gast, D. L. (1981). Applying delay procedure to the instruction of the severely handicapped. *Journal of the Association for the Severely Handicapped, 6,* 3–14.

Striefel, S., Bryan, K. S., & Aikins, D. A. (1974). Transfer of stimulus control from motor to verbal stimuli. *Journal of Applied Behavior Analysis, 7,* 123–135.

Touchette, P. E. (1971). Transfer of stimulus control: Measuring the moment of transfer. *Journal of the Experimental Analysis of Behavior, 15,* 347–354.

Touchette, P. E., & Howard, J. S. (1984). Errorless learning: Reinforcement contingencies and stimulus control transfer in delayed prompting. *Journal of Applied Behavior Analysis, 17,* 175–188.

Walls, R. T., Haught, P., & Dowler, D. L. (1982). Moments of transfer of stimulus control in practical assembly tasks by mentally retarded adults. *American Journal of Mental Deficiency, 87,* 309–315.

Walls, R. T., Dowler, D. L., Haught, P., & Zawlocki, R. J. (1984). Progressive delay and unlimited delay of prompts in forward chaining and whole task training strategies. *Education and Training of the Mentally Retarded, 19,* 276–284.

Wolery, M., Gast, D. L., Kirk, K., & Schuster, J. (1988). Fading extra-stimulus prompts with autistic children using time delay. *Education and Treatment of Children, 11,* 29–44.

Zane, T., Handen, B. L., Mason, S. A., & Geffin, C. (1984). Teaching symbol identification: A comparison between standard prompting and intervening response procedures. *Analysis and Intervention in Developmental Disabilities, 4,* 367–377.

CHAPTER 5

System of Least Prompts Procedure

Chapter Overview

Describing the System of Least Prompts Procedure
Effects of Using the System of Least Prompts Procedure
Steps for Using the System of Least Prompts Procedure
Sample System of Least Prompts Procedure Program
Summary Comments
Exercises
References

Key Terms

System of Least Prompts
Hierarchy
Levels
Least Intrusive to Most
   Intrusive
Target Stimulus
Controlling Prompt
Response Interval
Unprompted Correct
No Response Error
Unprompted Error

Prompted Correct
Prompted Error
Chained Responses
Discrete Responses
Gestural Prompt
Verbal Prompt
Pictorial Prompt
Model Prompt
Partial Physical Prompt
Full Physical Prompt

Questions to Be Answered by This Chapter

1. What is the system of least prompts procedure?
2. Is the system of least prompts procedure effective?

3. What are the recommendations for using the system of least prompts procedure?
4. What are the steps for using the system of least prompts procedure successfully?
5. How do you measure progress with the system of least prompts procedure?

This chapter describes the system of least prompts strategy, also known as the increasing assistance procedure, and includes a description of the procedural parameters, an overview of the strategy, and a summary of the literature documenting its effectiveness. The chapter also explains in detail successful implementation of the system of least prompts procedure and provides an example in which the strategy is used.

DESCRIBING THE SYSTEM OF LEAST PROMPTS PROCEDURE

The **system of least prompts** procedure is an instructional strategy with four procedural parameters. First, it uses a prompt **hierarchy** that consists of at least three **levels.** The first level is the opportunity to respond without prompts; the second level and all subsequent levels include prompts that are arranged from the **least intrusive to most intrusive** amounts of assistance. A **target stimulus** is provided at the first level of the hierarchy and communicates to students that they are to respond. This is followed by delivery of prompts that progressively provide more assistance or information. The final prompt in the system of least prompts hierarchy is a **controlling prompt,** one that ensures that students will perform the task correctly.

The second parameter is the presentation of the target stimulus at each level in the hierarchy. The target stimulus should accompany the presentation of each prompt. Initially, the target stimulus should be delivered alone, followed by the least intrusive prompt and the target stimulus, which in turn should be followed by the next most intrusive prompt and stimulus.

The third parameter is the use of a consistent amount of time to respond both before and after delivery of each prompt (Lent & McLean, 1976). The time inserted between the levels in the system of least prompts hierarchy is called the **response interval**. A trial should progress from presentation of the target stimulus alone, followed by a response interval, to presentation of the target stimulus and the least intrusive prompt, and another response interval. This sequence is repeated until students respond correctly.

The fourth parameter of the system of least prompts procedure is the reinforcement of all correct responses made by students regardless of when those correct responses occur in the hierarchy. In other words, students are rewarded for both types of correct responses: those following the delivery of the target stimulus alone and those following the delivery of a prompt(s).

The system of least prompts procedure begins with the presentation of the first level in the hierarchy (opportunity to respond without prompts). For example, Ms. Jackson is teaching Pete to put his materials away. She says, "It is time for workshop." She gives the target stimulus and allows Pete 5 seconds to begin putting away his materials. If he responds correctly to the target stimulus alone (**unprompted correct**),

Ms. Jackson delivers reinforcement. If Pete fails to respond (**no response error**) or makes an incorrect response (**unprompted error**) to the target stimulus, Ms. Jackson repeats the target stimulus ("It is time for workshop."), and delivers the first prompt ("Put your things away.")—which is the second level of the hierarchy. If Pete responds correctly following this prompt (**prompted correct**), Ms. Jackson provides reinforcement; if he is incorrect (**prompted error**) or makes no responses, Ms. Jackson delivers a second prompt—or the third level of the hierarchy. She repeats the task direction, "It is time for workshop"; delivers a partial physical prompt; and waits another 5-second response interval. This process is repeated until all the prompts in the hierarchy have been delivered or until the task is performed correctly.

The goal of the system of least prompts procedure is for students to perform the behavior correctly before a prompt is delivered (i.e., at the first level in the system of least prompts hierarchy). A flow chart showing the use of the system of least prompts procedure is presented in Figure 5.1.

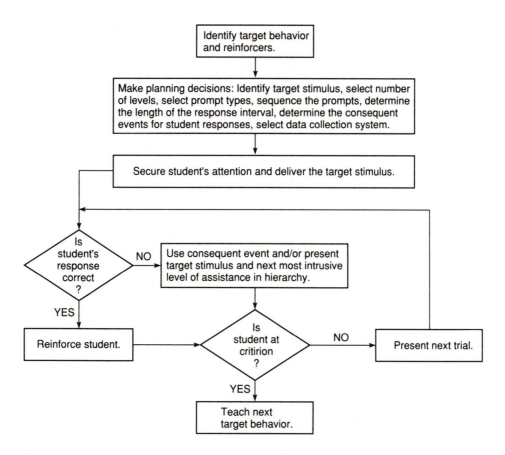

Figure 5.1. A flow chart for the system of least prompts procedure.

EFFECTS OF USING THE SYSTEM OF LEAST PROMPTS PROCEDURE

Students and Behaviors Taught

The system of least prompts procedure has been used successfully to teach students with a wide range of disabilities. The age range has included preschool (Banerdt & Bricker, 1978), elementary-aged, and adolescent-aged students (Freagon & Rotatori, 1982; Horner & Keilitz, 1975). However, the majority of research to date has been conducted with adults (18 years and older) (Browder et al., 1984; Cronin & Cuvo, 1979). The disabling conditions have included borderline or mild mental retardation (Martin et al., 1984), moderate retardation (Tucker & Berry, 1980), and severe retardation; however, most studies have focused on severe mental retardation (Aeschleman & Schladenhauffen, 1984; Coon, Vogelsberg, & Williams, 1981; Friedenberg & Martin, 1977; Giangreco, 1983).

The majority of skills taught with this procedure have required **chained responses,** that is, tasks in which a number of behaviors are sequenced together to form a more complex skill. Examples of chained tasks from various domains taught with the system of least prompts include playing a video game (Duffy & Nietupski, 1985), operating a washer and dryer (Cuvo, Jacobi, & Sipko, 1981), performing janitorial skills (Cuvo, Leaf, & Borakove, 1978), brushing teeth independently (Horner & Keilitz, 1975), and using tools in a vocational setting (Walls, Sienicki, & Crist, 1981). Although it is used more often with chained tasks, the procedure also has been effective with **discrete responses,** those skills that require a single behavior. The system of least prompts has been used to teach such skills as using expressive labeling during game playing (Bates & Renzaglia, 1982), using manual signs (Duker & Michielson, 1983; Duker & Morsink, 1984), identifying pictures receptively and expressively (Hupp et al., 1986), playing appropriately (Hopper & Wambold, 1978), using pronouns and prepositions in sentences (Konstantareas, 1984), and reading community shopping words (Gast et al., 1988).

Results of Using the System of Least Prompts Procedure

The system of least prompts procedure has been shown to be an effective procedure in teaching many different skills to students with varying disabilities. In a previous review of the system of least prompts literature, Doyle et al. (1988) found that in 85 percent of the studies reviewed, behaviors were taught to criterion when using this procedure. In terms of efficiency—such as total instructional time, number of sessions and trials to criterion, and errors or the number of prompts needed to achieve independent responding—this procedure is not always as efficient as other response prompting procedures. For example, in two studies with discrete tasks, progressive time delay required fewer trials, led to fewer errors, and involved less direct instructional time to criterion than the system of least prompts (Bennett et al., 1986; Godby, Gast, & Wolery, 1987). When compared to a constant time delay procedure, the system of least prompts was again found less efficient (Doyle et al., 1990; Gast et al., 1988; McDonnell, 1987; Schoen & Sivil, 1989). Although these results indicate that the system of least prompts procedure may be less efficient than the delay procedures, students "learn how to learn" with the procedure, thus increasing its efficiency (Doyle et al.,

1990). The system of least prompts strategy appears to be at least as efficient as the most-to-least prompts procedure in terms of number of errors and seconds to criterion (Glendenning, Adams, & Sternberg, 1983).

Recommendations for Practice

The system of least prompts procedure is a viable instructional option because it can be used with a wide range of students and is effective with many different types of skills. Thus, teachers should become fluent in using the strategy. However, it may be more difficult to use than error correction and constant and progressive time delay because of the number of planning decisions required. For example, a teacher must decide on the number and the type of prompts to use, making the procedure more difficult than the delay procedures because the teacher must identify a variety of prompts rather than the single controlling prompt. Also, arranging the prompts into a hierarchy of least intrusive to most intrusive is often difficult due to the fact that the intrusiveness of a prompt (amount of help provided) is related to both the task and the student's skills. For example, if an instructor is teaching bed making to two students, one who is imitative and one who is not, then the use of a model prompt will provide different amounts of help to each student.

It is important to individualize the prompt hierarchy for each student. For example, a model delivered to a nonimitative student may be appropriate at the beginning level in the hierarchy, whereas a model for the imitative student may be used in the final level. The sequence of prompts must place the most intrusive prompt at the final level of the hierarchy. The final prompt in the hierarchy is identical to the controlling prompt described for the time delay procedures; that is, it must ensure correct performance of the response. However, unlike the time delay procedures, the prompts in the system of least prompts procedure are faded by the student rather than by the teacher as the student responds correctly to one prompt and does not respond correctly to another. This self-fading of the more intrusive prompts eliminates the need for such teacher decisions as when to insert a delay interval, how long the delay interval should be, or even when to change to a different type or level of assistance. Additional teacher decisions are similar to other response prompting procedures.

With each of the procedures described in the preceding chapters, reinforcement follows correct responses that occur before and after the prompt. This also is done in the system of least prompts. However, a teacher will find it easier to decide on error consequences with the system of least prompts than with other response prompting procedures. Usually, the teacher interrupts errors and presents the next level in the hierarchy. As instruction occurs over time, the teacher delivers progressively less help, until the student makes correct responses to the target stimulus alone.

STEPS FOR USING THE SYSTEM OF LEAST PROMPTS PROCEDURE

As with any good program plan, a teacher must follow specific steps to ensure that the instructional procedure will be implemented reliably. The system of least prompts procedure is dependent on the completion of the following eight steps:

- Identify the stimulus that cues the student to respond.
- Select the number of levels in the hierarchy.
- Select the type of prompts to be used in the hierarchy.
- Sequence the selected prompt types from least assistance to most assistance.
- Determine the length of the response interval.
- Determine the consequences to be used for each student response.
- Select a data collection system.
- Implement, monitor, and adjust the program based on the student's data patterns.

Identify the Stimulus That Cues the Student to Respond

After selecting the target behaviors, the teacher's first step is identifying the stimulus or cue that signals the student to respond. This target stimulus can be (a) a task direction, such as "What is this?"; (b) a material or environmental manipulation, such as setting up a kitchen or showing the student a sink filled with dirty dishes and waiting for a response; or (c) an event that occurs naturally in the student's routine, such as a ringing fire alarm, a ringing phone, a school bus arriving at the student's home, or dirty dishes on the table. With the system of least prompts, the target stimulus is the signal that will eventually control the student's response.

This target stimulus is always the first level in the prompt hierarchy. It is often referred to as the independent, or no assistance, level because it allows the student to respond without prompting from the teacher. The type of target stimulus the teacher selects depends on both the student and the skill being taught. For example, two students are learning to load the dishwasher in a group home. One student has severe mental retardation and is told after each meal, "It is time to load the dishwasher"; this is an example of a task direction used as the target stimulus. The second student has moderate mental retardation and is expected to load the dishwasher after each meal without being told; for this student, the target stimulus is a naturally occurring event. In each case, the target response is loading the dishwasher, but the target stimulus is different. Whenever possible, a naturally occurring stimulus should serve as the target stimulus because it will increase the probability of generalization. Individuals in the natural environment are not likely to use artificial task directions. Thus, the teacher should observe and analyze times when the skill will be performed to identify the naturally occurring stimuli.

Regardless of the type of target stimulus used, it should be present in all levels of the prompt hierarchy. The teacher delivering an artificial target stimulus at each level in the hierarchy or ensuring that the same natural target stimulus sets the occasion for the desired response (such as successful completion of one step in a chain serving as the target stimulus for the next step) will facilitate acquisition of the target response. The repeated exposure to the target stimulus throughout the hierarchy ensures that the student's response is directly and closely related to the target stimulus (Doyle et al., 1988). Two examples of repeated exposures of the target stimulus in the system of least prompts hierarchy are shown in Table 5.1.

Select the Number of Levels in the Hierarchy

To be defined as a system of least prompts procedure, the prompt hierarchy must include the target stimulus alone (independent level) and at least two levels of prompts.

TABLE 5.1. Examples of Target Stimuli and the Presentation at Successive Levels in the System of Least Prompts Hierarchy

Level	Teacher Delivers Verbal Task Direction	Task Example
1	Task direction alone	"Wash the dishes."
2	Task direction followed by prompt type 1	"Wash the dishes." "Open the dishwasher."
3	Task direction followed by prompt type 2	"Wash the dishes." Teacher opens dishwasher.
4	Task direction followed by prompt type 3	"Wash the dishes." Teacher physically guides student to open dishwasher.

Level	Teacher Allows Natural Stimulus to Occur	Task Example
1	Natural event alone	Dirty dishes on the table.
2	Natural event followed by prompt type 1	Dirty dishes on the table. "Open the dishwasher."
3	Natural event followed by prompt type 2	Dirty dishes on the table. Teacher opens dishwasher.
4	Natural event followed by prompt type 3	Dirty dishes on the table. Teacher physically guides student to open dishwasher.

Therefore, the minimum number of levels is three. Although there is no maximum number of levels possible, the teacher should consider both task and student characteristics. If the skill is a discrete task, then two to three prompts are frequently used, because identifying more than three is difficult. For example, Mr. Harris is teaching Betty to respond in complete sentences when shown action pictures and given the task direction, "What is the boy doing?" He could use a hierarchy that has three levels: (a) the target stimulus, (b) the target stimulus plus a verbal prompt (i.e., "Tell me a sentence."), and (c) the target stimulus plus a model (i.e., "The boy is running."). Because the target response was an expressive task, other prompts (such as physical and gestural prompts) are neither possible nor practical. However, for other types of tasks, such as chained skills, it is easier to use more prompts resulting in a greater number of levels in the hierarchy. For example, Janet taught Alex to sweep under the tables at a restaurant using four prompts plus a target stimulus, for a total of five levels in the hierarchy. Her target stimulus was the naturally occurring event of customers finishing their meals and leaving the restaurant. The hierarchy began with (a) the natural event at level 1, (b) the natural event plus an indirect verbal prompt at level 2 (i.e., "What are you supposed to do?"), (c) the natural event plus a direct verbal prompt at level 3 (i.e., "Sweep the floor."), (d) the event plus the third prompt at level 4 (i.e., giving Alex the broom), and finally (e) the target stimulus and the fourth prompt at level 5 (i.e., physically guiding Alex to sweep the floor). Because chained tasks often consist of motor responses, physical and gestural prompts can be used in the hierarchy; thus, a greater total number of possible levels and combinations of prompts exists.

Another consideration when a teacher is selecting the number of levels is the student's characteristics. The greater the total number of levels, the longer the student must wait for the amount of assistance she needs to perform the correct response, especially during initial instruction. This long wait time for the "right amount of assistance" may increase the probability for her errors and disruptive behavior. If a student has difficulty maintaining attention to tasks for extended periods of time, then a hierarchy consisting of several levels is a poor choice for her. Likewise, if a student becomes disruptive when she makes errors, then the total number of levels in her hierarchy should be kept to a minimum. However, if a student needs extensive assistance or small changes in the amount of assistance to respond correctly, her hierarchy may need a greater number of levels.

A final consideraton is the availability of time for instruction. As a general rule, the greater the number of levels in the hierarchy, the longer the instructional sessions will be. This is particularly true during initial instruction with a new task. Because so many different skills have been taught to such varied populations using a wide range of hierarchies, no further recommendations can be made for the selection of the total number of levels. The number of prompts plus the target stimulus is, in part, an arbitrary decision.

Select the Types of Prompts to Be Used in the Hierarchy

The following are examples of the different types of prompts that have been used in the system of least prompts hierarchies:

- **Gestural prompt:** Point to an untied shoe.
- **Verbal prompt:** Say "Put your toys away."
- **Pictorial prompt:** Give the student written instructions on how to operate a washing machine.
- **Model prompt:** Demonstrate how to put the toothpaste on the toothbrush.
- **Partial physical prompt:** Touch a student's hand to indicate that a sponge should be picked up.
- **Full physical prompt:** Place a hand over the student's hand and guide the spoon to the student's mouth.

Many variations in the possible combinations of prompts have been used. Most commonly, different types of prompts are included in the same hierarchy. However, other variations include the presentation of multiple prompt types at each level and the use of a single type of prompt throughout the hierarchy. Three variations of prompt hierarchies are shown in Table 5.2.

As with the target stimulus and the number of prompts, the teacher should individualize the types of prompts according to both student and skill characteristics. For example, a student who does not imitate will, in general, not be able to use such prompts as verbal directions and models (Snell & Zirpoli, 1987). For such a student, varying the intrusiveness of physical guidance may be more effective. Further, if a teacher wishes to increase a student's imitation of a model, he could pair each of the physical prompts with a model of the skill to increase the probability that the student

TABLE 5.2. Combinations of Prompt Types at Levels in the System of Least Prompts Hierarchy

Level	Different Type Each Level	Multiple Types Each Level	Single Type Each Level
1	Target stimulus	Target stimulus	Target stimulus
2	Target stimulus Verbal prompt	Target stimulus Verbal prompt Gestural prompt	Target stimulus Physical prompt at shoulder
3	Target stimulus Model prompt	Target stimulus Verbal prompt Model prompt	Target stimulus Physical prompt at wrist
4	Target stimulus Physical prompt	Target stimulus Verbal prompt Model prompt Physical prompt	Target stimulus Physical prompt hand on hand

will become imitative. For a student who responds consistently to direct verbal instructions, verbal prompts—rather than models, gestures, or physical prompts— may be more appropriate. For example, a natural cue as the target stimulus followed by indirect verbal assistance and then more direct verbal prompts (i.e., those with more information) may be sufficient. However, the most common practice for a student with a moderate or severe disability is for a teacher to use a different type of prompt at each level in the hierarchy: for example, presentation of the task direction at level 1, a verbal prompt at level 2, a model at level 3, and a physical prompt in the final level of the hierarchy.

The skill being taught also should be considered when a teacher selects the prompt types. Although their recommendation was not empirically verified, Wolery and Gast (1984) suggested that the prompt type should match the modality of the skill being taught. For example, if the target response is verbal, then the teacher should select verbal prompts; if the target behavior is following instructions, then the teacher may find gestural or pictorial prompts more appropriate. It is clear, however, that some skills are best taught with specific prompt types. For instance, when teaching expressive language tasks, a teacher will find that various combinations of verbal and/or model prompts are easier to deliver than physical or gestural prompts. Further, if the skill is new or very difficult, the teacher needs to include physical guidance at some level of the hierarchy.

Sequence the Selected Prompt Types from Least Assistance to Most Assistance

Inherent in the definition of a system of least prompts procedure is the arrangement of the selected prompt types into a hierarchy of least assistance to most assistance. The hierarchy begins with presentation of the target stimulus, or the least amount of assistance available to the student; proceeds through the intermediate levels while delivering prompts that provide progressively more assistance; and ends with a prompt that ensures correct performance of the target behavior. The final order of prompts is again dependent on the student and the skill being taught. For example, Ginny is learning to clean her lunch tray. Mr. Marshall has selected three prompts: one model, one physical, and one verbal. To arrange the prompts in the least-to-most order, he must decide (a) which prompt provides Ginny with the least amount of assistance, (b) which prompt provides her with more information, and (c) which gives her the most amount of assistance. Mr. Marshall may consider Ginny's previous learning history by asking the following questions:

- Overall, which of these three prompt types has been used to teach Ginny new skills?
- Has she learned this type of *functional* skill before, or have other teachers concentrated on different types of skills?
- If she has learned a variety of tasks, what type of prompt has been the most successful?
- When a prompt is needed to elicit a previously learned response, what type of prompt is used most often?
- If this task has been successfully taught to other students with these three prompts, what was the least-to-most sequence?
- Does the student respond correctly when each prompt is used separately?

The answers to these questions will assist Mr. Marshall in developing the least-to-most sequence of the model, physical, and verbal prompts specific to Ginny and the task of cleaning her tray. Mr. Marshall has taught this skill to other students in his class; however, this is a new type of task for Ginny and one that is considered difficult. Mr. Marshall knows that Ginny will respond to verbal directions alone when the task is one that she can already do. He also knows that she will consistently imitate only simple behaviors, not complex chains of behavior. Ginny does not independently clean her tray and is not able to make the correct response consistently when Mr. Marshall delivers a verbal prompt or when he models the correct response. However, if he delivers a physical prompt, Ginny allows him to guide her through the task.

After reviewing the answers, Mr. Marshall decides that the first level in the hierarchy should consist of the target stimulus, in this case the natural event of finishing lunch. The second and third levels should consist of a verbal prompt and model prompt, respectively, because of Ginny's response to these prompts. The physical prompt, in this instance, is a controlling prompt for Ginny because she is able to clean her tray with Mr. Marshall's physical guidance. It is critical that the prompt in the final level be a controlling one. The selected prompt hierarchy for Ginny, ordered in the least-to-most sequence, is shown in Table 5.3.

Determine the Length of the Response Interval

In the system of least prompts procedure, an opportunity to respond follows the presentation of each level in the hierarchy; that is, after presentation of the target stimulus (first level), a teacher should give a brief amount of time for the student to respond

TABLE 5.3. The System of Least Prompts Hierarchy Selected for Ginny

Level	Assistance	Example
1	Target stimulus	Ginny has finished eating lunch.
2	Target stimulus Verbal prompt	Ginny has finished eating lunch. "Clear your tray."
3	Target stimulus Model prompt	Ginny has finished eating lunch. Mr. Marshall demonstrates clearing another tray.
4	Target stimulus Physical prompt	Ginny has finished eating lunch. Mr. Marshall places his hand on Ginny's hand and clears the tray.

independently. Following delivery of the target stimulus and each prompt, the teacher needs to allow the student the identical amount of time to respond. If the student responds correctly within the response interval at any level, the teacher provides reinforcement and terminates the trial. If the student responds incorrectly or does not respond, the teacher provides the next prompt and response interval. This sequence is continued until the teacher has delivered all of the prompts or until the student makes a correct response. The duration of the response interval is somewhat dependent on both the student and the task characteristics. For example, the length of a response interval for a student with a long response latency may need to be longer than the interval for a student with a short response latency. To define the response interval, the teacher should time how long it takes the student to complete similar tasks.

Another consideration when a teacher is selecting the response interval is the task being taught. This might include measuring other students' performance on the target task. If similar students can begin the task when given 5 seconds to respond, then 5 seconds may be a reasonable response interval for the target student. Some responses will require more time than others. Expecting a student to answer a question verbally within 5 seconds may be as reasonable as allowing 30 seconds for her to write the answer to the same question. When teaching skills of long durations, a teacher may find it necessary to define both the amount of time the student will be allowed to *begin* the response and how long the student will have to *complete* the response. For example, Mr. Perez is teaching Mary to set the table. He allows Mary 5 seconds to initiate each step in the task analysis. However, some steps take her longer to complete than others (e.g., folding a napkin takes her longer to do than placing a glass in the correct spot). Therefore, once she initiates, Mr. Perez allows 15 seconds for Mary to complete longer steps. As a general rule, the response interval should be approximately the same amount of time it takes a person with similar characteristics to complete the response.

Determine the Consequences for Each Student Response

Before beginning any instructional program, the teacher should know exactly what to do when the student performs correctly or incorrectly or does not respond.

Responding to Correct Responses.   With the system of least prompts procedure, a teacher should follow all correct responses with reinforcement, regardless of when in the hierarchy the response occurs. Reinforcement of both unprompted and prompted correct responses increases the probability that the intermediate prompts will acquire control of the student's responding. It is possible with this procedure to vary the amount or density of reinforcement for the two types of correct responses. In other words, Mr. Perez may use descriptive verbal praise when Mary correctly sets the table after a prompt, and he could deliver praise and an extra helping of dessert when she sets the table to the target stimulus alone. Differential reinforcement of the two types of correct responses does not usually occur at the beginning of instruction. It can be used when the student has received several instructional sessions and continues to wait for prompts rather than responding to the target stimulus alone. As with any instructional procedure, the amount and the type of reinforcement is dependent on the student and the skill being taught. Although the teacher reinforces all correct responses, only the unprompted corrects (those that occur to the target stimulus alone) count toward the criterion.

Responding to Incorrect Responses.   Any time the student makes an error in the system of least prompts hierarchy, the teacher should interrupt the incorrect response and deliver the next prompt. Similarly, the teacher should present the next prompt in the hierarchy if the student makes no response. Additional consequences can be used for errors. The teacher can use a mild verbal reprimand and an instruction to wait for assistance. For example, if, while setting the table, Mary puts the knife in the wrong place, Mr. Perez interrupts the incorrect response and says, "That is wrong. Wait and I'll help you set the table." He delivers the next prompt in the hierarchy, "Put the knife to the right of the plate," then waits for her response. Table 5.4 shows a sample of the consequences for both a discrete and a chained task with the system of least prompts procedure.

Select a Data Collection System

As discussed in the preceding chapters, it is important for the teacher to monitor the effectiveness of his instruction. Examining the student's performance on a daily basis will help the teacher decide when he needs to make changes. Figures 5.2 through 5.4 are sample data collection forms for the system of least prompts procedure.

Implement, Monitor, and Adjust the Program Based on the Student's Data Patterns

When using the system of least prompts, a teacher should display visually all unprompted correct responses (those correct responses made to the target stimulus alone). However, it is also possible for the teacher to graph the correct responses that occur at each prompt level in the hierarchy. The sample graphs shown in Figures 5.5 through 5.8 show the percent of unprompted corrects and prompted corrects and the level in the hierarchy where each correct response occurred. This information

TABLE 5.4. Sample Consequences Following Student Responding in Discrete and Chained Tasks

	Expressive Labeling—Discrete Task		Washing Hands—Chained Task
Teacher	Picture; "What is this?"; waits 3 seconds.	Teacher	"Wash your hands."; waits 5 seconds.
Student	"Dog."	Student	Picks up toothbrush.
Teacher	"What is this? Say the whole thing."; waits 3 seconds.	Teacher	"No, Wash your hands. Turn the water on."; waits 5 seconds.
Student	No response.	Student	Turns the water on.
Teacher	"What is this? This is a dog."	Teacher	Reinforces student; waits 5 seconds for next step.
Student	"This is a dog."	Student	Picks up toothpaste.
Teacher	Reinforces student; waits 3 seconds to deliver next trial.	Teacher	"No, Wash your hands. Wet your hands."; waits 5 seconds.
		Student	No response.
		Teacher	"Wash your hands."; models the correct response; waits 5 seconds.
		Student	Touches the faucet.
		Teacher	"No, Wash your hands."; physically prompts the correct response; reinforces student; waits 5 seconds for the next step.

will help the teacher determine if he needs to make changes in the procedure and will also assist him in determining if less intrusive prompts are acquiring stimulus control over the correct response. Several problems can arise. Possible solutions include the following:

- If the student consistently makes errors at the final level in the hierarchy, the teacher should select a new, more intrusive, controlling prompt.
- If the student consistently makes errors at an intermediate level of assistance, the teacher needs to increase the number of levels in the hierarchy (use an additional prompt), select a new type of prompt, or examine the difficulty of the task.
- If the student consistently waits for a prompt instead of attempting to respond to the target stimulus alone and instruction has been implemented for several sessions, the teacher should differentially reinforce prompted and unprompted correct responses or eliminate reinforcement for prompted corrects altogether.

Student ___Howard___ Instructor ___B. Johnson___ Date __10/30/91__ Session __3__

Task ___Sight word reading___

Trial	Stimulus	Level 1 Task Direction	Level 2 Prompt 1 Verbal	Level 3 Prompt 2 Picture	Level 4 Prompt 3 Model
1	Stop	O	O	O	+
2	Exit	O	−	O	+
3	Exit	O	O	O	+
4	Stop	O	O	+	
5	Exit	O	O	+	
6	Stop	−	O	+	
7	Stop	O	+		
8	Exit	O	O	+	
9	Exit	O	+		
10	Stop	+			
Summary Data	Stop	N = 1	N = 1	N = 2	N = 1
		20%	20%	40%	20%
	Exit	N = 0	N = 1	N = 2	N = 2
		0%	20%	40%	40%

Key: + = correct, − = incorrect, 0 = no response

Student ___JoAnn___ Instructor ___S. Clemens___ Date __1/18/91__

Task ___Instruction following___

Trial Number Stimulus	1	2	3	4	5	6	7	8	9	10
Student Responses	I	I	I	I	I	I	I	(I)	I	(I)
	(G)	G	(G)	G	G	(G)	(G)	G	(G)	G
	M	(M)	M	M	(M)	M	M	M	M	M
	P	P	P	(P)	P	P	P	P	P	P

Key: I = independent or unprompted, G = gestural, M = model, P = physical

Figure 5.2. The top data collection form is for teaching a discrete task using the system of least prompts procedure. Any number of levels or type of prompts can be substituted for those presented in this example.

The bottom data sheet can be used with discrete tasks. This form could be used to teach the student to follow instructions (e.g., "Open the door," Look out the window," "Close the drawer," "Pick up the box") in one ten-trial session or possibly one trial at a time distributed throughout the day. On this data sheet, a letter is circled to indicate the prompt needed by the student to perform the correct response on each trial.

Student _____Danielle_____ Instructor _____S. Meyer_____ Date _5/5/91_ Session _2_

Start time _____10:00_____ Stop time _____10:15_____ Total time __15_min.____sec.

Task _____Folding shirt_____

Trial 1 Task Analysis	Independent	Verbal	Model	Physical
1. Grasp/fold one-third away from body.	O	O	O	+
2. Grasp/fold one-third toward body.	O	−	O	+
3. Grasp/fold top to bottom.	O	−	−	+
4. Place shirt in basket.	O	+		
Trial 2 Task Analysis	Independent	Verbal	Model	Physical
1. Grasp/fold one-third away from body.	O	O	+	
2. Grasp/fold one-third toward body.	−	O	+	
3. Grasp/fold top to bottom.	−	O	O	+
4. Place shirt in basket.	O	+		
Trial 3 Task Analysis	Independent	Verbal	Model	Physical
1. Grasp/fold one-third away from body.	O	O	+	
2. Grasp/fold one-third toward body.	O	+		
3. Grasp/fold top to bottom.	O	O	+	
4. Place shirt in basket.	+			
Summary Data Corrects	N = 1	N = 3	N = 4	N = 4
	8.3%	25%	33.3%	33.3%
Incorrects	N = 2	N = 2	N = 1	N = 0
	16.7%	16.7%	8.3%	0%
No Response	N = 9	N = 6	N = 3	N = 0
	75%	50%	25%	0%

Key: + = correct, − = incorrect, 0 = no response

Figure 5.3. This data collection form is used in teaching chained tasks with the system of least prompts procedure. Any number of levels or type of prompts can be substituted for those presented in this example.

SAMPLE SYSTEM OF LEAST PROMPTS PROCEDURE PROGRAM

To design an effective instructional program using the system of least prompts procedure, a teacher must follow eight steps. The following example illustrates these steps:

Chrissie is a 13-year-old with severe mental retardation. Her teacher, Mr. Lindsay, has begun to focus on establishing self-help skills that are important to Chrissie's parents. One of those skills is washing her hair independently, with minimal supervision. Chrissie is already familiar with a sink, faucet, and towel since she has learned to wash her hands and brush her teeth. Mr. Lindsay used enthusiastic, descriptive,

Student _____Marcia_____   Instructor _____K. Walker_____   Task _____Sandwich making_____

Task Analysis Session	1	2	3	4	5					
Date	5/16	5/17	5/18	5/19	5/20					
1. Take bread from cabinet.	V	V	V	V	I					
2. Carry cold cuts from refrigerator.	M	V	I	I	I					
3. Pick up knife from drawer.	P	P	M	V	V					
4. Select mayonnaise from refrigerator.	P	M	M	M	V					
5. Open bread.	P	M	V	V	V					
6. Remove two slices of bread.	M	M	M	V	I					
7. Close bread and return.	P	P	M	V	V					
8. Open jar of mayonnaise.	P	P	M	M	V					
9. Spread with knife/both slices.	P	P	P	M	M					
10. Close mayonnaise jar and return.	P	M	M	V	I					
11. Open cold cut container.	P	M	V	V	I					
12. Place meat on one bread.	M	M	V	I	I					
13. Place other bread on meat.	M	M	I	I	I					
14. Close meat container and return.	M	M	V	V	V					
15. Remove plate from cabinet.	M	V	V	V	V					
16. Place sandwich on plate.	M	V	I	I	I					
17. Cut sandwich in half diagonally.	P	P	P	P	P					
18. Place knife in sink.	V	V	V	I	I					
Summary Data										
Number of I's	0	0	3	5	9					
Number of V's	2	5	7	9	7					
Number of M's	7	8	6	3	1					
Number of P's	9	5	2	1	1					

Key: I = independent or unprompted, V = verbal, M = model, P = physical

Figure 5.4. This is an example of a data sheet to be used with a chained task. For each step in the task, the code to represent the level where a student responded correctly is written in. Any chained task, number, or type of prompt can be substituted and used with this data sheet. This data sheet might be appropriate when teaching a task once a day during the time of day that the task would naturally be performed.

verbal praise to teach those skills, and he selects this as a reinforcer for hair washing. A sample of a possible sequence for teaching the hair-washing skill is found in Table 5.5.

Identify the Stimulus That Cues the Student to Respond

Mr. Lindsay and Chrissie's parents decided that Chrissie is unable to discriminate the natural cue of dirty hair to signal hair washing. Therefore, they have decided to use a task direction ("Wash your hair.") as the target stimulus for the first level in

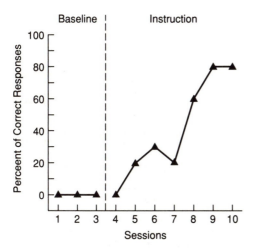

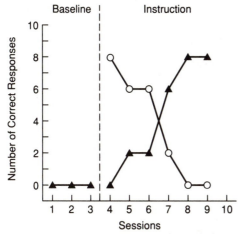

Figure 5.5. These are sample displays of data patterns for the system of least prompts procedure. Each graph can be used to summarize both chained and discrete tasks. The numbers along the left vertical axis represent the percent or number of correct responses that the student could achieve during a session or trial. Sessions or trials are represented along the bottom horizontal axis. The percent can be calculated or the number of correct responses can be counted for each session and plotted on a graph.

the hierarchy. Both teacher and parents agree that this is a reasonable signal based on the ease of delivery at each subsequent level and on Chrissie's level of functioning, and they believe that it is indicative of instructions parents give to nondisabled children.

Select the Number of Levels in the Hierarchy

Hair washing is a chained task, and Mr. Lindsay could identify several levels in the prompt hierarchy. However, due to the difficulty of the task—that is, (a) it is a new task, (b) it has ten steps in the task analysis, and (c) it will require a significant amount

Student _____Juan_____   Instructor ___S. Key___   Date _6/12/91_

Task _____Instruction following_____

Trial Number Stimulus	1 open	2 open	3 open	4 open	5 open	6 open	7 open	8 open	9 open	10 open
Student Responses	I	I	I	(I)	I	(I)	(I)	(I)	(I)	(I)
	G	G	(G)	G	(G)	G	G	G	G	G
	(M)	(M)	M	M	M	M	M	M	M	M
	P	P	P	P	P	P	P	P	P	P

Key: I = independent or unprompted, G = gestural, M = model, P = physical

Figure 5.6. This is a data display for a discrete task, made directly from Figure 5.3. The symbols on this graph represent the type of prompts available in the hierarchy. The student's trial-by-trial responses, which are circled during instruction, are then connected to form a graph. Criterion would be indicated by the number of consecutive circled *I*'s or unprompted correct responses.

TABLE 5.5. Sample Task Analysis for Chrissie's Hair Washing

Step Number	Task
1	Gather materials; go to sink.
2	Turn on water.
3	Wet hair.
4	Open shampoo bottle.
5	Squeeze shampoo into hand.
6	Rub shampoo into hair.
7	Rinse hair.
8	Turn off water.
9	Towel-dry hair.
10	Put shampoo bottle away.

of direct instructional time—and due to Chrissie's characteristics, Mr. Lindsay decides to use a total of four levels. These include the target stimulus ("Wash your hair.") and three prompts.

Select the Type of Prompts to Be Used in the Hierarchy

Mr. Lindsay has taught Chrissie a variety of discrete and chained tasks using all types of prompts. However, after he task-analyzed the skill of hair washing and considered Chrissie's characteristics, he selected a verbal prompt, a partial physical prompt, and a full physical prompt. Although he knows that the verbal prompt will not control the correct response on each step of the task, Mr. Lindsay suspects that Chrissie will

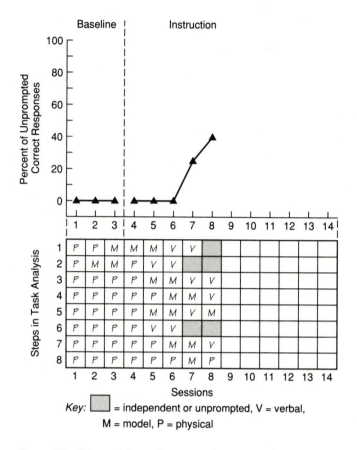

Figure 5.7. This graph is used to summarize percent of unprompted correct responses for a chained task and to provide information on the type of prompt that was required to produce a correct response for each step of the task analysis. On the upper portion of the graph, a percentage is calculated and the percent of unprompted correct responses for each session is plotted. On the grid at the bottom of the graph, the prompt that was needed for the student to respond correctly on each step of the task analysis is indicated and the steps that the student performed independently (to the task direction alone) are blackened in. This graph not only allows a teacher to record data and summarize student responding across the entire task but also provides information on how the student is progressing on each step of the task. In this way, difficult steps of the task can be identified and modification can be made if needed.

correctly complete a few of the steps with this level of assistance because of her familiarity with the towel, sink, and faucet. Also, he wants to increase Chrissie's responding to verbal prompts. Mr. Lindsay eliminated model prompts because he has had success in teaching Chrissie with models only when she could visually observe the response, and this would be awkward with some steps in the task analysis (e.g., washing his own hair in the classroom). Similarly, gestural or pictorial prompts would be impractical to use on such steps as working the shampoo through her hair or

Student _____Steve_____   Instructor _____Diane_____   Task _____Putting on pants_____

Task Analysis Session	1	2	3	4						
Date	2/2	2/3	2/4	2/5						
7. Straighten pants on body.	FP	PP	PP	PP						
6. Pull waistband to waist.	PP	PP	PP	G						
5. Stand up.	PP	G	I	I						
4. Place left foot through left pants leg.	FP	FP	PP	PP						
3. Place right foot through right pants leg.	FP	FP	FP	FP						
2. Sit in chair.	G	G	I	I						
1. Grasp waistband of pants with both hands.	PP	PP	G	I						
Summary Data	7	7	7	7	7	7	7	7	7	7
	6	6	6	6	6	6	6	6	6	6
	5	5	5	5	5	5	5	5	5	5
	4	4	4	4	4	4	4	4	4	4
Circle the Number of Correct	3	3	3	③	3	3	3	3	3	3
Unprompted Responses and Connect.	2	2	②	2	2	2	2	2	2	2
	1	1	1	1	1	1	1	1	1	1
	⓪	⓪	0	0	0	0	0	0	0	0

Key: I = independent, G = gestural, PP = partial physical, FP = full physical

Figure 5.8. This is another example that represents a combined data sheet and graph using the system of least prompts procedure. For each session, the prompt that was needed to produce the correct response is recorded, the number of unprompted correct responses is counted, and the number that occurred for that session is circled. The responses are then connected from session to session to form a graph.

rinsing her hair. Therefore, based on these characteristics of the task, Mr. Lindsay has selected two physical prompts in addition to the verbal prompt to teach Chrissie the hair-washing skill.

Sequence the Selected Prompt Types from Least Assistance to Most Assistance

The first level in the hierarchy will be the task direction, "Wash your hair." This is the target stimulus that will eventually control the entire task of hair washing. Based on Chrissie's performance in the classroom and the difficulty of the task, Mr. Lindsay has placed a verbal prompt specific to each step in the task analysis at the second level in the hierarchy. For example, step 1 in the task is gathering materials. The first level for this step will be "Wash your hair," and if an incorrect response or no response occurs, the second level will be "Wash your hair. Find the shampoo and towel and go to the sink." The third level in the system of least prompts hierarchy will be delivery of a partial physical prompt that provides more information to Chrissie than did the verbal prompt. Therefore, if Chrissie makes an incorrect response or no response to the task direction plus the verbal prompt, Mr. Lindsay will say, "Wash your hair," and nudge Chrissie's elbow to indicate that she is to find the materials. The fourth and final level in the hierarchy will be the delivery of the task direction plus a full physical prompt, hand-over-hand guidance. This will ensure that Chrissie will make the correct response to each step in the task analysis.

Determine the Length of the Response Interval

Mr. Lindsay decides that 5 seconds is enough time to initiate each of the steps in the task analysis. Therefore, he will begin counting to five after each level in the hierarchy. Because some of the steps in this task analysis will take longer to complete than others (e.g., gathering the materials, rubbing in the shampoo, and rinsing), Mr. Lindsay will allow a maximum of 30 seconds for Chrissie to complete each step.

Determine the Consequences for Each Student Response

For all correct responses, both unprompted and prompted, Mr. Lindsay will deliver descriptive verbal praise, "Chrissie, that is right. You found the shampoo and the towel," and a pat on the back. If Chrissie makes an error, Mr. Lindsay will interrupt the incorrect response and immediately provide the next level in the hierarchy. Likewise, if Chrissie makes no response during the 5-second response interval, Mr. Lindsay will present the next prompt in the hierarchy.

Select a Data Collection System

For each step in the task analysis, Mr. Lindsay will record the assistance that was necessary to produce the correct response, using the data collection sheet in Figure 5.9. He selects this data sheet because he can summarize and graph on the same form and will be able to see if less intrusive prompts are acquiring stimulus control during instruction. This will allow him to determine if he needs to change the number or type of prompts being delivered or if he should increase the number of instructional sessions per week.

Implement, Monitor, and Adjust the Program Based on the Student's Data Patterns

Mr. Lindsay will graph Chrissie's data on Figure 5.9. He will monitor and analyze the graph and make changes as needed.

Mr. Lindsay conducts the first session of hair washing as follows:

1. Mr. Lindsay guides Chrissie to the bathroom; presents the task direction, "Wash your hair"; and begins counting to five.
2. If Chrissie correctly performs the first step (i.e., gathering the materials), he delivers descriptive praise and a pat on her back. He then begins counting to five while waiting for Chrissie to perform the next step in the task analysis (i.e., turning on the water).
3. If Chrissie does not respond, does not complete the response within 30 seconds, or responds incorrectly, Mr. Lindsay again presents the task direction, "Wash your hair"; delivers the first prompt, "Find the shampoo and the towel"; and begins counting to five.

Student ____Sally____   Instructor ____S. Durner____   Task ____Hair washing____

Task Analysis Session	1	2	3	4						
Date	9/4	9/5	9/6	9/7						
1. Gather materials; go to sink.	FP	PP	V	I						
2. Turn on water.	V	V	I	I						
3. Wet hair.	FP	FP	PP	G						
4. Open shampoo bottle.	FP	PP	PP	G						
5. Squeeze shampoo into hand.	PP	PP	V	V						
6. Rub shampoo into hair.	PP	PP	PP	V						
7. Rinse hair.	PP	FP	PP	PP						
8. Turn off water.	V	I	I	I						
9. Towel-dry hair.	FP	PP	PP	G						
10. Put shampoo bottle away.	PP	PP	I	I						
Summary Data	10	10	10	10	10	10	10	10	10	10
	9	9	9	9	9	9	9	9	9	9
	8	8	8	8	8	8	8	8	8	8
	7	7	7	7	7	7	7	7	7	7
	6	6	6	6	6	6	6	6	6	6
	5	5	5	5	5	5	5	5	5	5
Circle the Number of Correct	4	4	4	(4)	4	4	4	4	4	4
Unprompted Responses and Connect.	3	3	(3)	3	3	3	3	3	3	3
	2	2	2	2	2	2	2	2	2	2
	1	(1)	1	1	1	1	1	1	1	1
	(0)	0	0	0	0	0	0	0	0	0

Key: I = task direction alone, V = verbal, PP = partial physical, FP = full physical, G = gestural

Figure 5.9. A data collection sheet selected for hair washing.

4. If Chrissie responds correctly following the first prompt at the second level in the hierarchy, Mr. Lindsay delivers descriptive verbal praise and a pat on her back and then waits a 5-second response interval for Chrissie to turn on the water. He does not deliver the task direction since he prefers that completion of the previous step in the task analysis serve as the signal for Chrissie to respond.

5. If Chrissie responds incorrectly or makes no response, Mr. Lindsay delivers the task direction and the second prompt (or third level) in the hierarchy (i.e., "Wash your hair" and the partial physical prompt). He then counts to five.

6. If Chrissie makes the correct response of gathering the materials, Mr. Lindsay delivers the same reinforcement as above and waits for Chrissie to turn on the water.

7. If Chrissie makes an incorrect response or no response, Mr. Lindsay gives the task direction and the full physical prompt (or fourth and final level)

in the hierarchy. Because the full physical prompt ensures a correct response, Mr. Lindsay praises Chrissie, gives her a pat on the back, then begins counting to five while waiting for Chrissie to make an independent response to the next step in the task analysis (i.e., turning on the water).

8. If Chrissie responds correctly within the 5-second response interval, Mr. Lindsay reinforces her and waits another 5 seconds for Chrissie to begin the third step in the task (i.e., wetting her hair).

9. If Chrissie does not respond, does not complete the response within 30 seconds, or makes an error, Mr. Lindsay delivers the task direction, "Wash your hair," and the first prompt specific to this step—that is, "Turn on the water." He again waits 5 seconds for a response from Chrissie.

10. If Chrissie turns the water on at this level in the hierarchy, Mr. Lindsay delivers praise and pats her on the back, then waits 5 seconds for a response on the next step of wetting hair.

11. If Chrissie makes an error, does not finish within 30 seconds, or does not respond, Mr. Lindsay delivers the task direction and the partial physical prompt, then again counts to five.

12. This sequence of presenting each level of assistance in the hierarchy based on student responding continues for each step in the task analysis.

Mr. Lindsay continues this procedure until Chrissie can complete the total task of ten steps to the initial task direction alone: "Wash your hair."

SUMMARY COMMENTS

- The system of least prompts procedure is a response prompting procedure that uses a hierarchy of prompts arranged in a sequence of least assistance to most assistance, and it has been effective in teaching a variety of responses to many different types of students.
- There are eight steps in the design of a system of least prompts procedure—each is dependent, in part, on student and task characteristics.
- The first level in the hierarchy, consisting of the stimulus that will eventually control the student's behavior, is often presented with each successive level in the hierarchy.
- All intermediate prompts provide the student with some information about the response being taught.
- The final level in the hierarchy consists of a controlling prompt that ensures that the student will correctly perform the task.
- The teacher must wait for a response from the student following each level in the hierarchy.
- The teacher should reinforce unprompted and prompted correct responses.
- The teacher does not fade the prompts; rather, the student selects the amount of assistance she needs to perform the correct response.

This chapter discussed the most effective and efficient means of implementing the system of least prompts procedure. Chapter 6 reviews the steps necessary for successful implementation of another response prompting procedure, most-to-least prompting. Although there are many similarities across the procedural parameters of these strategies, Chapter 6 illustrates such differences as the arrangement of prompts in terms of levels of assistance and the criterion for movement between levels in the hierarchies.

EXERCISES

1. Discuss the differences between implementing the system of least prompts procedure with a discrete versus a chained task.
2. Design a system of least prompts program for teaching putting on a coat using a three-level hierarchy and also a five-level hierarchy.
3. Discuss the implications for elimination of the target stimulus at varying levels of the hierarchy in terms of transfer of stimulus control to the target stimulus.
4. Design a system of least prompts program for Chrissie using a different hierarchy—include new prompt types, a different number of levels, and the use of differential reinforcement.

REFERENCES

Aeschleman, S. R., & Schladenhauffen, J. (1984). Acquisition, generalization, and maintenance of grocery shopping skills by severely mentally retarded adolescents. *Applied Research in Mental Retardation, 5,* 245–258.

Banerdt, B., & Bricker, D. (1978). A training program for selected feeding skills for the motorically impaired. *AAESPH Review, 3,* 222–229.

Bates, P., & Renzagila, A. (1982). Language instruction with a profoundly retarded adolescent: The use of a table game in acquisition of verbal labeling skills. *Education and Treatment of Children, 5,* 13–22.

Bennett, D. L., Gast, D. L., Wolery, M., & Schuster, J. (1986). Time delay and system of least prompts: A comparison in teaching manual sign production. *Education and Training of the Mentally Retarded, 21,* 117–129.

Browder, D.M., Hines, C., McCarthy, T. J., & Fees, J. (1984). A treatment package for increasing sight word recognition for use in daily living skills. *Education and Training of the Mentally Retarded, 19,* 191–200.

Coon, M. E., Vogelsberg, R. T., & Williams, W. (1981). Effects of classroom public transportation instruction on generalization to the natural environment. *Journal of the Association for the Severely Handicapped, 6*(2), 46–53.

Cronin, K. A., & Cuvo, A. J. (1979). Teaching mending skills to mentally retarded adolescents. *Journal of Applied Behavior Analysis, 12,* 401–406.

Cuvo, A. J., Jacobi, L., & Sipko, R. (1981). Teaching laundry skills to mentally retarded students. *Education and Training of the Mentally Retarded, 16,* 54–64.

Cuvo, A. J., Leaf, R. B., & Borakove, L. S. (1978). Teaching janitorial skills to the mentally retarded: Acquisition, generalization, and maintenance. *Journal of Applied Behavior Analysis, 11,* 345–355.

Doyle, P. M., Wolery, M., Ault, M. J., & Gast, D. L. (1988). System of least prompts: A literature review of procedural parameters. *Journal of the Association for the Severely Handicapped, 13*(1), 28–40.

Doyle, P. M., Wolery, M., Gast, D. L., Ault, M. J., & Wiley, K. (1990). Comparison of constant time delay and the system of least prompts in teaching preschoolers with developmental delays. *Research in Developmental Disabilities, 11,* 1–22.

Duffy, A. T., & Nietupski, J. (1985). Acquisition and maintenance of video game initiation, sustaining and termination skills. *Education and Training of the Mentally Retarded, 20,* 157–162.

Duker, P. C., & Michielson, H. M. (1983). Cross-setting generalization of manual signs to verbal instructions with severely retarded children. *Applied Research in Mental Retardation, 4,* 29–40.

Duker, P. C., & Morsink, H. (1984). Acquisition and cross-setting generalization of manual signs with severely retarded individuals. *Journal of Applied Behavior Analysis, 17,* 93–103.

Freagon, S., & Rotatori, A. F. (1982). Comparing natural and artificial environments in training self-care skills to group home residents. *Journal of the Association for the Severely Handicapped, 7,* 73–86.

Friedenberg, W. P., & Martin, A. S. (1977). Prevocational training of the severely retarded using task analysis. *Mental Retardation, 15*(2), 16–20.

Gast, D. L., Ault, M. J., Wolery, M., Doyle, P. M., & Belanger, S. (1988). Comparison of constant time delay and the system of least prompts in teaching sight word reading to students with moderate retardation. *Education and Training in Mental Retardation, 23,* 117–128.

Giangreco, M. F. (1983). Teaching basic photography skills to a severely handicapped young adult using simulated materials. *Journal of the Association for the Severely Handicapped, 8,* 43–49.

Glendenning, N. J., Adams, G. L., & Sternberg, L. (1983). Comparison of prompt sequences. *American Journal of Mental Deficiency, 88,* 321–325.

Godby, S., Gast, D. L., & Wolery, M. (1987). A comparison of time delay and system of least prompts in teaching object identification. *Research in Developmental Disabilities, 8,* 283–306.

Hopper, C., & Wambold, C. (1978). Improving the independent play of severely mentally retarded children. *Education and Training of the Mentally Retarded, 13,* 42–46.

Horner, R. W., & Keilitz, I. (1975). Training mentally retarded adolescents to brush their teeth. *Journal of Applied Behavior Analysis, 8,* 301–309.

Hupp, S. C., Mervis, C. B., Able, H., & Conroy-Gunter, M. (1986). Effects of receptive and expressive training of category labels on generalized learning by severely mentally retarded children. *American Journal of Mental Deficiency, 90,* 558–565.

Konstanareas, M. M. (1984). Sign language as a communication prostheses with language-impaired children. *Journal of Autism and Developmental Disorders, 14,* 9–25.

Lent, J. R., & McLean, B. M. (1976). The trainable retarded: The technology of teaching. In N. G. Haring & R. L. Schiefelbusch (Eds.), *Teaching Special Children* (pp. 197–230). New York: McGraw-Hill.

Martin, G., Cornick, G., Hughes, J., Mullen, H., & Ducharme, D. (1984). Training developmentally handicapped persons as supervisors in sheltered workshops. *Applied Research in Mental Retardation, 5,* 199–218.

McDonnell, J. (1987). The effects of time delay and increasing prompt hierarchy strategies on the acquisition of purchasing skills by students with severe handicaps. *Journal of the Association for the Severely Handicapped, 12(3),* 227–236.

Schoen, S. F., & Sivil, E. O. (1989). A comparison of procedures in teaching self-help skills: Increasing assistance, time delay, and observational learning. *Journal of Autism and Developmental Disorders, 19*(1), 57–72.

Snell, M. E. & Zirpoli, T.J. (1987). Intervention strategies. In M. E. Snell (Ed.), *Systematic instruction of persons with severe handicaps* (3rd ed.) (pp. 110–149). Columbus, OH: Charles Merrill.

Tucker, D. J., & Berry, G. W., (1980). Teaching severely multihandicapped students to put on their own hearing aids. *Journal of Applied Behavior Analysis, 13,* 65–75.

Walls, R. T., Sienicki, D. A., & Crist, K. (1981). Operations training in vocational skills. *American Journal of Mental Deficiency, 85,* 357–367.

Wolery, M., & Gast, D. L. (1984). Effective and efficient procedures for the transfer of stimulus control. *Topics in Early Childhood Special Education, 4(3),* 52–77.

CHAPTER 6

Most-to-Least Prompts Procedure

Chapter Overview

Describing the Most-to-Least Prompts Procedure
Effects of Using the Most-to-Least Prompts Procedure
Steps for Using the Most-to-Least Prompts Procedure
Sample Most-to-Least Prompts Procedure Program
Summary Comments
Exercises
References

Key Terms

Most-to-Least Prompts
Decreasing Assistance
Hierarchy
Most Intrusive to Least Intrusive
Controlling Prompt
Level
Response Interval
Prompted Correct
Prompted Error
Target Stimulus

Unprompted Correct
Unprompted Error
No Response
Criterion
Probes
Discrete Tasks
Chained Tasks
Forward Chaining
Backward Chaining
Total Task

Questions to Be Answered by This Chapter

1. What is the most-to-least prompts procedure?
2. Is the most-to-least prompts procedure effective?

3. What are the recommendations for using the procedure?
4. What are the steps to using the most-to-least prompts procedure successfully?
5. How do you measure progress with the most-to-least prompts procedure?

This chapter gives an overview of the most-to-least prompts procedure; describes the procedural parameters; summarizes its effectiveness with students who have disabling conditions; and provides a detailed explanation of the steps for implementing the most-to-least procedure, with an example.

DESCRIBING THE MOST-TO-LEAST PROMPTS PROCEDURE

The **most-to-least prompts** procedure, also known as the **decreasing assistance** procedure, is an instructional strategy that progressively fades the teacher's assistance from the point of the most amount of help needed to ensure correct responses to the point of the student's independent performance of the target behavior. There are three procedural parameters. First, the teacher selects a target stimulus and a minimum of two prompts to be placed into a prompt **hierarchy** that is arranged in sequence from the **most intrusive to least intrusive** amount of assistance. Wolery, Bailey, and Sugai (1988, p. 255) define *intrusiveness* as "the amount of control the teacher exerts over the student's behavior." In the most-to-least prompts procedure, the prompt that has the most control is delivered until the criterion level performance is obtained. This is followed by prompts that exert less control of the student's behavior. A **controlling prompt** that ensures a student will perform the target behavior correctly must be identified. The controlling prompt is always delivered at the first **level** in the most-to-least hierarchy. After the student meets criterion at the first level, the teacher presents prompts that progressively provide less information—i.e., second-level assistance, third-level assistance, and so forth. After each prompt, the student is allowed an opportunity to respond (**response interval**). A correct response at these levels in the hierarchy is a **prompted correct,** and each incorrect response following a prompt is a **prompted error.** The *final* level in the hierarchy does not contain a prompt; the teacher presents the **target stimulus** that signals the student to respond. If the student responds correctly to the target stimulus alone, it is an **unprompted correct** response. An incorrect response at this level is called an **unprompted error.** Any time the student does not respond to assistance delivered in the hierarchy, it is a **no response.**

The second procedural parameter is the identification of a **criterion** (e.g., percent or number of prompted correct responses) for moving from one level to another in the hierarchy. The student's reaching criterion at one prompt level results in the teacher using less intrusive prompts.

The third procedural parameter is ongoing assessment of the student's performance at less intrusive levels in the hierarchy. These **probes** consist of one or two test trials to assess whether the student can perform the target behavior with less assistance than is currently used during instruction. If the student makes a correct response with less assistance during a probe trial, the teacher can rearrange the hierarchy and use this less intrusive prompt during instruction.

The most-to-least procedure begins with the teacher presenting the first level in the hierarchy—simultaneous delivery of the target stimulus and the controlling prompt. The target stimulus cues the student that she is to respond, and the controlling prompt ensures that she will make the correct response. For example, Ms. Duffin is teaching Roger to vacuum his apartment, and she has selected a hierarchy of three levels: physical prompts, a model and gestural prompt, and the target stimulus alone. Initially, she delivers the target stimulus ("Vacuum the floors.") and the physical prompt (puts her hand on Roger's hand and places it on the vacuum cleaner). Ms. Duffin then allows Roger an opportunity to respond to the assistance delivered in level one. If he responds correctly, she reinforces him. If he responds incorrectly, she continues to use the first level of assistance. When Roger reaches the criterion set for the first level (e.g., two consecutive correct trials), Ms. Duffin conducts probe trials to test his performance to less intrusive levels of the hierarchy. She checks to see if he can vacuum (a) when she models the target behavior, (b) when she points to the vacuum cleaner and the floor, and (c) when she delivers the target stimulus alone. If a less intrusive prompt controls the target behavior, she uses that less intrusive prompt; otherwise, Ms. Duffin delivers the prompt originally selected for level two, accompanied by the target stimulus and an opportunity to respond. Ms. Duffin finds that Roger cannot respond correctly to any other form of assistance, so she presents the target stimulus and models the target behavior. She then waits 5 seconds for Roger to initiate the correct response. If Roger makes an incorrect response or does not respond, Ms. Duffin returns to the more intrusive level of assistance found in the first level. However, if he performs correctly, she continues to deliver the model prompt and the target stimulus until Roger has met criterion for moving to a less intrusive level and until she conducts a probe. Roger progresses through the hierarchy until he can respond to the target stimulus without assistance. A flow chart of the most-to-least prompts procedure is presented in Figure 6.1.

EFFECTS OF USING THE MOST-TO-LEAST PROMPTS PROCEDURE

Students and Behaviors Taught

The most-to-least prompts procedure has been used to teach students with varying disabilities. For example, the procedure has been effective with children who have autism and developmental disabilities (Duker & Morsink, 1984; Hinerman et al., 1982) and mild mental retardation (Kayser, Billingsley, & Neel, 1986). The majority of the research has been conducted with students exhibiting moderate, severe, or profound mental retardation (Colozzi & Pollow, 1984; Cuvo, Leaf, & Borakove, 1978; Duker & Michielson, 1983; Richmond & Lewallen, 1983). In addition, the age range in the most-to-least prompts investigations has included infants (Dunst, Cushing, & Vance, 1985), primary-aged students (Luiselli et al., 1978), and adolescents and adults (Cuvo, Jacobi, & Sipko, 1981; Wheeler et al., 1980).

A variety of behaviors have been taught with this procedure. The skills have included **discrete**, or single response, **tasks**—such as signing manually (Duker &

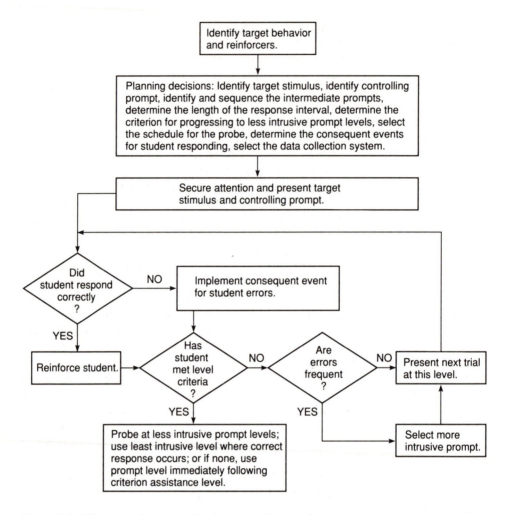

Figure 6.1. A flow chart for the most-to-least prompts procedure.

Michielson, 1983), turning the head (Dunst et al., 1985), answering questions (Luiselli et al., 1978), and expressively identifying letters and animals (Richmond & Lewallen, 1983). Other target behaviors have included **chained tasks**, tasks in which a number of behaviors are sequenced together to form a more complex skill—sorting garments (Cuvo et al., 1981), cleaning a rest room (Cuvo et al., 1978), and making a snack (Kayser et al., 1986).

Results of Using the Most-to-Least Prompts Procedure

The majority of research conducted with most-to-least prompts has used the procedure alone in teaching new skills; however, some investigations have used it in conjunction with another strategy. Duker and Michielson (1983) and Duker and Morsink (1984) taught manual signing using the system of least prompts and most-to-least prompts procedures. In the Cuvo et al. (1981) and Cuvo et al. (1978) studies, most-to-least prompts was used with the system of least prompts. The most-to-least hierarchy was used to teach those steps in the task analysis that had been identified as difficult or used with the steps that had a high probability of error responses.

The most-to-least prompts procedure also has been compared to other procedures. For example, Schoen, Lentz, and Suppa (1988) compared most-to-least prompting to graduated guidance when teaching self-help skills to preschoolers with disabilities and found the procedures equally effective. Day (1987) taught students with severe mental retardation using both most-to-least prompts and the system of least prompts procedures. Although both procedures produced an increase in correct responding, the most-to-least prompts resulted in greater improvement. The results are mixed for such efficiency measures as the number of sessions, errors, and such instructional time to criterion when the most-to-least prompts and system of least prompts procedures have been compared. For example, the system of least prompts can produce more rapid acquisition of the target behavior (Csapo, 1981) but result in a greater number of errors (Csapo, 1981; Day, 1987) than the most-to-least prompts procedure. In addition, the most-to-least procedure may promote more active responding on the part of students because they do not passively wait for a prompt as sometimes occurs with the system of least prompts procedure (Glendenning, Adams, & Sternberg, 1983). However, Walls et al. (1984) found no statistically significant differences between the two procedures in terms of errors or minutes of direct instructional time.

The most-to-least prompts procedure also has been compared to the stimulus shaping and trial and error procedures (Richmond & Bell, 1983), the stimulus fading procedure (Schreibman, 1975; Wolfe & Cuvo, 1978), and the stimulus fading and trial and error strategies (Strand & Morris, 1986). Although most-to-least prompts was found to be less effective than stimulus fading (Schreibman, 1975; Wolfe & Cuvo, 1978), the results were mixed in terms of efficiency. Stimulus fading and shaping produced fewer errors in two studies (Schreibman, 1975; Richmond & Bell, 1983), but no differences were found in the number of errors and trials to criterion in another study (Strand & Morris, 1986).

Recommendations for Practice

Because most-to-least prompts appears to be an effective procedure, it should be included as an instructional option for all teachers of students with disabilities. The number of teacher planning decisions makes it more complex than error correction, antecedent prompt and fade, and the time delay procedures. However, the procedure has several advantages since it deals with problems not easily addressed by other procedures; these advantages are shown in Table 6.1.

STEPS FOR USING THE MOST-TO-LEAST PROMPTS PROCEDURE

The most-to-least prompts procedure shares many steps with the procedures described in previous chapters. However, there are a number of additional steps that must be addressed for successful implementation of the most-to-least procedure. The

TABLE 6.1.Advantages for Use of the Most-to-Least Prompts Procedure

Problem	Most-to-Least Advantage
Student is not imitative or does not follow verbal directions.	The teacher may begin teaching with a prompt that is more intrusive than a model or a verbal prompt.
Student does not wait for a prompt.	The teacher delivers the necessary assistance before the student can respond.
Student makes a high number of errors.	The teacher delivers the necessary assistance before the student responds, selects a criterion for moving to new level, and can return to more intrusive assistance if error occurs at less intrusive levels.
The task is new and difficult.	The teacher first selects and then delivers a controlling prompt before the student responds and does not decrease the amount of assistance until the student can perform correctly with more intrusive prompts.
The task is a chained task that requires fluent movement.	The teacher selects and delivers the necessary assistance for each step in the chain, prompting fluent movement through the entire task.

11 steps listed below are defined and explanations or examples are included to ensure effective use of the procedure. In addition, the information contained in step one, reviewing the process for selecting a target behavior, can be used with other instructional procedures.

- Select and describe the target behavior.
- Identify the stimulus that signals the student to respond.
- Select the number of levels in the hierarchy.
- Select the type of prompts to be used in the hierarchy.
- Sequence the type of prompts from most assistance to least assistance.
- Determine the length of the response interval.
- Determine the criterion for progressing to a less intrusive level.
- Select the schedule for assessing the student's performance at less intrusive levels.
- Determine the consequences for each student response.
- Select a data collection system.
- Implement, monitor, and adjust the program based on the student's data patterns.

Select and Describe the Target Behavior

The success of the most-to-least prompts procedure is dependent on several steps. Initially, a detailed description of the target behavior is required. The behavior must be observable and measurable and defined as either a discrete or a chained task.

The definition of a discrete behavior is straightforward and requires little elaboration; examples are pointing to objects, identifying pictures, and following simple instructions (e.g., "Touch your nose."). With chained tasks, the teacher must determine (a) the number and sequence of steps in the chain, (b) whether to teach one step at a time, (c) if one step is taught at a time, whether to use forward or backward chaining, or (d) whether to use a total task approach and teach all steps simultaneously.

If the teacher uses **forward chaining,** he must identify the steps in the task analysis and provide instruction on the first step of the chain, followed by the second step, and so on until he has taught all the steps. He uses the most-to-least procedure to teach the first step, followed by prompting the student through the remaining steps in the task. The teacher uses the procedure until the student responds correctly to the target stimulus alone on step one. Once this criterion has been met, the teacher goes to the second step in the task using the most-to-least hierarchy and continues the sequence until the student performs the entire task independently.

In **backward chaining,** the steps in the task analysis are identical to those selected in the forward chaining example; however, teaching begins with the last step and progresses toward the first step in the chain (Snell & Zirpoli, 1987). For example, Mr. Habadi is using most-to-least prompts in a backward chaining sequence to teach Molly to make toast. The first step in the task analysis is plugging in the appliance and the last step is removing the bread when it pops up. Mr. Habadi physically guides Molly through all the steps in the task until he reaches the last step. He then uses the most-to-least prompts hierarchy to teach removing the toast. When Molly can remove the toast to the target stimulus alone, Mr. Habadi teaches the step that precedes the last step in the chain. He continues to use the most-to-least sequence of prompts, in a backward order of completing the skill, until Molly can perform the entire task without assistance.

A **total task** format also can be selected to teach a chained skill. In total task, all steps in the chain are taught simultaneously, as compared to one step at a time to criterion in the forward and backward chaining examples. If using the most-to-least procedure, the teacher progresses through the hierarchy on each step of the task analysis during each instructional session. Examples of the differences between these three formats are shown in Table 6.2.

Identify the Stimulus That Signals the Student to Respond

The second step in designing an instructional program is the teacher selecting the stimulus that signals the student to respond. The target stimulus can be a verbal task direction ("Wash your clothes."), a material cue (giving the student a notebook illustrating the steps for using the washing machine), or a naturally occurring event (no clean clothes in the student's closet).

In the most-to-least prompts procedure, the teacher always presents the target stimulus, in isolation, in the last level of the hierarchy. Therefore, the teacher does not deliver this stimulus in isolation until the student can perform the target behavior at the more intrusive levels. As described in previous chapters, the type of target stimulus selected is dependent on both the student and the skill characteristics. For example, Molly is learning to both wash and dry clothes independently. Her teacher

TABLE 6.2. Examples of Forward Chaining, Backward Chaining, and the Total Task Approach in Teaching a New Skill

Task Analysis	Forward Chaining	Backward Chaining	Total Task
Plug in toaster.	Teacher uses most-to-least hierarchy to teach step 1.	Teacher assists student through step 1.	Teacher uses most-to-least hierarchy to teach step 1.
Put bread in the toaster.	Teacher assists student through step 2.	Teacher assists student through step 2.	Teacher uses most-to-least hierarchy to teach step 2.
Push toast down.	Teacher assists student through step 3.	Teacher assists student through step 3.	Teacher uses most-to-least hierarchy to teach step 3.
Remove bread from toaster.	Teacher assists student through step 4.	Teacher uses most-to-least hierarchy to teach step 4.	Teacher uses most-to-least hierarchy to teach step 4.

analyzed the tasks and identified 12 steps for the washing task and 4 steps for drying. Because washing clothes has a greater number and more difficult steps, the target stimulus might be a task direction, such as "Wash the clothes." However, the target stimulus for drying the clothes could be a naturally occurring event, such as the washing machine stopping and clothes being wet.

With all types of target stimuli, the teacher presents the stimulus with each prompt in the most-to-least hierarchy so that it is closely paired with the student's response. This pairing facilitates the transfer of stimulus control from the prompt to the target stimulus; that is, it increases the probability that students will respond in the presence of the target stimulus alone. Examples of the repeated exposure of two different types of target stimuli in a most-to-least hierarchy are shown in Table 6.3.

Select the Number of Levels in the Hierarchy

When identifying the number of levels, the type of prompts, and the sequence of prompts, the teacher must consider the characteristics of both the student and the target behavior. Although some examples are included here, Chapter 5 presented more detailed examples and explanations. The types of prompts that have been used with the most-to-least procedure are identical to those used with the system of least prompts. Refer to Chapter 2 for complete definitions and examples of prompt types.

The total number of levels in a most-to-least hierarchy includes the target stimulus delivered alone plus the number of prompts in the hierarchy. Each hierarchy must contain a minimum of three levels: the controlling prompt, at least one intermediate prompt, and the target stimulus. For example, Mr. Habadi wants to teach Molly to follow instructions and make toast. Because following instructions is a discrete skill and

TABLE 6.3. Examples of Target Stimuli and Delivery at All Levels in the Most-to-Least Prompts Hierarchy

Level in Hierarchy	Teacher Delivers Verbal Target Stimulus	Task Example
1	Target stimulus followed by controlling prompt.	"Wash the clothes." Teacher physically guides student to complete task.
2	Target stimulus followed by less intrusive prompt.	"Wash the clothes." Teacher demonstrates task for student.
3	Target stimulus presented alone.	"Wash the clothes."

Level in Hierarchy	Teacher Allows Natural Target Stimulus to Occur	Task Example
1	Target stimulus followed by controlling prompt.	Washer stops and clothes are wet. Teacher physically guides student to complete task.
2	Target stimulus followed by less intrusive prompt.	Washer stops and clothes are wet. Teacher demonstrates task for student.
3	Target stimulus presented alone.	Washer stops and clothes are wet.

Molly can already follow a few simple instructions, he selects only two prompts and a target stimulus, for a total of three levels. However, because Molly has never been taught a chained skill and has no experience with kitchen appliances, he selects a target stimulus and three types of prompts—for a total of four levels in the hierarchy—to teach her how to make toast. In general, the greater the number of levels in the hierarchy, the more gradual the removal of prompts will be. This can result in greater amounts of instructional time but fewer student errors.

Select the Type of Prompts to Be Used in the Hierarchy

The first step the teacher must take when determining the type of prompts to be used in the most-to-least hierarchy is selecting the controlling prompt. To identify a controlling prompt, a teacher must present a number of different prompts and measure whether the student can perform the correct response. Mr. Habadi delivers a model prompt, a gesture, and a full physical prompt for each step in the task analysis. From the data on these test trials, Mr. Habadi selects a controlling prompt for Molly, one that consistently produces the correct response for each step. The remaining prompt types are based on the student and the task characteristics and the number of levels in the hierarchy (see Chapter 5). The most-to-least hierarchy can include the use of different types of prompts at each level in the hierarchy, multiple prompt types at each level of assistance, and a single prompt type throughout the hierarchy. Examples of prompts in most-to-least hierarchies appear in Table 6.4.

TABLE 6.4. Combinations of Prompt Types at Levels in the Most-to-Least Prompts Hierarchy

Level in Hierarchy	Different Type Each Level	Multiple Type Each Level	Single Type Each Level
1	Target stimulus Physical prompt	Target stimulus Verbal prompt Model prompt Physical prompt	Target stimulus Physical prompt—hand on hand
2	Target stimulus Model prompt	Target stimulus Verbal prompt Model prompt	Target stimulus Physical prompt—at wrist
3	Target stimulus Verbal prompt	Target stimulus Verbal prompt	Target stimulus Physical prompt—at shoulder
4	Target stimulus	Target stimulus	Target stimulus

Sequence the Selected Prompt Types from Most Assistance to Least Assistance

An important step in a most-to-least prompts program is the teacher arranging the selected prompts into a hierarchy of most assistance to least assistance. The hierarchy begins with the target stimulus paired with the controlling prompt, proceeds through the intermediate prompt levels, and ends with the target stimulus in isolation. The final arrangement is dependent on both the student and the target behavior. For example, Ms. Forster is trying to establish appropriate leisure skills with students in her classroom. She wants to teach Harold how to bait a hook, cast a line, and reel in a fish. Ms. Forster has selected a four-level hierarchy consisting of a verbal task direction, followed by three prompts—a model prompt, a partial physical prompt, and a full physical prompt. She cannot assume that one type of prompt will deliver more assistance to Harold than another. Ms. Forster has taught this task to other students, but Harold has had limited experience in learning such tasks, so she briefly observes Harold in the classroom and records the type of prompts delivered during scheduled activities. She finds that Harold rarely makes correct responses to verbal directions and responds correctly to models only after being taught a skill for several sessions. However, she notes that Harold cooperates with staff when they physically prompt him. Based on her observations, Ms. Forster decides that a full physical prompt will deliver the greatest amount of assistance, and she places this prompt at the first level in the hierarchy. Further, the second level will be the partial physical prompt, and the third level will be the model prompt. The final level in the hierarchy will be a verbal task direction alone. Ms. Forster's final hierarchy for Harold is shown in Table 6.5.

When teaching chained tasks, a teacher can use the same hierarchy of prompts with different steps (i.e., only one hierarchy is needed). If the teacher uses different hierarchies on different steps, then he must develop multiple hierarchies. The advantage of using one hierarchy is that there is less for the teacher to remember when implementing the program. The advantage of using multiple hierarchies is that the teacher can give more prompt levels on the more difficult steps and fewer prompt levels on the less difficult steps.

TABLE 6.5. The Most-to-Least Prompts Hierarchy Selected for Harold

Level in Hierarchy	Assistance	Example
1	Target stimulus; full physical prompt	"Put your line in the water." Ms. Forster places her hand on Harold's hand and guides Harold through the step.
2	Target stimulus; partial physical prompt	"Put your line in the water." Ms. Forster places her hand on Harold's elbow.
3	Target stimulus; Model prompt	"Put your line in the water." Ms. Forster demonstrates the step.
4	Target stimulus	"Put your line in the water."

Frequently, instruction begins with one hierarchy for all steps. As instruction progresses and probes are provided, the student will demonstrate that she needs less assistance on some steps than on others. In such cases, the teacher should provide the amount of assistance needed. For example, if a student can perform two steps at the verbal prompt level but needs a physical prompt on the other steps, then his teacher should change to the selection of multiple hierarchies for different steps. An example is shown in Table 6.6.

Determine the Length of the Response Interval

In the most-to-least prompts procedure, an opportunity for the student to respond follows the delivery of each prompt. For example, after the teacher presents the target stimulus and controlling prompt, he should allow the student a brief amount of time to respond; or, after presenting the target stimulus and a less intrusive prompt, the teacher should give the student another opportunity to respond. He continues to deliver both the target stimulus and assistance, followed by the same response interval throughout instruction. Sometimes it is not possible to allow an opportunity to respond. If the teacher has selected a full physical prompt at the first level of assistance, the prompt precludes an independent response from the student; the teacher places his hand on the student's hand and physically controls movement through the completion of the task. As described in previous chapters, the length of the response interval is dependent on the specific student and the difficulty of the task. Both variables should be considered when selecting the response interval.

Determine the Criterion for Progressing to a Less Intrusive Level

The movement of a student to a less intrusive level in the hierarchy is dependent on her attainment of a specified criterion of correct responding at a more intrusive level. The criterion should be set at a high level of accuracy to ensure that correct performance will be maintained when less assistance is delivered (Wolery et al., 1988). However, the criterion should not be so stringent that the efficiency of instruction is reduced. The criterion may be a specified percentage of correct responding (Cuvo

TABLE 6.6.   An Example of Possible Combinations of Hierarchies When Teaching a Chained
Task Using the Most-to-Least Prompts Procedure

Task Step	Level in Hierarchy	Same Hierarchy Across Steps	Different Hierarchy Across Steps
Put bread in toaster.	1	Target stimulus; full physical	Target stimulus; full physical
	2	Target stimulus; model	Target stimulus; partial physical
	3	Target stimulus; gesture	Target stimulus; gestural
	4	Target stimulus	Target stimulus
Push toast down.	1	Target stimulus; full physical	Target stimulus; partial physical
	2	Target stimulus; model	Target stimulus; model
	3	Target stimulus; gestural	Target stimulus
	4	Target stimulus	
Remove bread from toaster.	1	Target stimulus; full physical	Target stimulus; model
	2	Target stimulus; model	Target stimulus; gestural
	3	Target stimulus; gestural	Target stimulus
	4	Target stimulus	

et al., 1981), a specified number of consecutive correct responses (Colozzi & Pollow, 1984), or a certain number of minutes at each level of assistance (Dunst et al., 1985).

For example, Mr. Habadi selects 100 percent correct responding for three consecutive days as the criterion for movement between levels in the hierarchy when teaching Molly to make toast using a backward chaining format. He begins by physically prompting Molly through the first two steps in the chain, then presents the target stimulus and a full physical prompt for step 3. After three days of Molly allowing his guidance through the first three steps and physical prompts for step 4, Mr. Habadi delivers level-two prompts (the target stimulus and a model) and allows Molly 5 seconds to respond after step 4. When she can remove the bread from the toaster for three consecutive days with a model, Mr. Habadi moves to level three (the target stimulus and gestural prompt). He continues to deliver this level of assistance and the response interval until Molly is at criterion on step 3. Mr. Habadi then proceeds to level four (the target stimulus alone).

Select the Schedule for Assessing the Student's Performance at Less Intrusive Levels

When using the most-to-least prompts procedure, the teacher should assess the student's performance at the less intrusive levels of assistance. This probe consists of one or two test trials delivered periodically to determine if the student can perform the target behavior with less assistance than is being delivered during instruction. The test trials can be conducted at any time during the instructional program (e.g., once a week, every other session, following each session, or after a certain number of trials). In addition, test trials should be conducted when the student meets the criterion for moving to another level in the hierarchy. If teaching a chained task, the teacher should conduct a probe trial for each step in the task.

The test trials may indicate that the student can perform the target behavior with less assistance than originally planned, so the teacher can eliminate more intrusive prompts and deliver a less intrusive level. For example, Mr. Habadi began teaching Molly to plug in the toaster by using forward chaining, with the full physical prompt. When she met the criterion for moving to level two, he conducted six probe trials— two with the model, two with a gestural prompt, and two with the target stimulus alone. He found that Molly could not perform the target behavior when presented with the target stimulus alone, but could do so with the gesture. Based on the probe trials, he eliminated level two from the original hierarchy (the target stimulus and model prompt) and conducted instructional trials using a gesture and the target stimulus. Because he conducted the probe trials, he was able to save valuable instructional time by eliminating one level of assistance from the hierarchy. When Molly could remove the bread from the toaster with the target stimulus alone, Mr. Habadi began teaching step 3 in the task analysis. However, he returned to using the original prompts selected for each step in the task—the full physical, model, and gestural prompts.

Determine the Consequences for Each Student Response

Prior to instruction, the teacher needs to identify the consequences for each response. Possible responses include correct performance with assistance, correct performance to the target stimulus alone, errors made either with assistance or without assistance, and no responses by the student.

Responding to Correct Responses.   With the most-to-least prompts procedure, all correct responses are followed by reinforcement regardless of whether the student receives assistance. A correct response at levels with assistance (prompted correct) is reinforced, as is a correct response at the final level in the hierarchy (unprompted correct). The criterion for moving from one level to a less intrusive level is dependent on the number and percent of prompted correct student responses and the criterion for task completion depends on unprompted correct responses; only correct responses to the target stimulus alone should signal completion of training. As described in the previous chapters, the amount and type of reinforcement delivered for prompted and unprompted correct responses can be varied.

Responding to Incorrect Responses.   When using the most-to-least prompts procedure, there are three types of incorrect responses. It is possible for the student to make an error after the delivery of a prompt (prompted error) or after the presentation of the target stimulus alone (unprompted error), or the student may not respond at all (no response). If an error occurs following the delivery of the controlling prompt, the teacher should find a more intrusive prompt. However, if the error occurs following delivery at other levels of assistance, a variety of options are available:

- The teacher can ignore the error and go on to the next trial using the same level of assistance. However, if the student makes another error, the teacher can deliver a more intrusive prompt. This is an example of setting a criterion for returning to a more intrusive level of assistance (e.g., two consecutive errors results in the teacher backing up to a previously successful prompt).
- The teacher can deliver the controlling prompt following each student error, as an error correction procedure.
- The teacher can deliver the next most intrusive prompt for remaining trials in the session.
- The teacher can insert a new level in the hierarchy—one that is made up of multiple types of prompts. For example, this level could include delivery of the target stimulus, the prompt from the level where the error occurred, and the controlling prompt.

Regardless of the type of consequent event, the teacher should attempt to end a trial with the student making a correct response. That is, he should ensure that the student performs correctly with some level of assistance (a) before moving to a new trial for the same behavior or (b) before moving to teaching the next step in a chained target behavior.

Mr. Habadi selects the multiple types of assistance as the consequent event following any error or no response in making toast. Table 6.7 shows a sample of the use of multiple types of assistance for step 1 in making toast.

TABLE 6.7. An Example of a Consequent Event Following Student Errors When Teaching a Task with Forward Chaining Using the Most-to-Least Prompts Procedure

Task Step	Teacher and Student Behaviors		Example of Consequences
Step 1: Plug in toaster.	Teacher	Present level 1 assistance: Target stimulus and full physical prompt.	"Make toast." Teacher guides student's hand with his hand to plug in toaster.
	Student	Correct response.	Student allows teacher to guide her through completion of step 1.
	Student	Criterion level responding.	Student makes three correct responses on three consecutive days.
	Teacher	Go to level 2 assistance: target stimulus and model prompt. Wait 5 seconds.	"Make toast." Teacher plugs in another toaster. Counts silently to 5.
	Student	Prompted error.	Student begins to eat bread.
	Teacher	Present consequent event: target stimulus, model prompt, and full physical prompt.	"Make toast." Teacher plugs in another toaster. Delivers hand-on-hand guidance.
	Student	Correct response.	Student allows teacher to guide her through completion of step 1.
	Teacher	Return to level 2: target stimulus and model prompt. Wait 5 seconds.	"Make toast." Teacher plugs in a toaster. Counts to 5.

Select a Data Collection System

When a teacher is using the most-to-least procedure, he should collect data on the student's responses. Examination of the data on a daily basis will allow him to monitor the effectivenesss of the instructional program and assist in deciding if changes are needed. Sample data collection forms for the most-to-least prompts procedure are shown in Figures 6.2 and 6.3.

Implement, Monitor, and Adjust the Program Based on the Student's Data Patterns

Displaying these data on a graph will help the teacher determine if student progress is being made or if changes are necessary. Examples of student problems that may occur with the most-to-least prompts procedure and the teacher options available for solving the problems are described below.

- The student is making errors at the first level in the hierarchy:
  (a) Select a new controlling prompt that ensures a correct response.
  (b) Modify the task analysis if a chained task by adding another step.
  (c) Add more reinforcement for prompted correct responses.
- Less intrusive prompts are not producing correct responses, resulting in the frequent return to the controlling prompt.
  (a) Insert another prompt or level of assistance.
  (b) Modify the task analysis (e.g., add more steps).
  (c) Increase the criterion for moving from one level to another (e.g., two consecutive corrects at each prompt level to four consecutive prompted corrects).
  (d) Add to or change the correction procedure following errors.
  (e) Add more reinforcement for correct responses to less intrusive assistance.
- Each time a probe trial is conducted, the student responds correctly to a less intrusive prompt.
  (a) Modify the hierarchy, eliminating any levels of assistance that are not needed.
  (b) Use this level of assistance as the controlling prompt.

The changes mentioned above are made based on the teacher's examining the data collection sheets and the graph or visual representation of the data. Sample graphs are included in Figures 6.2 and 6.3.

SAMPLE MOST-TO-LEAST PROMPTS PROCEDURE PROGRAM

To design an effective instructional program to teach a new task using the most-to-least prompts procedure, a teacher must address each of the steps described above. The following example shows the 11 steps needed for teaching a chained skill with the most-to-least prompts procedure.

Student ___Dennis___   Instructor ___K. Boyd___   Date _11/14_   Session _4_

Task _____Instruction following_____

Trial	Stimulus	Prompts				Comments
		Physical	Model	Gestural	Independent	
1	Open the window.	+				
2	Close the door.	+				
3	Close the door.	+				
4	Open the window.	+				
5	Open the window.		+			
6	Close the door.		−			
7	Open the window.		+			
8	Open the window.			−		
9	Close the door.	+				
10	Close the door.	+				
Summary Data: Number of Corrects		6	2	0	0	
	Percent of Corrects	60	20	0	0	

Key: + = correct, − = error, 0 = no response

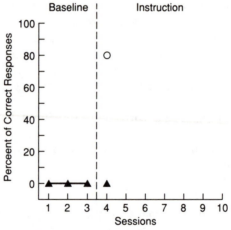

Key: ▲ = unprompted correct response,
○ = prompted correct response

Figure 6.2. This data collection form can be used for teaching a discrete task or a chained task using either forward or backward chaining with the most-to-least prompts procedure. The type of response is recorded under the appropriate assistance column. Then the individual step from the task analysis or discrete behavior is recorded in the stimulus column. This form allows the teacher to keep a record of the type of student responses made at the levels in the hierarchy, when the student has met the criterion between levels, and when the student has met the criterion for the specific step or discrete behavior.

  The line graph below the form allows the recording of the percentage of correct responses that occurred in the instructional session. Either unprompted corrects alone are recorded or both unprompted and prompted corrects are recorded, using a separate symbol for each type of response.

Student ___Karol___   Instructor ___L. Morris___   Task ___Making toast___

Steps Stimulus Session	1	2	3	4	5	6	7	8	9		
Date	9/6	9/7	9/8	9/9	9/10	9/13	9/14	9/15	9/16		
1. Plug in toaster.	P	P	P	P	P	P	P	P	P		
2. Bread in toaster.	P	P	P	P	P	P	P	P	P		
3. Push toast down.	P	P	P	P	P	P	P	M	I		
4. Remove toast.	P	P	P	P	M	I	I	I	I		
5. Butter toast.	M	V	I	I	I	I	I	I	I		
6.											
7.											
8.											
9.			·								
10.											

Summary Data

	10	10	10	10	10	10	10	10	10	10	10
	9	9	9	9	9	9	9	9	9	9	9
	8	8	8	8	8	8	8	8	8	8	8
	7	7	7	7	7	7	7	7	7	7	7
	6	6	6	6	6	6	6	6	6	6	6
	⑤	⑤	5	5	5	5	5	5	5	5	5
Circle Number of Prompted Corrects	4	4	④	④	④	4	4	4	4	4	4
	3	3	3	3	3	③	③	③		3	3
Darken Number of Unprompted Corrects	2	2	2	2	2				②	2	2
	1	1				1	1	1	1	1	1
			0	0	0	0	0	0	0	0	0

Key: M = model, V = verbal, I = independent, P = physical

Figure 6.3. This data collection form for the most-to-least prompts procedure can be used for teaching a chained skill using a total task format. The type of prompt used is recorded for each step in the task analysis. If multiple hierarchies are used (i.e., a different hierarchy for each step), prompts can be added to the key. This data sheet will show the effectiveness of the assistance selected in the hierarchy. For example, if on step 5 of the task the student consistently makes errors with a model prompt, it may indicate that the teacher should increase the criterion for movement from the physical prompt to the model prompt on this step, add the model to the controlling level in the hierarchy, or add a different prompt to the hierarchy for this step.

The bottom portion of the form can be used as a graph. The number of correct responses made with assistance are circled, and the number of correct responses made without a prompt are darkened.

Kim-Rae is a 17-year-old with severe mental retardation. Although she does not use vocalizations, she does use an augmentative picture system for communication. She follows simple instructions, receptively identifies a few survival words, and spontaneously selects new pictures to add to her communication system (e.g., favorite foods and activities). Kim-Rae has learned such community-based activities as riding a bus, ordering in a restaurant, shopping for groceries, and attending community leisure events. However, her teacher, Mr. Kitchen, has not been successful in finding her supported employment in the community or in getting her interested in the local vocational program. Because of her age, her parents and teacher are concerned about daily activities for Kim-Rae when she graduates. They identify several job placements for the upcoming school year, one of those being a neighborhood grocery store.

Select and Describe the Target Behavior

Mr. Kitchen talks to the store owners and finds that they are willing to allow a student placement if she has particular skills. They want their employee to sweep the floors, clean the counters, wash the store windows, and follow simple instructions for general picking up. Mr. Kitchen is certain that Kim-Rae will be able to perform these skills. However, her primary job responsibility will be to restock the shelves. Mr. Kitchen believes that this is the primary skill Kim-Rae should be taught. He task-analyzes the skill into ten steps and decides to teach these steps using the most-to-least prompts procedure and the total task approach; that is, he will teach all of the steps at the same time. He selects this procedure and total task because of previous success in teaching other chained skills, such as washing floors and sinks. These are the steps in the task analysis:

1. The student accepts a picture/word from her supervisor for the grocery item and finds the correct shelf;
2. obtains the grocery item from the shelf;
3. finds a basket;
4. goes to the storage room;
5. matches the item from the shelf to the box containing the item;
6. opens the box;
7. fills the basket;
8. finds the shelf where the item is displayed;
9. places the items on the shelf; and
10. returns to her supervisor for an additional work assignment.

Identify the Stimulus That Signals the Student to Respond

Mr. Kitchen interviews the store owners and asks if they would consider using a target stimulus other than the natural stimulus of empty shelves. They agree, so he selects a material or picture prompt as the target stimulus or task direction. The material target stimulus is an album consisting of photographs demonstrating the steps in the task—for example, the shelf that needs to be restocked. Kim-Rae will receive the album when she approaches her supervisors.

Select the Number of Levels in the Hierarchy

Because this is a chained task and multiple types of prompts have been effective with Kim-Rae in the past, it would be possible for Mr. Kitchen to identify any number of levels to teach the skill. However, because Kim-Rae has had experience in learning chained skills and the target stimulus is a picture, Mr. Kitchen decides that a three-level hierarchy—a controlling prompt, an intermediate prompt, and the target stimulus alone—is all that is necessary to teach this target behavior to Kim-Rae.

Select the Type of Prompts to Be Used in the Hierarchy

Mr. Kitchen examines both the student and the task characteristics. Kim-Rae is imitative and will follow some verbal directions, and the steps in the task analysis are not difficult. Therefore, he decides that Kim-Rae should not require physical prompting to perform any of the ten steps correctly. He selects a model of the correct response and a verbal prompt as the two prompts in the hierarchy.

Sequence the Selected Prompt Types from Most Assistance to Least Assistance

The first level in the hierarchy will be the target stimulus and the model prompt; Mr. Kitchen will demonstrate the correct response for Kim-Rae. Based on classroom performance, Mr. Kitchen knows that a model gives Kim-Rae more assistance then do verbal prompts alone. The intermediate level in this hierarchy will consist of the target stimulus and a verbal prompt; Mr. Kitchen will tell Kim-Rae exactly how to perform each step. The third and final level will be the target stimulus alone; Mr. Kitchen will present the photograph and printed word. This final level in the hierarchy is the stimulus that will eventually control the entire task of Kim-Rae's restocking the shelves in the grocery store. He decides to use the same type of prompts and hierarchy for each step in the task analysis. Mr. Kitchen also decides that he could add a physical prompt for any steps where a model was not sufficient.

Determine the Length of the Response Interval

Mr. Kitchen is aware of the importance of fluency in supported employment settings, so he has decided that he will allow Kim-Rae a maximum of 5 seconds to initiate each step in the task analysis. He will begin counting to five after each presentation of the target stimulus. Because some of the steps may take longer to complete than others (e.g., restocking the grocery items will take longer than getting the grocery item off of the shelf), Mr. Kitchen will allow a maximum of 30 seconds for Kim-Rae to complete each step; he will begin counting to 30 once Kim-Rae has started to respond.

Determine the Criterion for Progressing to a Less Intrusive Level

Mr. Kitchen is going to teach Kim-Rae to restock the shelves with a different grocery item, three times a day—one total task trial each session. He determines that the criterion for moving from one prompt level to another is two consecutive trials of 90 percent correct responses for the total task analysis. That is, Kim-Rae must respond correctly for two consecutive sessions with a prompt on nine of the ten steps.

Select the Schedule for Assessing the Student's Performance at Less Intrusive Levels

He decides that once Kim-Rae meets the criterion for movement between prompts he will assess her responses to the less intrusive levels of assistance. For example, if Kim-Rae responds correctly on nine of the ten steps with a model prompt for three consecutive sessions, Mr. Kitchen will test her with the verbal prompt (intermediate level) and the target stimulus alone (final level) for each task step. If she responds correctly to the target stimulus alone on any step, he will eliminate the less intrusive verbal prompt from the hierarchy for that specific step and retain the original hierarchy for the remaining steps.

Determine the Consequences for Each Student Response

For all correct responses, both prompted and unprompted, Mr. Kitchen will deliver descriptive verbal praise (e.g., "Wonderful job, Kim-Rae, you found the right box.") and add one point to her activities chart, which allows her to purchase leisure activities throughout the day. If Kim-Rae makes an error, Mr. Kitchen will interrupt, deliver a mild reprimand (e.g., "No, that is not the box you are looking for."), and deliver the controlling prompt before conducting a trial with the next step in the chain. This will ensure that she responds correctly on each step.

Select a Data Collection System

For each step in the task analysis, Mr. Kitchen will record the assistance that Kim-Rae needed to make the correct response during each instructional trial. The data collection sheet in Figure 6.3 will be used to collect data. He selects this data collection form because it also allows him to summarize the data and examine the types of prompts he is delivering. For example, if Kim-Rae makes an error during step 3 with a verbal prompt, he can deliver the controlling prompt and record an *M* for model in the student responding columns; this indicates that Kim-Rae needed the assistance provided by the model before she could make the correct response. This form will assist Mr. Kitchen in deciding if he needs to make changes based on the visual display of types of prompts, criterion for movement between levels, and student errors.

Implement, Monitor, and Adjust the Program Based on the Student's Data Patterns

Mr. Kitchen will simply connect the numbers of correct prompted responses Kim-Rae made each session that he circled and the number of unprompted corrects that he darkened on the bottom half of the data collection form in Figure 6.3.

Mr. Kitchen conducts the first two days (six trials) of training as follows:

1. Mr. Kitchen approaches Kim-Rae and hands her the photograph of the item that needs to be restocked (target stimulus), delivers the controlling model prompt for the first step in the task (finding the shelf that contains the grocery item that needs to be restocked), and begins counting to five.
2. If Kim-Rae initiates the correct response within the 5 seconds, he starts to count again, allowing her 30 seconds to imitate the model. If she responds correctly, he says, "That was great, Kim-Rae, you found the shelf," and explains that she has earned an activity point. At this first level in the hierarchy, Mr. Kitchen expects the model always to produce the correct response, although it is possible that Kim-Rae can make an error.

3. If Kim-Rae makes an error at this level, he will tell her what she did wrong—"No, that is not the right shelf."—and physically prompt the correct response (i.e., deliver more intrusive assistance).

4. Once she has found the correct shelf, Mr. Kitchen will deliver the target stimulus, model the second step in the task (getting the grocery item from the shelf), and begin counting to five. Each type of student response is followed by delivery of the identical consequent event described for step 1.

5. Mr. Kitchen continues to progress through each step in the task using the first level in the most-to-least hierarchy, until he has modeled each of the ten steps.

6. When Kim-Rae correctly imitates nine out of ten steps in the task analysis for two consecutive one-trial sessions, Mr. Kitchen will probe the remaining two levels in the hierarchy.

7. If Kim-Rae cannot correctly perform the task steps with less intrusive assistance, Mr. Kitchen will begin instruction in the next session using the second level in the hierarchy—the target stimulus and a verbal prompt for each step in the task analysis (e.g., "Look at your book, find this shelf.").

8. If Kim-Rae initiates a correct response within the response interval and completes it, Mr. Kitchen reinforces with descriptive verbal praise and an activity point.

9. If she does not initiate within 5 seconds or complete the correct response within 30 seconds on any of the ten steps, Mr. Kitchen delivers the first level—the target stimulus and the controlling model prompt and another response interval. He then teaches the next step in the task using the verbal prompt. Mr. Kitchen has decided that if Kim-Rae makes more than two errors in the session using the verbal prompt, he will return to the more intrusive first assistance level for all steps in the task and require Kim-Rae to reach criterion again before moving to less intrusive target stimulus/verbal prompt level.

10. When Kim-Rae has met criterion of two consecutive sessions of correct responding for nine of the ten steps with delivery of the target stimulus and the verbal prompt, Mr. Kitchen tests her responses to the target stimulus alone.

11. If Kim-Rae cannot perform correctly, he will use this level of assistance in the next instructional session for all steps in the task analysis until she can perform correctly.

In the total task approach to teaching chained behaviors, the task criterion is reached when the student can perform all steps in the chain with presentation of the target stimulus alone.

SUMMARY COMMENTS

*   The most-to-least prompts procedure is a response prompting procedure that uses a hierarchy of prompts arranged in a sequence of most assistance to least assistance.

- There are 11 steps in the design of a most-to-least prompts instructional program, and the design of each of the steps is dependent on the student and the task characteristics.
- The first level in the hierarchy consists of simultaneous delivery of the target stimulus and the controlling prompt, assistance that ensures a correct response from the student.
- All intermediate levels contain the target stimulus and prompts that progressively deliver less assistance as the student's responding comes under control of the target stimulus.
- The final level consists of the target stimulus alone. This stimulus is the level of assistance that the teacher wants eventually to control the student's behavior.
- If the type of prompt does not preclude the use of a response interval, the teacher allows the student the opportunity to respond following delivery of each level in the hierarchy.
- The teacher should determine not only the task criterion but also the criterion for movement between assistance levels in the hierarchy.
- All correct responses, both unprompted and prompted, should be reinforced.
- The teacher should attempt to ensure that an instructional trial ends with the student making a correct response—e.g., through error correction.
- Student responses to less intrusive prompts should be probed regularly to avoid unnecessary delivery of prompts.
- The procedure can be used to teach discrete tasks or chained skills using forward, backward, or total task approaches.
- The procedure has been effective in teaching a variety of tasks to a wide range of students.

Chapters 3 through 6 outlined the number of steps necessary for successful implementation of four response prompting instructional procedures. The next chapter discusses three additional strategies: antecedent prompt and test, antecedent prompt and fade, and graduated guidance. Although the literature illustrates that these procedures are used often, the steps for their implementation have not been well defined. Chapter 7 attempts to systematize the use of each of these procedures.

EXERCISES

1. Discuss the primary differences between the use of the system of least prompts and the use of the most-to-least prompting procedure.
2. Design a program using the most-to-least prompting procedure to teach Kim-Rae a discrete skill with one type of prompt in the hierarchy.
3. Using the information presented in Chapters 3 through 6, discuss the advantages and disadvantages of following specific procedures to teach chained and discrete skills.
4. Redesign Kim-Rae's program using a backward chaining format.
5. Discuss the implications for selecting a less stringent criterion for movement between levels in the most-to-least prompting procedure.

REFERENCES

Colozzi, G. A., & Pollow, R. S. (1984). Teaching independent walking to mentally retarded children in a public school. *Education and Training of the Mentally Retarded, 19*(2), 97–101.

Csapo, M. (1981). Comparison of two prompting procedures to increase response fluency among severely handicapped learners. *Journal of the Association for the Severely Handicapped, 6*(1), 39–47.

Cuvo, A. J., Jacobi, L., & Sipko, R. (1981). Teaching laundry skills to mentally retarded students. *Education and Training of the Mentally Retarded, 16*(1), 54–64.

Cuvo, A. J., Leaf, R. B., & Borakove, L. S. (1978). Teaching janitorial skills to the mentally retarded: Acquisition, generalization, and maintenance. *Journal of Applied Behavior Analysis, 11*(3), 345–355.

Day, H. M. (1987). Comparison of two prompting procedures to facilitate skill acquisition among severely mentally retarded adolescents. *American Journal of Mental Deficiency, 91*(3), 366–372.

Duker, P. C., & Michielson, H. M. (1983). Cross-setting generalization of manual signs to verbal instructions with severely retarded children. *Applied Research in Mental Retardation, 4*(1), 29–40.

Duker, P. C., & Morsink, H. (1984). Acquisition and cross-setting generalization of manual signs with severely retarded individuals. *Journal of Applied Behavior Analysis, 17*(1), 93–103.

Dunst, C. J., Cushing, P. J., & Vance, S. D. (1985). Response-contingent learning in profoundly handicapped infants: A social systems perspective. *Analysis and Intervention in Developmental Disabilities, 5*(½), 33–47.

Glendenning, N. J., Adams, G. L., & Sternberg, L. (1983). Comparison of prompt sequences. *American Journal of Mental Deficiency, 88*(3), 321–325.

Hinerman, P. S., Jenson, W. R., Walker, G. R., & Peterson, P. B. (1982). Positive practice overcorrection combined with additional procedures to teach signed words to an autistic child. *Journal of Autism and Developmental Disorders, 12*(3), 253–263.

Kayser, J. E., Billingsley, F. F., & Neel, R. S. (1986). A comparison of in-context and traditional instructional approaches: Total task, single trial versus backward chaining, multiple trials. *Journal of the Association for Persons with Severe Handicaps, 11*(1), 28–38.

Luiselli, J. K., Colozzi, G., Donellon, S., Helfen, C. S., & Pemberton, B. W. (1978). Training and generalization of a greeting exchange with a mentally retarded, language-deficient child. *Education and Treatment of Children, 1*(4), 23–29.

Richmond, G., & Bell, J. (1983). Comparison of three methods to train a size discrimination with profoundly mentally retarded students. *American Journal of Mental Deficiency, 87*(5), 574–576.

Richmond, G., & Lewallen, J. (1983). Facilitating transfer of stimulus control when teaching verbal labels. *Education and Training of the Mentally Retarded, 18*(2), 111–116.

Schoen, S. F., Lentz, F. E., Jr., & Suppa, R. J. (1988). An examination of two prompt fading procedures and opportunities to observe in teaching handicapped preschoolers self-help skills. *Journal of the Division for Early Childhood, 12*(4), 349–358.

Schreibman, L. (1975). Effects of within-stimulus and extra-stimulus prompting on discrimination learning in autistic children. *Journal of Applied Behavior Analysis, 8*(1), 91–112.

Snell, M. E., & Zirpoli, T. J. (1987). Intervention strategies. In M.E. Snell (Ed.), *Systematic instruction of persons with severe handicaps* (3rd ed.) (pp. 110–149). Columbus, OH: Charles Merrill.

Strand, S. C., & Morris, R. C. (1986). Programmed training of visual discriminations: A comparison of techniques. *Applied Research in Mental Retardation, 7*(2), 165–181.

Walls, R. T., Crist, K., Sienicki, D. A., & Grant, L. (1981). Prompt sequences in teaching independent living skills. *Mental Retardation, 19*(5), 243–246.

Wheeler, J., Ford, A., Nietupski, J., Loomis, R., & Brown, L. (1980). Teaching moderately and severely handicapped adolescents to shop in supermarkets using pocket calculators. *Education and Training of the Mentally Retarded, 15*(2), 105–112.

Wolery, M., Bailey, D. B., Jr., & Sugai, G. M. (1988). *Effective teaching: Principles and procedures of applied behavior analysis with exceptional students.* Boston: Allyn & Bacon.

Wolfe, V. F., & Cuvo, A. J. (1978). Effects of within-stimulus and extra-stimulus prompting on letter discrimination by mentally retarded persons. *American Journal of Mental Deficiency, 83*(3), 297–303.

CHAPTER 7

Antecedent Prompt and Test Procedure, Antecedent Prompt and Fade Procedure, and Graduated Guidance Procedure

Chapter Overview

Key Terms

Antecedent
Antecedent Prompt and Test
Transfer of Stimulus Control
Antecedent Prompt and Fade
Graduated Guidance
Controlling Prompt
Antecedent Prompt Trials
Probe Trials
Test Trials
Simultaneous Prompting
Faded

Shadowing
Discrete Tasks
Chained Tasks
Task Direction
Naturally Occurring Event
Response Interval
Correct Response
Incorrect Response
No Response
Intensity
Locus of Control

Questions to Be Answered by This Chapter

1. How are the antecedent prompt and test, antecedent prompt and fade, and graduated guidance procedures alike?
2. How do the three procedures differ?
3. Why might a student with severe disabilities not be successful in learning with the antecedent prompt and test procedure?
4. What are the ways that a teacher can fade prompts when using the antecedent prompt and fade procedure?
5. Why does the teacher not plan consequences for incorrect responses when using the graduated guidance procedure?

This chapter discusses three similar but independent instructional strategies: antecedent prompt and test, antecedent prompt and fade, and graduated guidance. Like the other instructional strategies described in the preceding chapters, these strategies involve the teacher presenting a response prompt with a stimulus that cues the student to respond, then removing the prompt in some way until the student responds to the stimulus alone. The strategies in this chapter are similar because they all present a response prompt as an **antecedent** event, or before students have the opportunity to respond; the purpose of the prompt is to assist them in performing the correct response. The strategies differ in the way that the response prompt is removed. Using the **antecedent prompt and test** procedure, the teacher presents a prompt and then removes the prompt altogether to test for **transfer of stimulus control** to the stimulus that cues the student to respond (i.e., target stimulus). Using the **antecedent prompt and fade** procedure, the teacher presents a prompt and then gradually removes it until the target stimulus being taught controls the response. Using the **graduated guidance** procedure, the teacher also presents a prompt but removes the prompt based on moment-to-moment decisions during each trial on whether to deliver, reduce, or remove a prompt.

This chapter explains each of these procedures in further detail, summarizes results from research, and presents and illustrates the steps for using each of the procedures.

DESCRIBING THE ANTECEDENT PROMPT AND TEST PROCEDURE

The antecedent prompt and test procedure involves a teacher initially presenting a **controlling prompt** (i.e., a prompt that ensures the student will perform the correct response) simultaneously with the stimulus that is being taught. These **antecedent prompt trials** are delivered for a specified number of trials or sessions. Following these trials, the teacher totally removes the prompt and provides **probe trials,** or **test trials,** that assess the student's ability to respond to the target stimulus alone. The prompt is totally removed rather than being removed gradually. For example, Mr. Johannsen is teaching Hannah how to count dollar bills in amounts from $1 to $5. For the first ten trials of a session, Mr. Johannsen models counting the dollar bills, randomly demonstrating each amount for two trials. Following these trials, Mr. Johannsen gives Hannah some bills; says, "Count the money"; and gives Hannah the opportunity to perform without the prompt. He then provides appropriate consequences for correct and incorrect responding.

Several variations of the procedure can be used. The teacher can give the prompted trials without requiring the student to make a response, or the teacher can provide the prompt and require that the student practice the response on each trial. Test trials without the prompt can be delivered in several ways: (a) immediately after the prompt trials, (b) a few seconds after the prompt trials, (c) prior to the prompt trials, (d) at the next session following the prompt trials, (e) for the rest of the day following a prompted trial, or (f) in a setting other than that where the prompted trials were delivered. Regardless of how test trials are given, the antecedent prompt and test procedure always includes the presentation of a prompt followed by test or probe trials in which the prompt has been totally removed. A systematic form of the antecedent prompt and test procedure is known as the **simultaneous prompting** procedure. This procedure has a limited research base but is a state-of-the-art antecedent prompt and test procedure. The sample antecedent prompt and test program presented in this chapter is representative of the methods used in studies examining the simultaneous prompting procedure. A flow chart for using the antecedent prompt and test procedure is shown in Figure 7.1.

DESCRIBING THE ANTECEDENT PROMPT AND FADE PROCEDURE

The antecedent prompt and fade procedure involves a teacher presenting a controlling prompt simultaneously with the stimulus that she is teaching and then removing the prompt gradually. A criterion for decreasing the prompt and levels of prompts ranging from most-to-least amount of assistance is *not* specified as it is in the most-to-least prompting procedure. Instead, the prompt is **faded** (i.e., gradually removed) based on the teacher's judgment about whether the student is "ready" to receive less assistance. The teacher continues to fade the prompt gradually until the student consistently responds correctly to the stimulus alone. The teacher can fade the prompts by decreasing the intensity of the prompt, changing the locus (i.e., position) of the prompt, decreasing the frequency of the prompts, or changing the prompt type. For example, Ms. Jacoby is teaching Dan to pull up his pants. Initially, she says, "Dan, pants up"; places her hands over Dan's hands; and guides him in pulling up his pants. Following several trials, when Ms. Jacoby decides that Dan is ready to receive less assistance, she says, "Dan, pants up"; places her hands over Dan's hands; and partially assists him in pulling up his pants. Following several trials using this prompt, Ms. Jacoby then says, "Dan, pants up," and gestures for Dan to pull up his pants. Ms. Jacoby continues to fade out the prompt by changing the prompt type when she decides that Dan is ready to receive less assistance. After delivering this sequence of prompts, she assesses whether he can pull his pants up independently. The use of the antecedent prompt and fade procedure is shown in the flow chart in Figure 7.2.

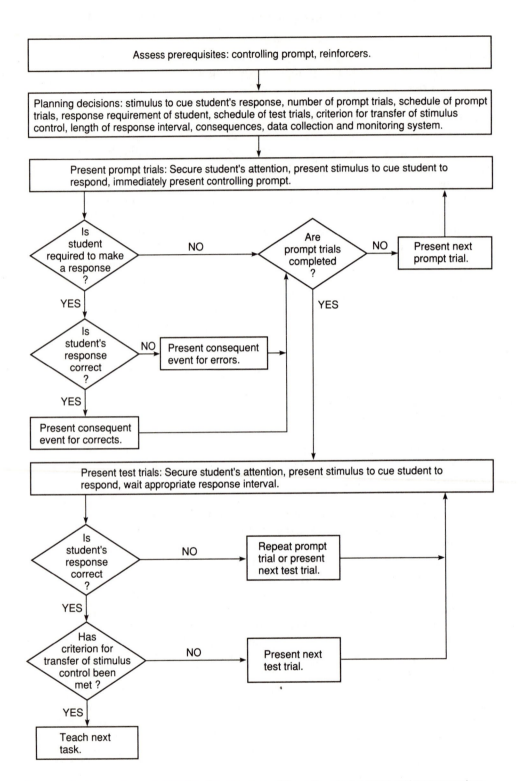

Figure 7.1. A flow chart representing the sequence of the antecedent prompt and test procedure.

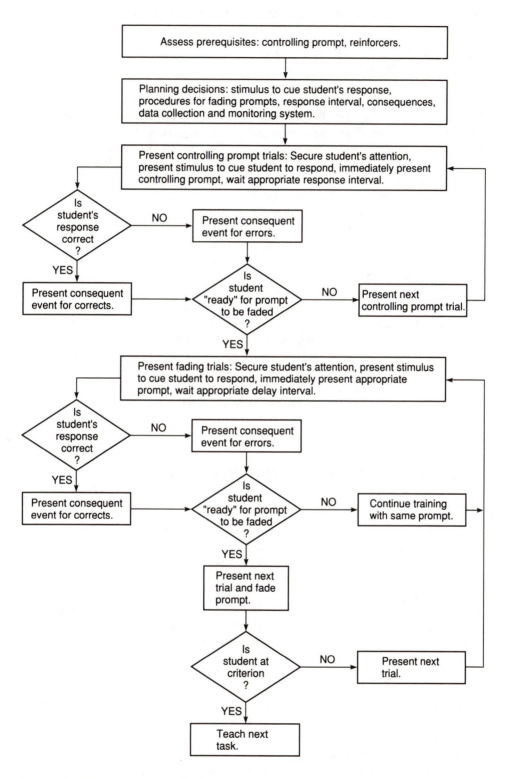

Figure 7.2. A flow chart representing the sequence of the antecedent prompt and fade procedure.

DESCRIBING THE GRADUATED GUIDANCE PROCEDURE

When using the graduated guidance procedure, as in the antecedent prompt and fade procedure, the teacher initially provides a controlling prompt and then gradually removes the prompt. The one component of this procedure that differentiates it from others, however, is that the teacher must make moment-to-moment judgments on the type and amount of prompt to provide or whether to provide any prompt based on the student's response. The teacher immediately delivers the type of prompt and the intensity of the prompt whenever she judges them to be necessary for ensuring a correct response, then immediately removes these prompts when she judges them to be unnecessary as the student begins to perform correctly. She continues to deliver or fade prompts as needed until she provides no prompts and the student responds to the task direction alone. For example, Ms. Chandler is teaching Delbert to wash dishes. Ms. Chandler uses full physical manipulation to get him to pick up a dish and place it in the sink. She continues to place her hands over Delbert's hands and uses full physical manipulation when he needs this amount of assistance, then immediately reduces or removes the physical guidance when it is not necessary to ensure correct responding. As instruction continues, she lightens her touch as Delbert begins to respond independently and provides more assistance when he begins to respond incorrectly or does not respond. During the steps of the dish-washing task in which Ms. Chandler does not need to provide a prompt, she continues to keep her hands near but not touching Delbert's hands while he is performing the task. Known as **shadowing,** this ensures that she can immediately provide a prompt when it is needed.

EFFECTS OF USING THE THREE PROCEDURES

Students and Behaviors Taught

Both the antecedent prompt and test and the antecedent prompt and fade procedures have been used extensively to teach many different types of skills to students with disabilities ranging from mild levels (Cooke & Apolloni, 1976; Frank & Wacker, 1986) to profound levels (Spangler & Marshall, 1983; Sternberg, McNerney, & Pegnatore, 1985). The majority of tasks taught with the antecedent prompt and test procedure have been **discrete tasks,** tasks involving a single response, such as reading sight words (Fink & Brice-Gray, 1979; Schuster, Griffen, & Wolery, in press), following instructions (Dehaven, 1981), labeling pictures (Rowan & Pear, 1985), and identifying abstract symbols (Howard et al., 1989). **Chained tasks,** tasks that involve several responses put together to form a more complex skill, also have been taught with this procedure and include performing assembly tasks (Crist, Walls, & Haught, 1984), using the phone (Smith & Meyers, 1979), and riding a bus (Welch, Nietupski, & Hamre-Nietupski, 1985). Most tasks taught with the antecedent prompt and fade procedure have been discrete tasks, but chained tasks also have been taught. Discrete tasks have included responding expressively to questions (Clark & Sherman, 1975), receptively identifying body parts (Koegel & Rincover, 1977), and following instructions

(Whitman, Zakaras, & Chardos, 1971). Chained tasks have included self-feeding (Knapcyzk, 1983), crossing streets (Marchetti et al., 1983), and assembling a saw chain (O'Neill & Bellamy, 1978). Unlike the other procedures, graduated guidance has been used exclusively with chained tasks, including dressing (Azrin, Schaeffer, & Wesolowski, 1976; Richmond, 1983), toileting (Foxx & Azrin, 1973), self-feeding (Azrin & Armstrong, 1973), and ascending stairs (Cipani, Augustine, & Blomgren, 1982). This procedure has most often been used with students who have severe to profound mental retardation. All ages of participants—ranging from preschoolers to adults— have been taught using the antecedent prompt and test and the antecedent prompt and fade procedures. The majority of the graduated guidance research has been conducted with adults (Azrin & Armstrong, 1973), although two research studies have taught self-help skills to preschoolers (Richmond, 1983; Schoen, Lentz, & Suppa, 1988).

Results of Using the Procedures

Some comparative investigations involving the antecedent prompt and test procedure have been conducted (Ault et al., 1989). One investigation involved graduated guidance, but no investigations have compared the antecedent prompt and fade procedure to other instructional strategies. Antecedent prompt and test, however, has been compared to error correction and to stimulus fading. In four studies comparing antecedent prompt and test to an error correction procedure (i.e., the prompt was presented only following errors), antecedent prompt and test yielded fewer errors in all studies (Ellis, Walls, & Zane, 1980; Haught, Walls, & Crist, 1984; Walls, Zane, & Thvedt, 1980; Zane, Walls, & Thvedt, 1981). In addition, Zane et al. (1981) found that the antecedent prompt and test procedure required fewer minutes of instruction time than did error correction; Ellis et al. (1980) and Walls et al. (1980) found no differences between the two procedures in instruction time. Dorry (1976) found the antecedent prompt and test procedure, when compared to stimulus fading, to be less effective. Two studies have compared the antecedent prompt and test procedure called simultaneous prompting to the delay procedures. Howard et al. (1989) compared simultaneous prompting with the progressive time delay procedure in teaching abstract symbols to adolescents with moderate retardation. The authors found both procedures to be effective, with no consistent difference in acquisition rates. Schuster et al. (in press) compared simultaneous prompting with a constant time delay procedure in teaching sight words to elementary students with moderate retardation. Their results indicated that both procedures were effective, with overall data showing the simultaneous prompting procedure to require fewer trials and sessions to criterion, take less instructional time, and to have lower student errors than the constant time delay procedure. When compared to a most-to-least prompting procedure, graduated guidance was found to be equally effective in teaching face washing and drinking from a water fountain to preschool students with Down syndrome (Schoen et al., 1988).

Recommendations for Practice

The antecedent prompt and test procedure is a relatively simple procedure because it requires use of one prompt followed by complete removal of that prompt. Although the procedure's effectiveness has been shown with students who have a variety of disabling conditions, those with more severe disabilities may need a procedure that involves more gradual fading of prompts. The antecedent prompt and fade procedure, which provides a way to remove prompts more gradually, can be used with all kinds of prompts and tasks. The disadvantage of this procedure is its reliance on the teacher making judgments about when to fade prompts. Since no systematic criterion is used, prompts may be faded too quickly or slowly, thus impeding learning. If a teacher has had experience with this procedure or has taught a particular student for a prolonged period of time, this procedure would be appropriate; however, if he is not familiar with the procedure or the student, he may need a more systematic means of fading prompts. Graduated guidance, although used most frequently with chained tasks, can be applied to discrete skills. As with antecedent prompt and fade, much of the success of the procedure lies in the teacher making judgments about what prompts to deliver and when to deliver then. It has been used successfully with students with profound retardation, but it has not been studied as extensively as some other procedures. It is recommended that the teacher be familiar with each student and with the delivery of prompts before selecting graduated guidance.

STEPS FOR USING THE ANTECEDENT PROMPT AND TEST PROCEDURE

These are the eight steps a teacher needs to follow to design an effective antecedent prompt and test instructional program:

- Identify the stimulus that cues the student to respond.
- Identify the controlling prompt.
- Determine the antecedent prompt trial procedures.
- Determine the testing procedures.
- Determine the length of the response interval.
- Determine the consequences for each student response.
- Select a data collection system.
- Implement, monitor, and adjust the program based on the student's data patterns.

Identify the Stimulus That Cues the Student to Respond

The first step in designing an antecedent prompt and test program is for the teacher to decide what stimulus will cue the student that it is time to respond (i.e., the stimulus being taught). The teacher may want to (a) tell the student directly to perform a task by using a **task direction;** (b) use other stimuli, such as pointing to the student when it is time for him to respond, setting out materials for the student to use, or holding up a new stimulus; or (c) use a **naturally occurring event** to cue the student that a response is needed. For example, a pile of dirty clothes cues a student that the laundry needs to be done. Whatever stimulus the teacher uses, she should identify it prior to instruction and use it consistently throughout programming.

Identify the Controlling Prompt

With the antecedent prompt and test procedure it is necessary for the teacher to identify only one prompt. Since only one prompt is delivered and then totally removed, it is necessary that the teacher use a controlling prompt, one that ensures a correct response by the student. Before beginning instruction, the teacher must assess different types of prompts to identify a prompt that provides the least amount of assistance possible but also controls the student's responding. The majority of controlling prompts that have been used in antecedent prompt and test investigations have been model prompts (Sarber et al., 1983; Lowe & Cuvo, 1976).

Determine the Antecedent Prompt Trial Procedures

Once the teacher has identified the controlling prompt, she must determine how to conduct antecedent prompt trials (simultaneous presentation of the target stimulus and the controlling prompt).

Schedule Prompt Trials.   Flexibility can be used in scheduling prompt trials as long as at least one prompt trial is delivered before a test trial is presented. They can occur one time only at the beginning of instruction on a new task, once a day during each instructional session, or at the beginning of a day throughout which observations of behavior will occur.

Identify the Number of Prompt Trials.   A determination also must be made on how many antecedent prompt trials will be delivered. In order for her method of instruction to be defined as an antecedent prompt and test procedure, the teacher must initially present at least one antecedent prompt trial, but she can deliver more prompt trials. For example, Mr. Ryan is teaching Susan to make social contacts with her playmates. During the first play period of the day, Mr. Ryan models greeting behaviors for Susan with various peers for at least ten trials. The number of antecedent prompt trials that he presents is an arbitrary decision. No research has been conducted to determine an optimal number of prompt trials. Mr. Ryan may prefer to deliver one prompt trial, several trials, or several sessions of prompt trials before providing test trials. When teaching a task unfamiliar to a student, a difficult task, or a student with a severe disability, the teacher may need to deliver more trials before removing the prompt. He may also identify a criterion for moving to test trials based on a certain number of correct consecutive prompted trials.

Identify the Student's Response Requirement.   When delivering prompt trials, the teacher must determine whether a response will be required from the student. The teacher may deliver a prompt trial and expect no response from the student or may require that the student perform the correct response following prompt trials. For example, when Mr. Ryan greets playmates, he requires that Susan imitate the correct response on each trial. Again, the decision on whether to include a response requirement from the student during probe trials is an arbitrary one. A response requirement, however, may be beneficial when teaching a difficult task or a student with a severe disability. However, the efficiency of instruction can be enhanced by not requiring a response because trials can be conducted more quickly.

Determine the Testing Procedures

Following the prompt trials, the teacher assesses transfer of stimulus control from the prompt to the stimulus being taught by providing test or probe trials. These trials are presented without the prompt.

Schedule Test Trials.   Test trials can be presented immediately following the prompt trials, a few seconds or minutes after the prompt trials, prior to the prompt trials, in one or several sessions or days following the prompt trials, or in a different setting than the one used for the prompt trials. The requirements for test trials are that they occur any time after the delivery of one or more prompt trials and that they involve the complete removal of the prompt. For example, Mr. Ryan models greeting responses to Susan's playmates and has her imitate. During the second play period of the day, he presents the task direction, "Go play with your friends," and observes the number of greetings Susan makes without prompts. Again, flexibility can be used in determining when these trials are delivered.

Criterion for Determining Mastery.   The purpose of the probe or test trials is for the teacher to assess the student's ability to respond without a prompt to the stimulus that cues the student to respond or to determine if transfer of stimulus control has occurred. Because of this, the teacher must be careful in determining a criterion for mastery when using this procedure. Obviously, Mr. Ryan will not want to stop instruction on the same day Susan demonstrates independent greeting responses during the second play period since he does not know if she will be able to perform the behavior when prompt trials are not presented during the first play period. Therefore, in setting his criterion for mastery he will want to present test trials in a way that ensures a true test of skill acquisition. Mr. Ryan decides that for three days he will conduct prompt trials during the first play period, then give a test trial during the second play period. After these days he will provide only the test trial during both play periods. When Susan is able to greet students during these test-trial-only sessions for three consecutive play periods, he will assume that she has learned the task.

Determine the Length of the Response Interval

When providing trials, the teacher must identify a certain amount of time that the student will be given to respond following the stimulus that cues the response and the prompt. This **response interval** should be used consistently throughout instruction and should be a reasonable amount of time for the student to respond. For example, Ms. Smith is teaching Gordon to answer the question "What is your name?" She wants to identify an amount of time that is reasonable for a person to answer this question; therefore, she decides that she will give Gordon 5 seconds to answer the question. Sometimes longer response intervals are needed to give a student time to begin or initiate a response, and the teacher should also identify the amount of time the student will be given to complete a response. For example, Mr. Ryan may give Susan 30 seconds to initiate a greeting response with a playmate during the play period.

Determine the Consequences for Each Student Response

Before implementing the antecedent prompt and test procedure, the teacher needs to identify the consequences that he will deliver when the student makes a correct, an incorrect, or no response. A **correct response** indicates that the student responded correctly within the response interval; an **incorrect response** indicates that the student responded incorrectly within the response interval; and a **no response** indicates that the student did not respond at all within the response interval.

Responding to Correct Responses.   When planning consequences for correct responding, the teacher must ask himself at least these three questions: (a) Do I want to reinforce correct responses for both prompt and test trials?, (b) Do I want to reinforce prompt and test trials in the same way?, and (c) How will I reinforce correct responses? Because prompt trials require a response from the student, the teacher should decide before instruction begins if he wants to reinforce both prompt and test trials. Most research that has been conducted using the antecedent prompt and test procedure has used reinforcement for correct responses during both prompt and test trials (Gersten et al., 1982). There are no rules for providing reinforcement during these trials, but consequences should be planned before training begins. If a student response is required during prompt trials, the teacher needs to decide if prompt and test trials will receive the same consequence for correct responding. He may provide the same reinforcement for both types of trials, provide more reinforcement for prompt trials, or provide more reinforcement for test trials. In addition, several correct prompted trials may be the criterion for moving to test trials, and several correct test trials may be the criterion for moving to another stimulus. Correct responses to the test trials are the only responses that count toward criterion. The teacher must identify specific reinforcers for each student using a reinforcer preference test prior to instruction.

Responding to Incorrect Responses.   The teacher should also have a plan for providing consequences for incorrect responses that occur during prompt and test trials. Most investigators using the antecedent prompt and test procedure corrected the student's error by guiding the student to complete the correct response (DeHaven, 1981) or by telling the student the correct answer (Fink & Brice-Gray, 1979). If the student makes incorrect responses during test trials, the transfer of stimulus control has not occurred, and the teacher should continue prompt trials during the next trial or session (Olenick & Pear, 1980).

Select a Data Collection System

As in other instructional programs, the teacher must collect student responding data on a daily basis to monitor progress and make effective modifications in the program when they are necessary. If student responses are not required during prompt trials, the teacher may not need to collect data during these trials; however, he may find it helpful to collect data on the delivery of the prompt trial even if a response was not required so that a record is kept of prompt trials that were delivered. A sample data collection sheet to be used with this procedure is shown in Figure 7.3.

Implement, Monitor, and Adjust the Program Based on the Student's Data Patterns

A sample line graph that presents a visual analysis of a student's progress is shown in Figure 7.4. Since the student's response to test trials is the target response, the teacher should plot the responses to these trials on the graph so he can determine when the student meets criterion. The student's responses to prompted trials can also be plotted to monitor progress during training trials.

Several modifications in the procedure may be needed when the student does not progress as expected. If many errors or no responses occur during prompt trials, the teacher should identify a prompt that will consistently control the student's behavior. Similarly, if the student makes excessive errors during test trials or shows several days of no improvement, the teacher should present more prompt trials before delivering test trials or should use an instructional procedure that gradually fades prompts.

Student ____S.T.____   Instructor ____P. G.____   Date __2/28__ Session __4__

Start time ____8:45____   Stop time ____8:52____   Total time ____7'____

Task _____Identifying coins_____

Trial/ Step	Stimulus/Task Analysis	Trial Type (Circle one)	Student Responding		
			Correct	Incorrect	No Response
1	Penny	Prompt (Test)			✓
2	Quarter	Prompt (Test)			✓
3	Penny	(Prompt) Test	✓		
4	Quarter	(Prompt) Test	✓		
5	Quarter	(Prompt) Test	✓		
6	Penny	(Prompt) Test	✓		
7	Penny	(Prompt) Test	✓		
8	Quarter	(Prompt) Test	✓		
9	Penny	(Prompt) Test	✓		
10	Quarter	(Prompt) Test	✓		
Number of Prompt Trial Responses			8	0	2
Percent of Prompt Trial Responses			100	0	100
Number of Test Trial Responses			0	0	0
Percent of Test Trial Responses			0	0	0

Key: ✓ = occurrence

Figure 7.3. On this data collection sheet, a circle is placed around the word *Prompt* or *Test* to identify each trial as a prompt or a test trial. Then the stimuli or the task analysis is placed in the appropriate column. A check mark is placed in the appropriate Student Responding column for each trial. For prompt trials in which a student response is not required, NA can be placed in the Student Responding column.

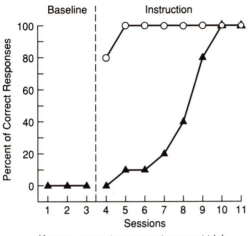

Figure 7.4. This graph represents sample data from an antecedent prompt and test instructional program in which prompt and test trials occur every session.

SAMPLE ANTECEDENT PROMPT AND TEST PROCEDURE

The teacher should consider eight steps to design an effective antecedent prompt and test program. The following example illustrates the use of these steps.

Barry is a 9-year-old with a bilateral hearing loss and moderate mental retardation. Ms. Gwinn, his teacher, wants to teach Barry the numerals 1-12 on the clock face. Barry uses a total communication system (i.e., speech and manual signs) to communicate, and Ms. Gwinn has successfully taught him numerous other discrimination tasks. Barry is able to consistently imitate some sounds and most motor movements. Ms. Gwinn has identified praise as a reinforcer for Barry and decides to teach him two numerals at a time to criterion before teaching two more numerals.

Identify the Stimulus That Cues the Student to Respond

Ms. Gwinn decides to use the verbal and signed task direction "What number?" to signal Barry to respond. She eventually wants Barry to be able to identify the numerals as they appear on any clock face, so she uses a variety of different kinds of clocks found in his natural environment and points to each numeral that she wants Barry to identify.

Identify the Controlling Prompt

Since Barry can imitate manual signs, Ms. Gwinn will use a verbal and signed model as the controlling prompt. This is the prompt that she knows will control Barry's responding and also provide the least amount of assistance possible.

Determine the Antecedent Prompt Trial Procedures

Because she wants to minimize Barry's errors, Ms. Gwinn decides to teach him two numerals at a time. She will provide him with 20 prompt trials every day, 10 for each of the numerals. She wants to be sure that Barry is attending as she presents prompt trials, so she requires that he imitate the response immediately after her model.

Determine the Testing Procedures

Ms. Gwinn wants to monitor Barry's progress closely, so she provides four test trials on a daily basis, two trials on each of the two numerals. Test trials consist of Ms. Gwinn providing the task direction ("What number?") and recording Barry's response. She delivers no prompts. She presents test trials immediately prior to prompt trials in every session so that she will assess Barry on what he learned during prompt trials on the preceding day of instruction. She will present no test trials prior to prompt trials on the first day of instruction because no prompt trials occurred on the preceding day. When Barry responds with 100 percent correct responses for three consecutive days during test trials, he will meet the criterion. Ms. Gwinn will then teach two new numbers while continuing to review the original numbers.

Determine the Length of the Response Interval

Because Ms. Gwinn wants Barry to tell time relatively quickly, she gives him 4 seconds to respond following each prompt or task direction.

Determine the Consequences for Each Student Response

Ms. Gwinn praises Barry when he makes a correct response during both prompt and test trials. When he makes an incorrect response or no response during both types of trials, Ms. Gwinn corrects him by physically guiding him to make the correct manual sign response.

Select a Data Collection System

Ms. Gwinn uses a data collection sheet like the one shown in Figure 7.3 to collect both prompt and test data. She uses the test trial data to determine if Barry has met the criterion but also monitors the prompt data to ensure that Barry is not making errors during prompt trials.

Implement, Monitor, and Adjust the Program Based on the Student's Data Patterns

Ms. Gwinn uses the daily test trial data to record the percent of Barry's correct responses for each session. Each day a session consists of test trials followed by prompt trials until Barry meets the criterion.

STEPS FOR USING THE ANTECEDENT PROMPT AND FADE PROCEDURE

The antecedent prompt and fade procedure is similar to the antecedent prompt and test procedure. Both procedures have the teacher initially present a prompt before the student has an opportunity to respond. In antecedent prompt and fade, however, the teacher uses a more gradual removal of the prompts. These are the seven steps a teacher must follow when planning an antecedent prompt and fade program:

- Identify the stimulus that cues the student to respond.
- Identify the controlling prompt.
- Specify the procedures for fading prompts.
- Identify the response interval.
- Determine the consequences for each student response.
- Select a data collection system.
- Implement, monitor, and adjust the program based on the student's data patterns.

Identify the Stimulus That Cues the Student to Respond

As with other instructional strategies, the first step in designing an antecedent prompt and fade program is for the teacher to determine the stimulus that signals the student that it is time to respond.

Identify the Controlling Prompt

To ensure that the student receives the amount of assistance necessary to complete a response correctly, the teacher must identify a controlling prompt. This will be the prompt that she will use during initial trials of the program.

Specify the Procedures for Fading Prompts

Once the teacher has identified the controlling prompt, she begins initial instructional sessions by presenting this prompt so that the student performs the correct response. This prompt is used for a specific number of trials or sessions until she decides whether the student is ready for the prompt to be reduced.

Determine the Schedule for Fading Prompts.   Unlike the most-to-least prompts procedure, the antecedent prompt and fade relies on the teacher's judgment to determine when prompts are faded, rather than specifying a criterion that the student must reach before a prompt is faded. The teacher needs to be familiar with the student's response patterns so that she can accurately determine when the student needs less assistance. She can use a certain number of trials or sessions as a guide in determining when to fade prompts; generally, when the teacher thinks that the student's responding is progressing, she should fade the prompt.

Determine the Method for Fading Prompts.   Prompts are faded so that the level of assistance provided is gradually reduced. The teacher does this by decreasing the **intensity** of the prompt, changing the **locus of control** of the prompt, reducing the frequency of the prompt, or changing the prompt type. If prompts are to be faded by intensity, the teacher uses the same prompt throughout instruction but changes the strength or force of it over trials. For example, when teaching a motor response, a teacher first presents full physical guidance by firmly holding her hands over the student's hands. As the prompt is faded, she gradually lightens her grip until she does not touch the student at all. Changing the intensity of a teacher model can also be used to fade prompts. For example, Ms. Halloway is teaching Yusuf to clap his hands when she says, "Clap your hands." Currently, he responds correctly when she claps very loudly and exaggerates her movements greatly. After several trials of using this prompt, Ms. Halloway gradually decreases the loudness of her hand clapping and the exaggeration of her movements until Yusuf claps without the model.

The teacher can also reduce prompts by altering the locus of control—changing the placement of guidance on the student's body from a prompt that provides the most assistance to a prompt that provides less assistance. For example, when teaching a motor task, a teacher should physically guide the student by placing her hands over the student's hands and guiding him through the entire task. As instruction continues, the teacher reduces the prompts by moving her place of guidance to the student's wrists, then forearms, elbows, upper arms, shoulders, and so forth, until she does not touch the student at all.

The teacher can also fade a prompt by reducing the frequency of its delivery. For example, Mr. Fields is teaching Jennifer to sweep the floor of her job site with a broom. Jennifer is able to complete the task correctly if Mr. Fields watches her and verbally instructs her on sweeping. At the beginning of instruction, Mr. Fields verbally instructs Jennifer continuously during the entire sweeping task. Over time, he slowly reduces the number of verbal instructions as Jennifer begins to respond more and more independently, until she can sweep the floor without assistance.

If the teacher uses more than one prompt type, then she can fade the prompts by determining a number of prompts that provide the student with varying degrees of assistance. For example, if Mr. Fields is teaching Jennifer to sweep the floor by changing the type of prompt, he might fade the prompts in this order: full physical guidance, partial physical guidance, model, gestural, verbal instruction, indirect verbal instruction, and no assistance. Several prompt types are used, but the assistance provided by the prompts is decreased as instruction continues. When deciding how to fade prompts, the teacher should consider the student's response patterns and what prompts have been used successfully in the past. Prompts can be faded using these fading methods separately or in combination. The plan for how prompts will be faded should be specified prior to beginning instruction.

Identify the Response Interval

Following delivery of each prompt, the teacher needs to give the student a certain amount of time to respond. This response interval, usually brief, consists of an amount of time that appears reasonable for the student.

Determine the Consequences for Each Student Response

Following delivery of each prompt in the antecedent prompt and fade procedure, the teacher records the student's response. Student responses should be scored as correct, incorrect, or no response. A correct response indicates the student performed the task correctly within the response interval; an incorrect response indicates the student responded incorrectly within the response interval; and a no response indicates the student did not respond within the allotted response interval. The teacher records the student's responses to each prompt and to the task direction alone. Correct responses to the task direction alone (i.e., when no prompt is presented) are the responses that count toward criterion.

Responding to Correct Responses.   Whenever the student makes a correct response, regardless of what prompt the teacher delivered, she should reinforce the student. The teacher should always identify reinforcers for each student prior to implementation of instruction through the use of reinforcer preference testing. The student should receive considerable reinforcement and errors should remain low since the prompt is faded only when the student is ready to receive less assistance. The student is reinforced for correct responses with each prompt used.

Responding to Incorrect Responses.   Investigations using the antecedent prompt and fade procedure have employed different consequences for incorrect responding. These have included verbal reprimands (Barrera, Lobato-Barrera, & Sulzer-Azaroff, 1980), verbal reprimands plus time-out (Clark & Sherman, 1975), and correcting the student using full physical guidance (Remington & Clarke, 1983). Consequent events should be selected based on each student. However, to reduce errors, the teacher should fade a prompt only when the student responds correctly and should provide more assistance when errors begin to occur. The teacher may choose to return to the controlling prompt and begin the fading procedures again, deliver the controlling prompt for a certain amount of time and then return to the prompt that was being used when errors began to occur, or move back to the prompt that was successful immediately prior to when errors occurred.

Select a Data Collection System

To know what prompt to deliver and when to fade or increase assistance, the teacher needs to collect daily data on the prompt that is being delivered and student's responses to each prompt. Sample data collection sheets for the antecedent prompt and fade procedure are included in Figure 7.5.

Implement, Monitor, and Adjust the Program Based on the Student's Data Patterns

When using the antecedent prompt and fade procedure, the teacher must make sure that she is not fading prompts too quickly or too slowly. The line graph presented in Figure 7.6 illustrates one way to graph training data. If the teacher fades the prompts too quickly, the student will begin to make errors and will need to be provided with

Student _____B.C._____   Instructor _____D.M._____   Task _____Stuffing envelopes_____

Stimulus/Task Analysis	Time	9:00	9:00	9:02	9:01					
	Session	1	2	3	4					
	Date	6/1	6/2	6/3	6/4					
1. Pick up envelope.		V	V	I	I					
2. Insert letter.		P	P	M	M					
3. Seal envelope.		P	P	P	P					
4. Put on address label.		M	M	M	V					
5. Put on return address label.		M	M	M	M					
Summary Data										
Number of P's		2	2	1	1					
Number of M's		2	2	3	2					
Number of V's		1	1	0	1					
Number of I's		0	0	1	1					

Key: P = physical, M = model, V = verbal, I = independent

Student _____Saul_____   Instructor _____Rikhoff_____   Date _____10/21_____ Session _____5_____

Start time _____8:30_____   Stop time _____8:45_____   Total time _____15'_____

Prompt _____Firm pressure/wrists_____   Task _____Taking off T-shirt_____

Trial/ Step	Stimulus/Task Analysis	Student Responding		
		Correct	Incorrect	No Response
1	Grasp left sleeve.	✓		
2	Pull over left arm.	✓		
3	Grasp right sleeve.	✓		
4	Pull over right arm.	✓		
5	Grasp collar, pull over head.	✓		
Number of Responses		5		
Percent of Responses		100		

Key: ✓ = occurrence

Figure 7.5. The top data collection sheet is used when prompts may change from trial to trial or when the teacher wants to use different prompts on different steps of the task analysis. Any prompt can be used with this data sheet, and the teacher can easily see over time if the prompts are successfully being faded or if no student change is occurring. The bottom data sheet is used when prompts will be faded slowly. The one prompt that is used for the entire session is indicated at the top of the sheet. During subsequent sessions, based on the data from this session, the prompts can be decreased, increased, or sustained.

a prompt that gives him more assistance until the prompt can be faded successfully. If the student continues to make errors with this prompt, then the teacher must add one or more prompts to allow the fading to occur more gradually. If the teacher fades the prompts too slowly, the student may know how to do the behavior independently

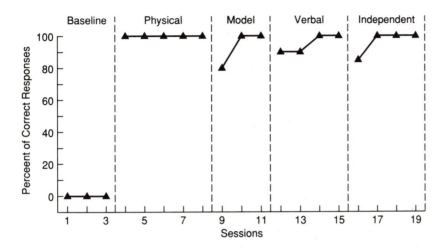

Figure 7.6. This sample graph from an antecedent prompt and fade program allows monitoring on how the student is performing on each of the prompts. If the prompts are being faded correctly, correct responses should be at high levels for each prompt.

but is never given the opportunity to do so. In this case, valuable instruction time is wasted and the student may become bored. Therefore, it is necessary for a teacher to periodically (e.g., every other day, once a week) present trials without prompts to assess the student's learning. If the student is unable to correctly perform the task independently, the teacher returns to the training procedures; however, if the student is able to perform the task independently, then she can begin instruction on another task.

SAMPLE ANTECEDENT PROMPT AND FADE PROCEDURE

There are seven steps a teacher needs to follow when using an antecedent prompt and fade procedure. The following example illustrates the use of these steps.

Saul is a 5-year-old with severe disabilities. His teacher, Mrs. Rikhoff, who has taught Saul for 2 years, wants to teach him to take off a pullover T-shirt. Since she is familiar with teaching Saul using prompts, she decides to use the antecedent prompt and fade procedure. Saul does not consistently follow a model or a verbal direction, but he has successfully learned other chained tasks—such as hanging his coat on a hook and getting a drink of water from the fountain. Mrs. Rikhoff developed a task analysis for teaching the dressing task and will simultaneously teach all the steps of the task.

Identify the Stimulus That Cues the Student to Respond

Since Mrs. Rikhoff will be at school when teaching Saul to take his T-shirt off, the naturally occurring stimulus of getting ready for bed or bath is not practical.

Therefore, she decides to use a verbal direction, "Saul, shirt off," as the stimulus to cue him to respond.

Identify the Controlling Prompt

Since Saul does not consistently follow a model, Mrs. Rikhoff will use full physical guidance as the controlling prompt.

Specify the Procedures for Fading Prompts

Mrs. Rikhoff knows that Saul learns best when his prompts are gradually faded. She will consequently remove the physical guidance prompt by fading both the intensity of the prompt and the locus of control. She decides to use the following fading steps: firm pressure to guide Saul's hands, then light pressure to his hands; firm pressure to guide Saul at his wrists, then light pressure at his wrists; firm pressure at Saul's elbows, then light pressure at his elbows; and firm pressure at Saul's upper arms, then light pressure at his upper arms. She uses each prompt for at least one session or until Saul responds with 100 percent accuracy when she uses each prompt. Twice a week she asks Saul to take his T-shirt off without providing any prompts so that she can assess his ability to perform the task without prompts.

Identify the Response Interval

For each step in the task analysis, Mrs. Rikhoff gives Saul 5 seconds to initiate each step and 10 seconds to complete each step.

Determine the Consequences for Each Student Response

Every time Saul makes a correct response, regardless of the prompt she uses, Mrs. Rikhoff praises Saul. At the end of each trial, Mrs. Rikhoff praises him, helps him put his T-shirt back on, and allows him to get a drink from the water fountain. If Saul responds at less than 100 percent for three consecutive days when she uses a prompt, Mrs. Rikhoff increases the assistance to the prompt that she used immediately prior to when Saul's errors began to occur.

Select a Data Collection System

Since Mrs. Rikhoff uses one prompt only each session, she uses a data collection sheet like the one found on the bottom of Figure 7.5.

Implement, Monitor, and Adjust the Program Based on the Student's Data Patterns

Mrs. Rikhoff graphs Saul's data on a line graph to monitor his performance closely with each prompt and to monitor trials she delivers without prompts. If Saul makes excessive errors, she fades the prompts more gradually by fading the pressure of her grip more slowly and using more positions on Saul's arm to guide him.

STEPS FOR USING THE GRADUATED GUIDANCE PROCEDURE

Like the antecedent prompt and fade procedure, graduated guidance involves a teacher presenting a prompt and then gradually removing it. The difference between the procedures is that with graduated guidance, the teacher makes moment-to-moment decisions about whether to deliver the prompt, reduce the prompt, or remove the prompt based on the student's response at the time. Therefore, the amount of prompt changes the teacher can make in any graduated guidance instructional session are often greater than with other response prompting strategies. These are the six steps for designing a graduated guidance instructional program:

- Identify the stimulus that cues the student to respond.
- Identify the controlling prompt.
- Specify the procedures for fading prompts.
- Determine the consequences for each student response.
- Select a data collection system.
- Implement, monitor, and adjust the program based on the student's data patterns.

Identify the Stimulus That Cues the Student to Respond

As with other procedures, the teacher must identify a stimulus that will signal to the student that he is required to respond.

Identify the Controlling Prompt

As with the other instructional strategies discussed in this chapter, the teacher must identify a prompt that will always control the student's behavior, thus ensuring that the student will perform the task correctly and giving himself a starting point from which to fade the prompts.

Specify the Procedures for Fading Prompts

Before beginning instruction, the teacher determines how he will fade the prompts or how he will deliver less assistance when the student begins to respond correctly. As in the antecedent prompt and fade procedure, he can fade the prompts by decreasing the intensity of the prompt, changing the locus of control, decreasing the frequency of the prompt, providing less assistance by changing the prompt type, or removing the prompt altogether. The teacher fades the prompts based on immediate, moment-to-moment decisions related to how the student responds. When the student begins to respond correctly to one type of prompt or responds independently, the teacher immediately fades or removes the prompt but always provides enough assistance to ensure a correct response.

Determine the Consequences for Each Student Response

Prior to implementing a graduated guidance program, the teacher must determine what consequences he will deliver based on the student's responding.

Responding to Correct Responses. The teacher reinforces the student for correct responses regardless of what prompt he is using at the time.

Responding to Incorrect Responses. In essence, the teacher does not allow incorrect and no responses. As soon as the student begins to make an incorrect or no response, the teacher should interrupt the response and immediately provide enough assistance to ensure a correct response. However, if the student resists the prompt at the end of a chain, no reinforcement should be given. For example, Coach Petrillo has been teaching Rhonda to perform repetitions of touching her toes using a task analysis and the graduated guidance procedure. After several weeks of instruction, Rhonda is performing the majority of the task analysis with Coach Petrillo shadowing Rhonda's arms as they move through the task. He verbally praises Rhonda for each of the steps she performs correctly. Immediately when Rhonda begins to move her arms in the incorrect direction, Coach Petrillo provides enough assistance (e.g., lightly guides her arms) for Rhonda to respond correctly on the step of the task analysis.

Select a Data Collection System

Because the decision to deliver, reduce, or remove prompts occurs rapidly during a session, it is difficult for a teacher to collect data on every student response. One alternative is for the teacher, at the end of each trial, to record a prompted trial if he delivered any prompts or an unprompted trial if the student responded independently during the entire trial. In this way, he can keep track of how many days of prompting occur.

Implement, Monitor, and Adjust the Program Based on the Student's Data Patterns

When implementing a graduated guidance program, the teacher must adjust the prompts immediately while conducting the trial. If the student begins to respond independently, the teacher reduces or removes the prompt. If the student begins to respond incorrectly or does not respond, the teacher presents a prompt that provides the amount of assistance necessary to ensure correct responding.

SAMPLE GRADUATED GUIDANCE PROCEDURE

There are six steps for a teacher to follow when using a graduated guidance procedure. The following example illustrates the use of these steps.

Martha is a 21-year-old with severe mental retardation. Mr. Brown, her teacher, wants to teach Martha to use a cassette tape player. Martha follows few verbal instructions and inconsistently follows a model. Mr. Brown has identified music as a reinforcer for Martha, and her family wants her to develop a leisure skill that she can perform independently in her free time at home. He develops a task analysis and will simultaneously teach all the steps of playing the tape player.

Identify the Stimulus That Cues the Student to Respond

Mr. Brown wants Martha, without the need for a task direction from a peer or adult, to play the tape player when she has free time. Therefore, he identifies the naturally occurring stimulus of free time and the tape player being in Martha's view as the stimulus to cue Martha to listen to the player.

Identify the Controlling Prompt

Mr. Brown knows that the prompt that will consistently ensure Martha's correct performance is full physical guidance. He begins instruction by using hand-over-hand guidance with firm pressure.

Specify the Procedures for Fading Prompts

Mr. Brown fades the pressure of his hand-over-hand guidance as instruction continues. During each trial, when Martha begins to respond correctly, he loosens his grip on her hand or removes his grip altogether. Any time Martha responds independently, Mr. Brown keeps his hands within a few inches of Martha's (i.e., shadowing) so that he can deliver a prompt immediately if one is needed. As Martha responds independently over time, Mr. Brown begins to move his hands slowly farther and farther away from hers, until she responds correctly without his presence.

Determine the Consequences for Each Student Response

When Martha responds correctly, regardless of the prompt he uses, Mr. Brown praises her. At the end of each trial, as long as Martha was compliant during the session and did not resist prompting, she is allowed to listen to a cassette tape.

Select a Data Collection System

Mr. Brown records each day if Martha required prompts during the trial or if she responded independently.

Implement, Monitor, and Adjust the Program Based on the Student's Data Patterns

Since Mr. Brown does not have specific data on Martha's responding, he will need to rely on his judgment as to her progress. If he thinks that he has not reduced his prompts for several consecutive days, then he may need to break the task into finer steps or choose a more systematic method of instruction and data collection so that Martha's responses can be monitored more closely.

SUMMARY COMMENTS

- When using the antecedent prompt and test, antecedent prompt and fade, and graduated guidance procedures, the teacher provides a prompt prior to the student's response, then removes the prompt.

- Each procedure has been effective in teaching students with a variety of disabilities.
- The antecedent prompt and test procedure requires a teacher to present a prompt during instructional trials, then later to test the student's ability to perform the target behavior without the prompt.
- The antecedent prompt and fade procedure requires a teacher to present a controlling prompt, then gradually remove the prompt.
- The graduated guidance procedure involves the teacher presenting a prompt, then making moment-to-moment decisions as the trial is in progress to deliver, reduce, or remove prompts.
- These are the steps for using the antecedent prompt and test procedure: (a) identify the stimulus that cues the student to respond; (b) identify the controlling prompt; (c) determine the antecedent prompt trial procedures; (d) determine the test trial procedures; (e) determine the length of the response interval; (f) identify the consequences to be delivered; (g) select a data collection system; and (h) implement, monitor, and adjust the program based on the student's data patterns.
- These are the steps for using the antecedent prompt and fade procedure: (a) identify the stimulus that cues the student to respond; (b) identify the controlling prompt; (c) specify the procedures for fading prompts; (d) determine the length of the response interval; (e) identify the consequences for each student response; (f) select a data collection system; and (g) implement, monitor, and adjust the program based on the student's data patterns.
- These are the steps for using the graduated guidance procedure: (a) identify the stimulus that cues the student to respond; (b) identify the controlling prompt; (c) specify the procedures for fading prompts; (d) identify the consequences for each student response; (e) select a data collection system; and (f) implement, monitor, and adjust the program based on the student's data patterns.

This chapter described three response prompting procedures: antecedent prompt and test, antecedent prompt and fade, and graduated guidance. In all of these strategies, the teacher presents a prompt with a stimulus that cues the student to respond, then removes it until the student responds to the stimulus being taught alone. The next chapter describes four instructional strategies that differ from all other strategies presented in Chapters 3–7 because they are considered naturalistic strategies: incidental teaching, mand-model, naturalistic time delay, and transition-based teaching. These are called naturalistic strategies because they are used within the student's ongoing natural environment or setting where the skills occur. Three of the procedures were developed specifically for teaching language; transition-based teaching can be used to teach a variety of skills, including language.

EXERCISES

1. Discuss two ways to schedule test trials using the antecedent prompt and test procedure. Describe the advantages and disadvantages of both.
2. Write an example of a hypothetical student and skill for which the antecedent prompt and test procedure would be appropriate. Include the student's age and

functioning level, the experience of the instructor, the student's learning history, the skill to be taught, and the setting.

3. Explain why the antecedent prompt and fade procedure is not considered as systematic as is the most-to-least prompting procedure.
4. James is an institutionalized adolescent. During his day, he has several instructors who teach him the same skill. For example, the instructor who works the first shift is teaching James to brush his teeth, and the second-shift instructor is teaching him the same skill. They choose the antecedent prompt and fade procedure to teach this skill. Is this a wise choice? Explain your answer.
5. For a classic example of the use of graduated guidance, read N. H. Azrin and P. M. Armstrong, "The 'Mini-Meal'—A Method for Teaching Eating Skills to the Profoundly Retarded," *Mental Retardation, 11*(1) (1973): 9–13.
6. List the advantages and disadvantages of using a graduated guidance procedure.

REFERENCES

Ault, M. J., Wolery, M., Doyle, P. M., & Gast, D. L. (1989). Review of comparative studies in the instruction of students with moderate and severe handicaps. *Exceptional Children, 55,* 346–356.

Azrin, N. H., & Armstrong, P. M. (1973). The "mini-meal"—a method for teaching eating skills to the profoundly retarded. *Mental Retardation, 11*(1), 9–13.

Azrin, N. H., Schaeffer, R. M., & Wesolowski, M. D. (1976). A rapid method of teaching profoundly retarded persons to dress. *Mental Retardation, 14,*(6), 29–33.

Barrera, R. D., Lobato-Barrera, D., & Sulzer-Azaroff, B. (1980). A simultaneous treatment comparison of three expressive language training programs with a mute autistic child. *Journal of Autism and Developmental Disorders, 10,* 21–37.

Cipani, E., Augustine, A., & Blomgren, E. (1982). Teaching profoundly retarded adults to ascend stairs safely. *Education and Training of the Mentally Retarded, 17,* 51–54.

Clark, H. B., & Sherman, J. A. (1975). Teaching generative use of sentence answers to three forms of questions. *Journal of Applied Behavior Analysis, 8,* 321–330.

Cooke, T. P., & Apolloni, T. (1976). Developing positive social-emotional behaviors: A study of training and generalization effects. *Journal of Applied Behavior Analysis, 9,* 65–78.

Crist, K., Walls, R. T., & Haught, P. A. (1984). Degrees of specificity in task analysis. *American Journal of Mental Deficiency, 89,* 67–74.

DeHaven, E. (1981). Teaching three severely retarded children to follow instructions. *Education and Training of the Mentally Retarded, 16,* 36–48.

Dorry, G. W. (1976). Attentional model for the effectiveness of fading in training reading-vocabulary with retarded persons. *American Journal of Mental Deficiency, 81,* 271–279.

Ellis, W. D., Walls, R. T., & Zane, T. (1980). Preresponse and error-correction prompting procedures for learning complex assembly tasks. *Contemporary Educational Psychology, 5,* 30–40.

Fink, W. T., & Brice-Gray, K. J. (1979). The effects of the teaching strategies in the acquisition and recall of an academic task by moderately and severely retarded preschool children. *Mental Retardation, 17,* 8–12.

Foxx, R. M., & Azrin, N. H. (1973). *Toilet training the retarded: A rapid program for day and nighttime independent toileting.* Champaign, IL: Research Press.

Frank, A. R., & Wacker, D. P. (1986) Analysis of a visual prompting procedure on acquisition and generalization of coin skills by mentally retarded children. *American Journal of Mental Deficiency, 90,* 468–472.

Gersten, R. M., White, W. A. T., Falco, R., & Carnine, D. (1982). Teaching basic discriminations to handicapped and nonhandicapped individuals through a dynamic presentation of instructional stimuli. *Analysis and Intervention in Developmental Disabilities, 2,* 305–317.

Haught, P. Walls, R. T., & Crist, K. (1984). Placement of prompts, length of task, and level of retardation in learning complex assembly tasks. *American Journal of Mental Deficiency, 89,* 60–66.

Howard, V. F., Spellman, C. R., Lacy, L. S., Day, R. M., & Cress, P. J. (1989). *A comparison of delayed prompting and simultaneous prompting using adolescents with mental retardation.* (Manuscript submitted for publication.)

Knapczyk, D. R. (1983). Use of teacher-paced instruction in developing and maintaining independent self-feeding. *Journal of the Association for the Severely Handicapped, 8,* 10–16.

Koegel, R. L., & Rincover, A. (1977). Research on the difference between generalization and maintenance in extra-therapy responding. *Journal of Applied Behavior Analysis, 10,* 1–12.

Lowe, M. L., & Cuvo, A. J. (1976). Teaching coin summation to the mentally retarded. *Journal of Applied Behavior Analysis, 9,* 483–489.

Marchetti, A. G., McCartney, J. R., Drain, S., Hooper, M., & Dix, J. (1983). Pedestrian skills training for mentally retarded adults: Comparison of training in two settings. *Mental Retardation, 21,* 107–110.

Olenick, D. L., & Pear, J. J. (1980). Differential reinforcement of correct responses to probes and prompts in picture-name training with severely retarded children. *Journal of Applied Behavior Analysis, 13,* 77–89.

O'Neill, C. T., & Bellamy, G. T. (1978). Evaluation of a procedure for teaching saw chain assembly to a severely retarded woman. *Mental Retardation, 16,* 37–41.

Remington, B., & Clarke, S. (1983). Acquisition of expressive signing by autistic children: An evaluation of the relative effects of simultaneous communication and sign-alone training. *Journal of Applied Behavior Analysis, 16,* 315–328.

Richmond, G. (1983). Shaping bladder and bowel continence in developmentally retarded preschool children. *Journal of Autism and Developmental Disorders, 13,* 197–204.

Rowan, V. V., & Pear, J. J. (1985). A comparison of the effects of interpersonal and concurrent training sequels on the acquisition, retention and generalization of picture names. *Applied Research in Mental Retardation, 6,* 127–145.

Sarber, R. E., Halasz, M. M., Messmer, M. C., Bickett, A. D., & Lutzker, J. K. (1983). Teaching menu planning and grocery shopping skills to a mentally retarded mother. *Mental Retardation, 21,* 101–106.

Schoen, S. F., Lentz, F. E., Jr., & Suppa, R. J. (1988). An examination of two prompt fading procedures and opportunities to observe in teaching handicapped preschoolers self-help skills. *Journal of the Division for Early Childhood, 12,* 349–358.

Schuster, J. W., Griffen, A. K., & Woler, M. (in press). Comparison of simultaneous prompting and constant time delay in teaching grocery words to students with moderate mental handicaps. *Journal of Behavioral Education.*

Smith, M., & Meyers, A. (1979). Telephone-skills training for retarded adults: Group and individual demonstrations with and without verbal instruction. *American Journal of Mental Deficiency, 83,* 581–587.

Spangler, P. F., & Marshall, A. M. (1983). The unit lay manager as facilitator of purposeful activities among institutionalized profoundly and severely retarded boys. *Journal of Applied Behavior Analysis, 16,* 345–349.

Sternberg, L., McNerney, C. D., & Pegnatore, L. (1985). Developing co-active imitative behaviors with profoundly mentally handicapped students. *Education and Training of the Mentally Retarded, 20,* 260–267.

Walls, R. T., Zane, T., & Thvedt, J. E. (1980). Trainer's personal methods compared to two structured training strategies. *American Journal of Mental Deficiency, 84,* 495–507.

Welch, J., Nietupski, J., & Hamre-Nietupski, S. (1985). Teaching public transportation problem-solving skills to young adults with moderate handicaps. *Education and Training of the Mentally Retarded, 20,* 287–295.

Whitman, T. L., Zakaras, M., & Chardos, S. (1971). Effects of reinforcement and guidance procedures on instruction-following behavior of severely retarded children. *Journal of Applied Behavior Analysis, 4,* 283–290.

Zane, T., Walls, R. T., & Thvedt, J. E. (1981). Prompting and fading guidance procedures: Their effect on chaining and whole task teaching strategies. *Education and Training of the Mentally Retarded, 16,* 125–135.

CHAPTER 8

Naturalistic Teaching Procedures

Chapter Overview

Key Terms

Incidental Teaching

Child-Directed
  Interaction

Verbal Request

Nonverbal Request

Mand-Model

Mand

Adult-Directed
  Interaction

Naturalistic Time Delay

Transition-Based Teaching

Functional
  Communication

Augmentative
  Communication

Natural Environment

Focusing

Verify

Request for an
  Elaboration

Target Stimulus

Response Interval

Unprompted Corrects

Prompted Corrects

No Response

Unprompted Error

Prompted Error

Routines

Transitions

Questions to Be Answered by This Chapter

1. What are the naturalistic teaching procedures?
2. Are the naturalistic teaching procedures effective?
3. What are the recommendations for using the naturalistic procedures?
4. What are the steps for using these procedures effectively?
5. How do you measure progress with the naturalistic teaching procedures?

Chapter 8 describes four teaching procedures: incidental teaching, mand-model, naturalistic time delay, and transition-based teaching. Three of these procedures (incidental teaching, mand-model, and naturalistic time delay) were developed specifically for increasing language and communication skills rather than for use across skill domains. Transition-based teaching may be used to teach a variety of skills, including language. Each of the procedures has been effective in establishing new skills with training occurring in the natural environment. Although these procedures are described in the literature, many individuals who should be using them have not been trained to do so (Schwartz, Anderson, & Halle, 1989). Because of the demonstrated effectiveness of the procedures across varying populations and settings, each should be included in the repertoires of teachers or other caregivers. This chapter describes the procedures and their effectiveness, explains the steps necessary for using the procedures, and provides an example of each strategy.

DESCRIBING THE NATURALISTIC TEACHING PROCEDURES

Incidental Teaching Procedure

Hart and Risley (1975) define **incidental teaching** as a procedure used to increase communication or language skills through interactions between students and adults in natural settings. There are several steps in planning an incidental teaching episode. The initial step is for the teacher to define the target communication or language response. Second, the teacher arranges the environment to increase the probability that the student will interact or use the target behavior. Third, the teacher selects the prompt that may be needed to elicit the desired response from the student. Fourth, the teacher identifies the consequent events that follow student responses. Fifth, the teacher chooses a data collection system appropriate for monitoring the effectiveness of the procedure.

After arranging the environment, the teacher waits for the student to approach. An approach by the student is defined as a **child-directed interaction,** which can occur as either a **verbal request** (the student speaks or uses some form of augmentative communication system) or a **nonverbal request** (the student points, cries, or looks at an object) as he or she approaches the adult. The purpose of the request may be to gain access to a toy or an activity, receive assistance, seek information, or ask permission. However, once the initiation occurs, the teacher must make a series of decisions:

- If this initiation should be used as a teaching opportunity, the teacher focuses on the student and verifies the topic.
- The teacher requests an elaboration of the student's response.
- The teacher allows the student time to respond.
- If the student responds correctly, the teacher reinforces the student with access to the item that the student has requested.
- If the student does not respond or responds incorrectly, the teacher provides a prompt that will ensure the correct target response from the student.
- The teacher allows the student time to respond following delivery of the prompt.
- If the student responds correctly following delivery of the prompt, the teacher provides access to the item that the student has requested.

With this procedure, the interaction should be brief, the prompts should be effective, and the interaction should result in positive consequences for the student. A flow chart demonstrating the use of the incidental teaching procedure is shown in Figure 8.1.

Mand-Model Procedure

As with incidental teaching, the **mand-model** procedure was designed to increase language and functional communication skills in the natural environment. The first step in planning to use the mand-model procedure is for the teacher to define the target response. The second step involves the teacher selecting a target stimulus to cue the student that it is time to respond. However, unlike incidental teaching, the adult does not wait for the student to initiate an interaction; rather, the teacher directs the interaction by approaching the student involved in a preferred activity and providing a **mand**—a non-yes/no question, request, or command. This **adult-directed interaction** is especially useful with students who do not initiate interactions with others or who initiate relatively few interactions. Therefore, the third step in implementing this procedure is for the teacher to decide when the adult-directed approach will occur. The fourth step is the teacher identifying a prompt that will ensure correct student performance of the target behavior. The final step in planning this procedure is the teacher selecting a system for data collection. The mand-model procedure, developed by Rogers-Warren and Warren (1980), increases the number of opportunities that the student will be given to use language and communication behaviors. It also results in more reinforcement of the student's communication behaviors in the natural environment. Once the teacher has defined the target language or communication response, defined the cue that will signal the student to respond, selected the prompt and the data collection system, and identified times when the student can be approached, he performs the mand-model procedure as below:

- The teacher observes the student engaged in an activity.
- The teacher approaches the student.
- The teacher interrupts the student's activity and delivers a mand that is related to the activity.

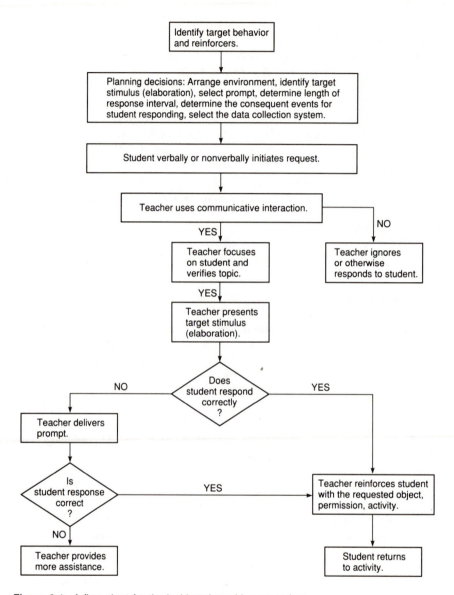

Figure 8.1. A flow chart for the incidental teaching procedure.

- The teacher allows the student time to respond.
- If the student makes a correct response, the teacher allows the student to continue the activity.
- If the student makes no response to the mand or makes an incorrect response, the teacher prompts the student to respond correctly by providing a model of the correct behavior.

- The teacher allows the student time to respond.
- If the student makes the correct response following delivery of the model prompt, the teacher allows the student access to the activity.

Although the mand-model procedure is implemented in the natural environment, it is more intrusive than the incidental teaching procedure because it uses adult-directed rather than student-initiated teaching opportunities. However, the teacher must identify the student's interests or focus of attention to minimize the intrusiveness of the interaction. A flow chart of the steps in the mand-model procedure is included in Figure 8.2.

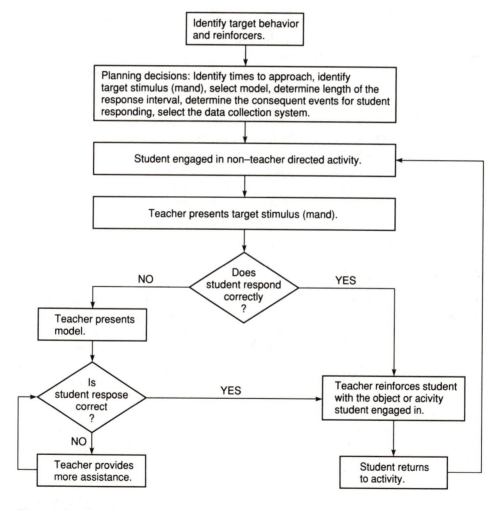

Figure 8.2 A flow chart for the mand-model teaching procedure.

Naturalistic Time Delay

The **naturalistic time delay** procedure, as described by Halle, Marshall, and Spradlin (1979), is used during existing routines in the natural environment and allows students to initiate communicative exchanges. Although it includes prompts if the student does not respond correctly, it relies on naturally occurring routines in the environment to signal the student to initiate requests for assistance, access to objects, or permission.

The initial steps include the teacher selecting the target response, the target stimulus, the prompt to ensure correct performance of the target response, and a data collection system. Finally, the teacher analyzes the student's environment to identify times when the student needs either materials or assistance. Once these steps are completed, the teacher implements the procedure as below:

- The teacher places himself close to the student and withholds materials or assistance.
- The teacher ensures that the student is aware of his availability by looking "expectantly" at the student.
- Simultaneous with the above two steps, the teacher waits silently for a period of at least 5 seconds for the student to indicate the need for assistance, permission, or materials.
- If the student makes the correct response, the teacher delivers praise and the natural consequences in the form of the requested materials or assistance.
- If the student makes an incorrect or no response, the teacher delivers a prompt providing the student with a model of the correct behavior.
- The teacher allows the student time to respond.
- If the student responds correctly following the prompt, the teacher provides access to the item that the student has requested.

A flow chart of the naturalistic time delay strategy is shown in Figure 8.3.

Transition-Based Teaching

Transition-based teaching was designed to teach new skills during transitions that exist between activities in the daily schedule. With this procedure, the teacher can control a teaching opportunity by (a) the adult (e.g., the teacher presents a direct instructional trial during the transition following the group language session and before gross motor activities begin) or by (b) the child (e.g., the teacher delivers a training opportunity when the student approaches and asks a question during free play). Unlike the other naturalistic procedures, this procedure was designed to teach a variety of skills, including nonlanguage behaviors. This procedure can increase the efficiency of the programs currently being used in the classroom by distributing trials across time. Once the teacher has selected the transitions, the target behavior, the target stimulus, the prompt to ensure correct responding, and the system for monitoring the students' progress, he implements the procedure as below:

- The teacher waits (a) for the transition to occur (e.g., the bell rings for students to leave the lunch table and go back to the classroom) or (b) for a student initiation signaling a transition (e.g., the student requests using the restroom).

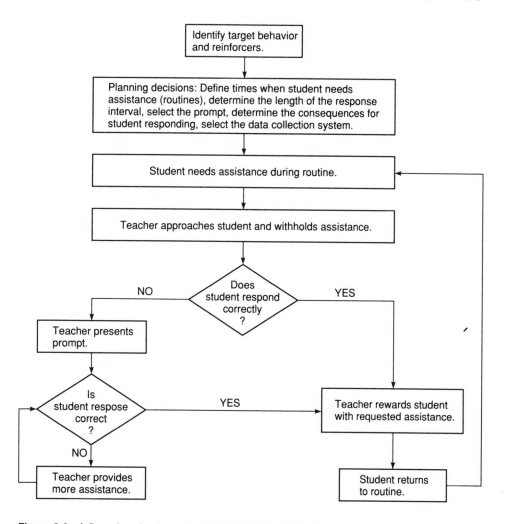

Figure 8.3. A flow chart for the naturalistic time delay teaching procedure.

- The teacher presents a target stimulus.
- The teacher allows the student time to respond.
- If the student responds correctly, the teacher allows the student to continue in the transition.
- If the does not student respond correctly, the teacher presents a controlling prompt to ensure a correct response.
- If the student responds correctly to the prompt, the teacher allows continuation of the transition.

A flow chart of the transition-based teaching procedure is shown in Figure 8.4. The similarities and the differences of the four procedures are shown in Table 8.1. For more detailed descriptions, see Kaiser, Alpert, and Warren (1987) and Warren and Kaiser (1988).

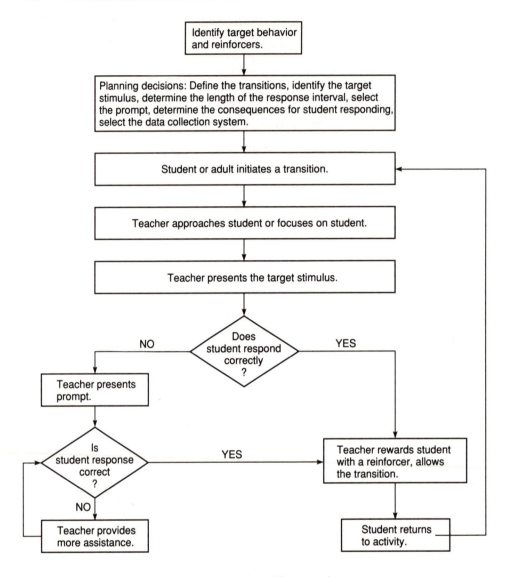

Figure 8.4. A flow chart for the transition-based teaching procedure.

EFFECTS OF USING THE NATURALISTIC TEACHING PROCEDURES

Students Taught

The incidental teaching procedure has been effective with young children. For example, Cavallaro and Bambara (1982) and Hart and Risley (1974, 1975, 1980) used this procedure with preschool students who had developmental delays and were from economically disadvantaged environments. The procedure also has been used with three- to six-year olds exhibiting such disabilities as Down syndrome, cerebral palsy,

TABLE 8.1. A Summary of Differences Between the Naturalistic Teaching Procedures

Naturalistic Procedure	The Procedure Was Designed to . . .	Instruction Begins By . . .	The Procedure Is Effective When . . .
Incidental teaching	increase language or communication responses related to student requests.	a student approaching the adult; the adult requests elaboration.	adult arrangement of the environment and request for the elaboration results in target behavior.
Mand-model	increase language or communication responses related to student activity.	an adult approaching a student during an activity; the adult delivers a mand.	adult interruption and delivery of a mand results in target behavior.
Naturalistic time delay	increase language or communication responses related to student routines.	an adult approaching a student during natural routines; the adult withholds assistance.	the routine, the availability of the adult, and the withholding of assistance result in target behavior.
Trasition-based teaching	increase skills from any domain; does not have to be related to the transition.	an adult or a child signaling a transition; the adult delivers task direction.	the transition and adult delivery of a task direction result in target behavior.

hearing impairments, and language delays (Cavallaro & Poulson, 1985) and autism (Neef, Walters, & Egel, 1984). With the incidental teaching procedure, teaching opportunities are a result of child-directed initiations. If those initiations do not occur, then the effectiveness of the procedure is decreased. It follows that the incidental teaching procedure would be a poor choice for a student who typically does not initiate interactions with adults. The effectiveness of the incidental teaching procedure with such a student is not known.

The mand-model procedure, however, because of its adult-directed approach, has been implemented with students who display infrequent initiations. Although effective with young children and preschoolers with speech and language impairments (Rogers-Warren & Warren, 1980; Warren, McQuarter, & Rogers-Warren, 1984), it also has been effective with adolescents and adults with moderate and severe mental retardation and 12- to 15-year-olds with autism (McGee, Krantz, & McClannahan, 1985).

Naturalistic time-delay, too, has been effective with a variety of populations. For example, Halle et al. (1979) used this procedure with 11- to 15-year-olds diagnosed as either severely or profoundly retarded. It also has been successful in establishing new skills with preschoolers who were developmentally delayed (Halle, Baer, & Spradlin, 1981).

The transition-based teaching procedure has not been disseminated in the literature, although one study used the procedure effectively with preschoolers who had developmental delays (Wolery, Doyle, Gast, Ault, & Lichtenberg, 1991).

Behaviors Taught

A variety of language behaviors have been taught with these procedures. With incidental teaching, these skills have ranged from increasing the spontaneous use of one-word verbalizations indicating a child's request (such as "More.") (Cavallaro &

Poulson, 1985) to communicating in complex compound sentences (such as "The little hand is on five.") (Hart & Risley, 1975). In addition, such language skills as correct yes/no responding to instructor questions (Neef et al., 1984) and correct use of prepositions (McGee et al., 1985) have been taught.

Rogers-Warren and Warren (1980) initially designed the mand-model procedure to increase the rates of verbalizations with students who displayed moderate and severe language delays. The verbalizations required of the students varied from one-word statements to whole sentences, depending on each student's capabilities. Later, Warren et al. (1984) increased the mean length of utterances after first establishing a stable rate of vocalizations. Their students were taught to answer in whole sentences when approached by an adult and told, "Tell me what you are doing and give me a whole sentence." The mand-model procedure also has been used to teach reading sight words (Fabry, Mayhew, & Hanson, 1984). The words were taught during a time when students were exchanging their tokens for backup reinforcers. A word was placed on the back of each token, and the adult initiated a teaching trial when she asked the student to read the word as the exchange occurred.

Naturalistic time delay was originally used by Halle et al. (1979) to increase the spontaneous requests for food by students with severe mental retardation. This procedure increased the number of requests for food items and facilitated generalization to other meal times and to other staff. The success of naturalistic time delay in increasing spontaneous language also resulted in training teachers to implement the procedure (Halle et al., 1981). Teachers were taught to "delay their offers of help in naturally occurring situations" (p. 389). Learning to use the time delay procedure during times such as lunch, free play, and scheduled activities increased the number of opportunities for evoking student language behaviors.

Wolery, Doyle, Gast, Ault, and Lichtenberg (1991) compared the effectiveness and efficiency of a progressive time delay procedure to the transition-based teaching procedure while teaching lowercase letters and numerals. The progressive time delay procedure was implemented in one-on-one instructional sessions using a massed trial format. Single transition-based teaching trials occurred at varied times (e.g., leaving the table after a snack to go to free play or on arrival in the morning while hanging up a jacket). The procedures were equally effective, and the transition-based teaching procedure resulted in near errorless learning and was slightly more rapid than progressive time delay when acquisition was measured by the number of errors and trials through criterion.

Recommendations for Practice

Functional communication refers to language behaviors that are instantly reinforced; that is, the student makes his wants and needs known and acquires those wants and needs without delay or further interpretation. This means that the student should be taught to use a communication system appropriate to his level of functioning across physical needs and cognitive abilities; and teachers, classroom aides, families, or anyone in contact with the student should understand the system and comprehend the communicative intent of the behavior. The procedures described in this chapter are designed to teach functional communication skills but can be used to increase a wide range of spontaneous language behaviors from the simple (one-word requests) to the complex (complete sentences with adjectives, prepositions, and so on). However, with these procedures the behavior expected from the student is generally related to her activity of the moment. By applying teaching procedures to language responses related to the student's activity, the teacher ensures the functionality of the language response. In addition, the naturalistic procedures can be used with a student who is not able to "speak" in two-word phrases or complete sentences or even say understandable single words. Some of the research has been conducted with such students by using each of the procedures in conjunction with **augmentative communication** systems (e.g., manual signs, picture boards, and Bliss symbols). This chapter does not describe such systems (see Miller & Allaire, 1987), but illustrates how spontaneous use of whatever communication system is in place can be increased.

Traditionally, language intervention with students who have moderate and severe disabilities has been done in one-on-one or small-group direct instructional sessions. This approach requires systematic scheduling and may be conducted by a speech pathologist or teacher. A great deal of preparation time and arrangement is frequently required on the part of the teacher. Such instruction uses behavioral strategies and produces progress in those sessions. However, generalization of the acquired language behaviors to settings outside of the isolated instructional settings frequently does not occur. The naturalistic teaching strategies were developed to facilitate generalization and were later used to facilitate acquistion. Current best practice suggests that these procedures can be used to establish both acquisition and generalization of communicative skills.

To establish generalization and functional communication, the teacher implements the naturalistic teaching procedures in the student's **natural environment**—the home, classroom, cafeteria, gym, community setting, or any setting where the student is expected to communicate. To conduct training in the natural environment, the teacher must arrange or physically change the setting to increase the probability of the student communicating. For example, she might reduce the number of available toys during free play to increase the student's requests for toys or fail to provide assistance when it is usually given. If language or functional communication training occurs in the environments where the specific skills are needed, then the probability that the acquired skills will maintain and be used in these settings is increased.

STEPS FOR USING THE INCIDENTAL TEACHING PROCEDURE

Incidental teaching is the oldest of the naturalistic teaching procedures. Originally, it was used to establish generalization of skills learned in structured language sessions (Hart & Risley, 1968); later, it was used to teach new language behaviors (Hart & Risley, 1974, 1975). These are the 11 steps for planning to use this procedure:

- Define the target behavior.
- Arrange the environment.
- Decide to use the initiation.
- Focus on the initiation and verify the topic.

- Identify the signal to respond.
- Determine the length of the response interval.
- Select the type of prompt that will ensure a correct response.
- Use the response interval.
- Determine the consequences for each student response.
- Select a data collection system.
- Implement, monitor, and adjust the program based on the student's data patterns.

Define the Target Behavior

Before using the incidental teaching procedure, a teacher must identify the type of target behavior. For example, he may want to increase the use of verb-noun combinations ("want eat" and "go store"), evoke complete sentences ("I want to eat." and "I want to go to the store."), replace gestures with one-word requests ("eat" and "store"), or increase the amount of spontaneous language throughout the day. For instance, Ms. Castille decides to increase the use of one-word vocal responses from Juan, who currently gestures to indicate his needs.

Arrange the Environment

With the incidental teaching procedure, teaching opportunities are controlled by the student; it is used only when the student initiates a communicative exchange. Consequently, the environment must be arranged to increase the probability that the student will initiate to the teacher allowing an incidental teaching opportunity to occur. Potential environmental changes, listed in Table 8.2, can be used separately or combined.

TABLE 8.2. Manipulations of the Environment for Increasing Communicative Initiations

Strategy	Description
Use interesting materials.	Provide novel or new materials that are likely to result in comments or questions by the student.
Place desired materials in view but out of reach.	During free-time activities, place desired objects out of student's reach or on a "must ask" shelf.
Use materials with which the student will require assistance.	Provide the student with materials that he will need help using and recognize that need for help (e.g., asking a student to carry boxes that are too heavy or giving him materials that require the teacher to open the box in which those materials are contained).
Provide inadequate amounts of materials.	While the student is performing a given activity, give him only part of the materials needed (e.g., if the student is setting the table, give him everything but the plates).
Sabotage the materials or the activity.	Structure the materials or the activity so that the student will initiate a response (e.g., interrupt the activity and re-start it only after an initiation occurs).
Violate the student's expectations.	If the student expects an event to occur, delay the event or do the opposite (e.g., walk to the refrigerator to get the juice for snack but do not open the refrigerator door).

[Based on a presentation in Kaiser (1987).]

Decide to Use the Initiation

If the student initiates a communicative interaction, the teacher's next step is to decide whether to use this opportunity for teaching, depending, of course, on the context. If a student is in danger or needs medical help, obviously this is not an appropriate time for a teacher to use the procedure. Likewise, if several students initiate at once or if the teacher has other immediate demands, using the incidental teaching procedure may not be possible.

Focus on the Initiation and Verify the Topic

If the teacher decides to use a student initiation as an opportunity to implement the incidental teaching procedure, the next step is for her to investigate the content of the student's request. She does this by first **focusing** on the student—that is, orienting toward and giving the student her undivided attention. Second, she must **verify** the topic of the student's initiation. For example, Ms. Castille may observe Juan looking at and pointing to the water fountain and ask, "Is that what you want?" Completion of this step will ensure that the student's initiations will be reinforced with the assistance, permission, or object he requested. Frequently, the student's intent is obvious; in such a case, the teacher would simply focus on that student.

Identify the Signal to Respond

The next step is for the teacher to select the type of **request for an elaboration** of the communicative behavior. This request is the **target stimulus** because it signals the student to respond with more complex communicative behavior. The request for elaboration is dependent on both the student's and the task's characteristics. For example, it may be (a) a verbal task direction to signal the student to respond—"Give me a sentence" if the teacher is attempting to increase the mean length of utterances; (b) "Show me what you want" if the teacher is establishing the use of an augmentative system; or (c) "Say it out loud" while the teacher increases the use of one-word target responses, as in Juan's example. The request for an elaboration or the target stimulus may also be nonverbal. For example, after focusing on Juan and verifying the request, Ms. Castille could shrug her shoulders and hold out her hands to indicate that she needs more information before she provides the requested assistance.

When a student initiates an interaction, the teacher should be certain that the target behavior and request for elaboration are related to the specific activity, want, or need in the initiation. For example, when Juan approaches her and points to the water fountain, Ms. Castille requests an elaboration of the gesture that indicates that Juan is thirsty—"Say it out loud." It would be inappropriate for the teacher to attempt to obtain a response unrelated to getting a drink.

Determine the Length of the Response Interval

Once the teacher identifies the target stimulus and presents the request for an elaboration, she must allow the student time to respond to the request. This is done by her providing 5–10 seconds for a response. This **response interval** can be of any duration appropriate to both the student and the task, but it should be consistent for each teaching opportunity. For example, after delivering the target stimulus, "Say it out loud," Ms. Castille gives Juan 4 seconds to respond.

Select the Type of Prompt That Will Ensure a Correct Response

If the student does not respond correctly during the response interval, the teacher delivers a prompt. This step is necessary to ensure that the student will be rewarded during each teaching episode. The prompt should provide the student with enough assistance to perform the target behavior correctly if the demand for elaboration is not effective in producing the correct response. In general, this procedure has been effective when a model prompt has been used to produce the target behavior. This type of prompt might be (a) a vocal model of the correct response, (b) a signed model of the target behavior, or (c) a gesture or a point to a picture or symbol when using augmentative communication systems. Although another type of prompt (such as a physical prompt) might be used with augmentative systems, it would not be practical with most types of target behaviors taught with this procedure. Therefore, incidental teaching might be most effective with those students who are able to imitate the teacher's model prompt. For example, if Juan does not make the correct response when Ms. Castille asks for an elaboration of the gesture to indicate thirst, then she can present a model of the target response, "Water," which ensures Juan's correct performance of the target behavior.

Use the Response Interval

The teacher gives another opportunity for the student to respond if the student used the prompt to make the correct response. For example, if a teacher allows 4 seconds for a response when the student first approaches and delivers a request for elaboration, she should also allow 4 seconds following her delivery of the prompt.

Determine the Consequences for Each Student Response

Before beginning instruction, the teacher needs to define the consequences for correct, incorrect, and no responses.

Responding to Correct Responses.   The teacher must reinforce all correct responses. This includes (a) **unprompted corrects,** correct responses that occur to the request for elaboration alone, and (b) **prompted corrects,** correct responses that occur following the prompt. If the student makes a correct response, he is given the permission, assistance, or object that he requested. For example, if Juan says, "Water," before the model or following delivery of the model, he will be allowed to get a drink from the fountain. However, only the unprompted correct responses, or those that occur to the request for elaboration alone, count toward the criterion. Sometimes the amount of reinforcement delivered for the two types of correct responses may vary. For example, Juan has been reinforced with a drink each time he has said "Water," either before or after the prompt. Ms. Castille would like Juan to consistently say, "Water," to the target stimulus alone, so she makes the decision to reinforce prompted correct responses with praise and unprompted corrects with praise and a drink. The differential reinforcement of the two types of correct responses results in Juan responding correctly before the prompt and reaching the criterion level performance.

Responding to Incorrect or No Responses.   If the student does not respond (**no response**) or makes an error before the prompt (**unprompted error**), the teacher delivers a prompt. However, if the student does not respond or responds incorrectly after the prompt (**prompted error**), the teacher has a number of options:

- She can repeat the same prompt and allow another opportunity to respond.
- She can deliver an error correction procedure—telling the student what she did wrong.
- She can simply ignore the prompted error, record the student's response, and walk away from the student.

It is important for teachers to remember that the purpose of this procedure is to encourage student communication of specific wants, allowing the student to be rewarded with the object, permission, or activity that she requested. If the controlling prompt is not effective and the student makes a prompted incorrect response, it is the teacher's responsibility to deliver enough information in the consequent event to ensure that the student will make the correct response. This is the case in each of the consequent events outlined above. The decision that is made regarding the type of consequent event that follows the student prompted errors is an arbitrary one that depends on the characteristics of the task and the student.

Select a Data Collection System

To monitor the effectiveness of the instructional procedure, the teacher needs to collect data each time a teaching opportunity occurs. The progress of the student can be measured through the use of a data collection sheet that contains situational information—such as the student's name, the date, the instructor, the description of the response, the time of day, or the place the trial occurred. In addition, the teacher should record student performance on each of the teaching trials. This information may be stated as the percentage or number of correct or incorrect responses. An example of a data collection sheet that might be used with the incidental teaching procedure is shown in Figure 8.5. Because the incidental teachng procedure is child-directed, data collection can be cumbersome. Although the target response is defined (e.g., making one-word statements), it is difficult for a teacher to determine beforehand when a student will initiate contact. Therefore, when the student initiates a communicative interaction, the teacher records the verified request in abbreviated narrative form (e.g., "He asked for a drink.").

Implement, Monitor, and Adjust the Program Based on the Student's Data Patterns

In addition to collecting the data on a daily basis, the teacher should display these data on a line graph to help determine if student progress is being made or if changes are necessary. For example, if the student is not making errors but the percentage

Student _____Johnny_____   Instructor _____B. McKenzie_____

Task _Increase student request for object, activity, or permission using initial consonant sound._

Trial Number	Time	Task Direction	Record the Target Responses	Elaboration			Model		
				+	−	0	+	−	0
1	8:30	Want help?	Coat off	✓			✓		
2	9:30	Want more?	More juice		✓		✓		
3	11:00	Want?	Bathroom	✓					
4	1:30	Want?	Marker	✓					
5	3:30	Want help?	Coat on		✓			✓	
Number of Responses				2	1	2	2	1	

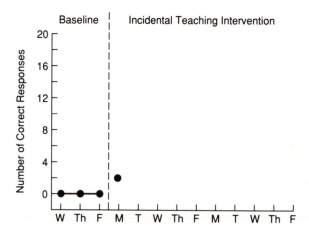

Figure 8.5. The top portion of this figure is a data collection form that allows a teacher to record when the teaching opportunity occurred, the request for an elaboration, and the actual target response. The amount of assistance a teacher needed to provide can be recorded with check marks in the appropriate columns.

The sample graph below the form shows the number of correct responses that occurred without the prompt (model). For each day, only those correct responses that occurred to the request for elaboration alone are graphed.

or number of unprompted corrects is low, this might indicate that differential reinforcement of unprompted and prompted correct responses is needed. This is done by the teacher providing more reinforcement for correct responses that occur before the prompt than for the correct responses that occur after delivery of the prompt. If the student is making an excessive number of errors, there are a number of possible explanations and solutions:

- The teacher can select a new controlling prompt; although students learning with this procedure are usually imitative, a model may not provide enough information if the task is difficult. For example, instead of a teacher model of pointing to a symbol on a communication board, the teacher may deliver a physical prompt by placing her hand on the student's hand and guiding it to the target symbol.

- The teacher can deliver another type of prompt in addition to the model. For example, she can deliver the correct sign with a hand-on-hand physical prompt to form the sign or say "M" and place the student's fingers on her lips.
- The teacher can select a hierarchy of prompts by beginning with a prompt that provides the student with minimal information and using more intrusive prompts if errors occur.
- The teacher can modify the task by requiring an easier communication response from the student.

The teacher implements the changes mentioned above based on the student's pattern of responding shown on his graph. A sample line graph for the incidental teaching procedure is included in Figure 8.5.

SAMPLE INCIDENTAL TEACHING PROCEDURE

There are 11 steps in preparing to use the incidental teaching procedure. The following example shows those steps.

Jerry is a 16-year-old with severe mental retardation. He is able to follow simple commands, work unsupervised for periods of 10-15 minutes, and move independently around the school grounds. His speech therapist reports to his teacher, Mrs. O'Leary, that Jerry can imitate most words when presented with a model. Mrs. O'Leary has observed this in the speech therapy room, but Jerry has not spontaneously used these words in other situations. He does not use expressive language to communicate the need for assistance, permission, or materials.

For example, the highlight of Jerry's morning is his break time following training in lawn and garden maintenance. As Jerry enters the cafeteria and sits down, the cafeteria staff comment on his good work habits and give him a cold drink and some fruit. Mrs. O'Leary assesses Jerry and finds that he can label several liquids (e.g., Coke, milk, and water) and most fruits (e.g., grapes, orange, apple, and banana). Mrs. O'Leary decides that Jerry should ask for a drink and fruit during his break by using, "(Name of liquid or fruit), please." In addition to this target response, she selects "Tell me what you want" as a request for elaboration. To alter his environment, she arranges for the cafeteria staff to continue their conversational comments to Jerry but not deliver drinks or snacks. Since Jerry is imitative, she decides to use a model prompt. Mrs. O'Leary also decides to use the form shown in Figure 8.5 to collect data. Mrs. O'Leary asks the cafeteria staff to use each communicative initiation by Jerry as a teaching episode.

The new environmental arrangement at break results in Jerry walking to the cafeteria staff and pointing to the refrigerator. They look at Jerry expectantly; ask, "Is this what you are pointing at?" (verifying the topic of the request); and present the request for an elaboration, "Tell me what you want." Jerry is allowed 5 seconds to make the correct target response. If he names a drink or fruit in response to the target stimulus, the cafeteria staff reinforce him with descriptive praise, "Oh, you want a drink," and give him the requested item. If he makes an incorrect or no response, they model the name of the drink or fruit and provide another 5-second response interval. The model prompt ensures that Jerry will make the correct response and receive the item he requests. After a week of Jerry approaching the staff, the staff waiting for the communicative behavior and requesting elaboration of Jerry, the environmental arrangement alone controlled Jerry's response. Jerry now walks into the break room, approaches the staff, and labels the drink or snack that he wants.

STEPS FOR USING THE MAND-MODEL TEACHING PROCEDURE

If the arrangement of the environment alone results in increased opportunities to encourage new language skills through student communicative initiations, then the incidental teaching procedure can be used. However, changing the environment may not increase student initiations. When initiations do not occur or occur infrequently, the opportunity to use the incidental teaching procedure does not exist. The mand-model procedure is a viable alternative in such cases. These are the nine steps for using the mand-model procedure.

- Define the target behavior.
- Identify times to approach the student.
- Interrupt the activity.
- Identify the signal to respond.
- Determine the length of the response interval.
- Select the type of prompt that will ensure a correct response.
- Use the response interval.
- Determine the consequences for each student response.
- Select a data collection system; implement, monitor, and adjust the program based on the student's data patterns.

Define the Target Behavior

The first step in the mand-model procedure is for the teacher to define the target behavior. The types of responses possible are as varied as those described for the incidental teaching procedure: asking a student to label the objects with one-word responses, use a particular grammatical form (e.g., noun-verb), or use complete sentences. However, the specific target behaviors must be related to the student's focus of attention.

Identify Times to Approach the Student

The next step is for the teacher to identify times during the student's schedule when it is appropriate and convenient to request the target response related to that activity. The teacher should initiate contact with the student rather than waiting for the child's initiation. For example, Mr. Post watches Michelle during free play, walks over to

Michelle when she is engaged in the play activity, and asks her questions about the toys. The differences between adult- and child-initiations may be especially important with students who never or rarely initiate contact with adults (e.g., those students who would go without dessert if it were contingent on their spontaneously requesting it or those students whose communicative behaviors do not increase because they are given objects, permission, or assistance without having to ask for them). Placing the contact in the hands of the adult can increase the number of teaching opportunities.

Interrupt the Activity

After identifying the time to approach the student, the teacher must interrupt the student's activity. This may be done in a variety of ways depending on the activity. For example, the teacher can remove an object with which the student is playing, stop the student from continuing an activity, or prevent the student from beginning an activity. Also, the teacher may join in the student's activity and insert the question.

Identify the Signal to Respond

The next step is the teacher selecting a target stimulus, or a mand, that signals the student to respond. Mands include non-yes/no questions (e.g., "What are you doing?", "With whom are you playing?", and "What do you want?") and commands (e.g., "Tell me what this is." and "Tell me the whole sentence."). The mand is the stimulus that the teacher wants to control the target response eventually. For this procedure to be effective, the mand or target stimulus must be related to the student's activity. Research with this procedure shows that asking questions about the student's activities increases the probability that the target behavior will occur. For example, when Mr. Post secures Michelle's attention during play and says, "Tell me what you are doing," he has interrupted her activity and delivered a mand related to her activity that cues her to respond.

Determine the Length of the Response Interval

Following delivery of the mand, Mr. Post gives Michelle an opportunity to respond. He does this by waiting 4 seconds for a response. Giving the student an opportunity to respond independently allows the teacher to determine whether the student can make the correct response to the target stimulus alone (mand) or whether he needs more information (model) to respond correctly.

Select the Type of Prompt That Will Ensure a Correct Response

The mand or target stimulus does not always evoke the target behavior. If the student does not respond correctly during the response interval, the teacher delivers a prompt that ensures the target response; in the mand-model procedure, that prompt is a model of the target response. The model is usually vocal, but it may be pointing to a picture or making a manual sign. However, in most cases the mand-model procedure is used with students who are imitative.

Use the Response Interval

After the teacher delivers the model, he should give the student a short interval to imitate the model. The length of the response interval is consistent for all mand-model opportunities; the student is given the same amount of time to respond following the model prompt as was allowed following the mand.

Determine the Consequences for Each Student Response

As with incidental teaching, the teacher's next step is to select consequent events that are to follow each possible type of student response.

Responding to Correct Responses.   If the student responds correctly to the mand (unprompted correct), the teacher praises her, provides her with any materials that were withheld, and allows her to continue with the activity. For example, as a teacher reads a story to preschoolers, he stops and asks the children to name characters in the story (e.g., "Who ran after the pig?"). If a child responds correctly, the teacher praises the student and resumes reading; a correct response to the mand results in allowing the student to continue the activity. The use of the natural consequent event for correct performance illustrates the importance of focusing on the student's activity. The student's communicative responses should increase because he is allowed to return to an already preferred activity. When a student makes a correct response to the model (prompted correct), the teacher delivers the natural consequent event (i.e., the student can continue with the activity). All correct responses, both prompted and unprompted, are reinforced with the natural consequent event.

Responding to Incorrect or No Responses.   Because the mand does not always provide enough assistance to control the student's response, the student may make an incorrect response (unprompted incorrect) or not respond at all during the response interval (no response). When this happens, the teacher should give the model. If the preschooler in the previous example simply looks at the book when the teacher stops reading and asks the question, then the teacher tells the child the correct answer ("Wolf."). If the student does not respond or responds incorrectly after the model (prompted incorrect), the teacher can use options similar to those described in the incidental teaching section.

Select a Data Collection System; Implement, Monitor, and Adjust the Program Based on the Student's Data Patterns

The same data collection rules and information for monitoring progress used with the incidental teaching procedure apply to the mand-model strategy. The teacher's data collection should be continuous in order for him to monitor the effectiveness of the procedure in establishing new language skills with the student. A sample data collection form and line graph for the mand-model procedure are shown in Figure 8.6.

Student _____ Tenika _____ Instructor _____ Laura _____ Date ___ Thurs. 11/24 ___

Task _Student will point to picture in notebook when teacher presents mand "Tell me what you want."_

Trial Number	Record When Trial occurred	Record the Picture Response	Student Responding					
			Mand			Model		
			+	−	0	+	−	0
1	Arrival	Classroom		✓				
2	Free play	Doll			✓	✓		
3	Snack	Juice	✓					
4	Art	Crayon	✓					
5	Departure	Coat	✓					
Number of Responses			3	1	1	1		
Percent of Responses			60	20	20	20		

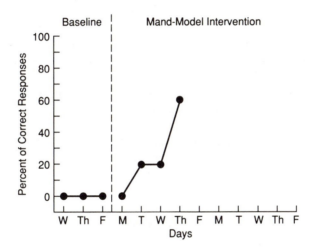

Figure 8.6. This data collection form for the mand-model procedure can be used to record both situational data and unprompted and prompted student responding data. Because the mand-model procedure is adult-directed, a teacher can plan ahead and record the time and target response for each initiation before beginning the day's instruction.

The sample graph below the form shows the percentage of correct responding that occurred without the model. Following the daily summary of student performance, only the correct responses to the mand without the prompt are plotted.

SAMPLE MAND-MODEL TEACHING PROCEDURE

The following example illustrates the steps in the mand-model teaching procedure.

Susie, a 3-year-old, has severe receptive and expressive language delays along with moderate hearing loss. She receptively identifies photographs of objects and people in her environment; she points to pictures of her cup, toothbrush, preferred foods, favorite toys, and family members in a notebook; and she has motor imitation. Although she points to these photographs during one-on-one instructional sessions and imitates manual signs for each photo, she does not use manual signs to label or request these objects. Her teacher, Mr. Robinson, decides to use the free play period to teach Susie to manually sign the names of known objects. He uses the data collection form and graph found in Figure 8.6 to monitor Susie's progress.

As Susie plays with a favorite doll, Mr. Robinson observes the activity, interrupts her play, signs, and says, "What are you playing with?" He allows her 4 seconds to sign "Doll." If Susie signs "Doll" correctly, Mr. Robinson delivers praise (e.g., "Good girl, you showed me the doll.") and allows her to continue playing with the doll. If she does not respond or responds incorrectly, Mr. Robinson models the sign for doll and gives her another 4 seconds to respond. When Susie signs correctly, he praises her and allows her to continue to play with the doll. Initially Susie needs the model prompt to make the correct sign; however, after about a week she signs "Doll" to his question alone.

STEPS FOR USING THE NATURALISTIC TIME DELAY TEACHING PROCEDURE

When using the naturalistic time delay procedure, the teacher must control the time and the place of instruction by (a) identifying beforehand the times, routines, and situations in which the student needs assistance or materials; (b) making herself available to the student at those times; and (c) withholding the assistance that she usually gives. These are the nine steps for this procedure:

- Define the response.
- Identify times when the student needs assistance.
- Approach the student and withhold assistance.
- Identify the signal to respond.
- Determine the length of the response interval.
- Select the type of prompt that will ensure a correct response.
- Use the response interval.
- Determine the consequences for each student response.
- Select a data collection system; implement, monitor, and adjust the program based on the student's data patterns.

Define the Response

As with the incidental teaching and mand-model procedures, the target response for the naturalistic time delay procedure is a language or functional communication response. For example, Jimmy is currently working in a local factory. When he completes a task, he wanders around the work area trying to gather materials for the next job until his supervisor assists him in selecting a new job. A target response could be a verbal request for help.

Identify Times When the Student Needs Assistance

With the naturalistic time delay procedure, the teacher examines the student's schedule to identify times when teaching episodes can be conducted. These times are **routines** when the student needs help and specific assistance is usually given—for example, when the teacher assists the student in fastening his buttons after swimming, making lemonade at snack time, gathering materials for an activity, or finding an item when shopping.

Approach the Student and Withhold Assistance

Once the routine has been selected, the teacher approaches the student, ensures that the student is aware of her availability, and withholds the assistance that the student needs and she usually gives. For example, Jimmy's supervisor walks over to Jimmy as he is leaving his work station. He stands next to Jimmy and looks "expectantly" at him (has a questioning look) or gestures with his hands. However, he does not help Jimmy find new work materials.

Identify the Signal to Respond

In the naturalistic time delay procedure, the approach, the availability of the adult, and the withholding of assistance all function as the naturally occurring target stimulus. They signal students to use communicative responses. In this manner, the procedure differs from the incidental teaching and mand-model procedures; rather than rely on a verbal request for an elaboration or a mand, the teacher can rely on a naturally occurring stimulus to signal the student to respond.

Determine the Length of the Response Interval

At the point when the student becomes accustomed to receiving help, the teacher withholds that assistance for a specified amount of time—generally, a minimum of 5 seconds. For example, the supervisor might walk over to Jimmy as he is finishing his task, ensure that Jimmy is aware of his presence, and wait silently for 5 seconds for Jimmy to request help in finding the materials he needs for his next job.

Select the Type of Prompt That Will Ensure a Correct Response

The next step in planning to use the naturalistic time delay procedure is for the teacher to select a prompt that will ensure a correct response if the student fails to make the target response when assistance is withheld. As with the incidental teaching and mand-model procedures, this prompt is often a model of the target response. For example, if Jimmy does not request help during the response interval, the supervisor says, "New job, please." It is possible with naturalistic time delay to use an indirect verbal prompt (e.g., "Tell me what you want." or "What?" or "Can I help you?") or a gestural prompt (e.g., the teacher shrugging his shoulders and holding out his hands to indicate that he does not know what the student needs). However, when teaching students with severe disabilities or difficult target behaviors, these types of prompts may not give the student the necessary information to perform the correct response.

Use the Response Interval

Delivery of the prompt is followed by another response interval. In the example with Jimmy, the supervisor delivers the model ("New job.") and waits another 5 seconds for Jimmy to imitate the model.

Determine the Consequences for Each Student Response

Before using the naturalistic time delay procedure, the teacher selects the consequent events that will follow all types of student responses.

Responding to Correct Responses.   If the student requests assistance without a prompt (unprompted correct), the teacher provides reinforcement in the form of praise and the requested materials or assistance. As with other naturalistic procedures, the natural consequences should be used. For example, a verbal request from Jimmy ("New job, please.") during the response interval results in the vocational teacher finding more work for Jimmy. If the student makes a correct response following the prompt (prompted correct), the teacher provides the requested help or materials. For example, Jimmy's supervisor helps him gather all of the materials needed for his next task if Jimmy waits for the prompt and then imitates the model. Only correct responses occurring before a prompt count toward the criterion for acquisition of the target behavior.

Responding to Incorrect or No Responses.   If the student does not respond (no response) or responds incorrectly before the prompt (unprompted incorrect), the teacher delivers the prompt. Student errors after the prompt (prompted incorrects) are followed by the consequent events suggested in the incidental teaching section of this chapter.

Select a Data Collection System; Implement, Monitor, and Adjust the Program Based on the Student's Data Patterns

A sample data collection form and line graph for the naturalistic time delay procedure are shown in Figure 8.7. The suggested procedural changes are the same as shown with the incidental teaching procedure.

SAMPLE NATURALISTIC TIME DELAY TEACHING PROGRAM

The steps for the effective use of naturalistic time delay are outlined in the following example.

Tracy is a 9-year-old with Down syndrome and moderate mental retardation. She can read 20–30 words, identify coins by value, and participate in daily community-based training activities. She communicates in two- and three-word sentences with adults and peers in her home and classroom. However, in community settings Tracy does not use expressive language to communicate requests. Tracy's teacher, Mr. Leonard, decides that for community training to be effective, Tracy should initiate

Student ___Sandy___   Instructor ___D. Moses___   Date ___Wed. 3/26___

Task _Student to request for object, permission, or assistance with two- to three-word sentence._

Trial Number	Time Assistance Was Withheld	Target Behavior	Student Responding					
			Unprompted Response			Model Response		
			+	−	0	+	−	0
1	Bus riding	"How much?"			✓	✓		
2	McDonald's	"I want____."			✓	✓		
3	Shopping	"Where is____."			✓	✓		
4	Movie	"One ticket."			✓	✓		
5	Ballet class	"Will you help?"			✓	✓		
Number of Responses			0	0	5	5	0	0
Percent of Responses			0	0	100	100	0	0

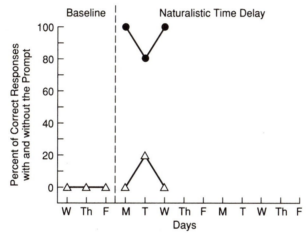

Key: △ = correct response to adult-directed approach alone,
● = correct response to adult-directed approach plus model

Figure 8.7. This data collection form for naturalistic time delay can be used to record the situational data, the setting, when assistance was withheld, and the correct response appropriate at that time. Check marks are used to record the type of student response. Because the naturalistic time delay procedure is adult-directed, a teacher can plan ahead and describe the approach and the correct response for each instructional trial before beginning the day's instruction.

The sample graph below the form shows the percentage of correct responding that occurred both with and without the model prompt. Following the daily summary of student performance, the correct responses to the adult-directed approach alone and the correct responses to the approach plus the delivery of the model are graphed.

requests in those activities. He selects grocery shopping to begin using naturalistic time delay. Mr. Leonard selected Tracy's using two- to three-word sentences to ask for assistance as the target behavior.

As Tracy enters the store, Mr. Leonard asks if she has her grocery list, requests that she read the grocery words, and tells her that she can begin shopping. After Tracy reads the words, he waits 5 seconds for Tracy to initiate shopping or request assistance in finding the food item. If Tracy knows where the item is located, she goes to the correct grocery aisle. However, if Tracy does not know where to find the food and she makes a correct response (asks, "Where is (name of food)?"), then Mr. Leonard shows her the grocery aisle where that food can be found. If Tracy makes an incorrect or no response, Mr. Leonard gives her a verbal model of the correct response (i.e., "Where is (name of food)?"), and waits an additional 5 seconds for Tracy to imitate the model. When Tracy repeats the three-word phrase, Mr. Leonard shows her where the food is located.

After several shopping trips, Tracy begins to read her list and spontaneously ask where the unknown items on the list are located. She does this in response to the naturally occurring event of entering the store without having to wait for an approach or the 5-second response interval from Mr. Leonard. Mr. Leonard also notes that on two occasions Tracy approached a stock boy and a store clerk to ask for help in finding a food item.

STEPS FOR USING THE TRANSITION-BASED TEACHING PROCEDURE

Transition-based teaching does not have an extensive research base. It was not developed as a procedure to encourage generalization but rather as a way to build acquisition and fluency of new tasks during times when training does not normally occur. The procedure is conducted in the natural environment during times that exist between scheduled activities. However, the instruction does not have to be related to the activities that precede or follow the teaching trial. These are the nine steps for using this procedure:

- Define the response.
- Define the transitions.
- Approach the student or focus on student initiation.
- Identify the signal to respond.
- Determine the length of the response interval.
- Select the type of prompt that will ensure a correct response.
- Use the response interval.
- Determine the consequences for each student response.
- Select a data collection system; implement, monitor, and adjust the program based on the student's data patterns.

Define the Response

This procedure can be used to teach a variety of behaviors, including language and functional communication skills. Although described as "naturalistic" because it is implemented at times that occur naturally in the student's environment, the target behavior does *not* have to be related to the student's wants, needs, or focus of attention. For example, when a student requests more juice during snack, the teacher can first require that he identify a photograph, read a word, or point to a letter of the alphabet before she rewards him with juice. As another example, Ellen is learning to identify the value of coins. Her teacher, Mr. West, decides that he does not have the time to conduct a one-on-one instructional session with Ellen since other students in the class can already identify these coins. Therefore, he decides to teach her the coin values using transition-based teaching.

Define the Transitions

The second step is for the teacher to identify the times throughout the day when transitions occur. **Transitions** are the times that exist between ongoing activities in the student's daily schedule. The transitions can be either adult- or child-directed; that is, a signal indicating that a transition-based instructional trial can take place is either prearranged by the adult, by always implementing a trial as the student enters the classroom in the morning, or initiated by the student when she asks for a new toy during free play. For example, Mr. West defines Ellen's transitions as the times between moving from one work area to another in her homeroom, the times between moving from one classroom to another, and the times when she approaches him to request assistance. When identifying transitions, the teacher should also decide on the total number of transitions that he will use as teaching opportunities.

Approach the Student or Focus on Student Initiation

Once the teacher has identified the target responses and transitions, he can either approach the student during the transition or wait for the student to initiate an interaction. When the transition occurs, he focuses on (e.g., gives attention to) and secures the student's attention.

Identify the Signal to Respond

After securing the student's attention, the teacher delivers a task direction or target stimulus. The task direction is similar to the request for elaboration in incidental teaching, the mand in mand-model procedure, and the naturally occurring routine in the naturalistic time delay procedure. It signals the student that a response is expected. The target stimulus in transition-based teaching is dependent on the behavior being taught (e.g., "What is this?" or "Tell me the color." or "Read the word." or "Show me the picture."). For example, Mr. West shows Ellen the coins and asks, "How much?"

Determine the Length of the Response Interval

Following delivery of the task direction, the teacher's next step is to allow the student time to respond. The response interval can be of any duration, depending on the characteristics of the response or the student. Usually it is 3–5 seconds. As with the other instructional procedures, the teacher waits silently for the student to respond during the response interval.

Select the Type of Prompt That Will Ensure a Correct Response

If the student does not respond or responds incorrectly, the teacher delivers a controlling prompt that gives the student the information needed to do the task correctly. For example, if a teacher is asking a student to identify photographs of objects receptively and the student makes no response to the task direction, she may use a model that points to the correct photograph. Because this procedure can be used to teach many different behaviors, a teacher can employ a variety of prompts. For example, if Ellen does not respond when Mr. West delivers the task direction, he delivers a model of the correct response ("Twenty-five cents.")

Use the Response Interval

Following delivery of the prompt, the teacher allows the student another opportunity to respond. Again, this response interval is 3-5 seconds. For example, when Mr. West delivers the model, he waits another 4 seconds for a response.

Determine the Consequences for Each Student Response

Before using the transition-based teaching procedure, the teacher selects the consequent events that will follow all types of student responses.

Responding to Correct Responses.   If the student responds correctly without a prompt (unprompted correct), the teacher provides reinforcement in the form of praise and allows the student to continue in the transition. As with other naturalistic procedures, the student receives the natural consequences that follow language or functional communication responses in the natural environment. If the student makes the correct response following the prompt (prompted correct), the teacher also provides reinforcement. However, only correct responses that occur before prompts count toward the criterion.

Responding to Incorrect or No Responses.   If the student does not respond (no response) or responds incorrectly before the prompt (unprompted incorrect), the teacher delivers the prompt. Student errors after the prompt (prompted incorrects) are followed by the consequent events suggested in the incidental teaching section of this chapter.

Select a Data Collection System; Implement, Monitor, and Adjust the Program Based on the Student's Data Patterns

A sample data collection form and line graph for the transition-based procedure are shown in Figure 8.8.

Student _____Jed_____ Instructor _____Douglas_____ Date ___10/12___

Task ___Student to identify orally (read) survival signs_____

Trial Number	Time of Transition	Type Circle	Written Stimulus	Student Responding	
				Before Prompt	After Prompt
1	9:00	C (A)	Exit	0	+
2	9:20	(C) A	Fire	0	+
3	10:15	(C) A	Exit	–	
4	12:00	C (A)	Fire	+	
5	1:30	C (A)	Fire	+	
6	1:50	C (A)	Exit	+	
Number of Responses				3	2
Percent of Responses				50	33.3

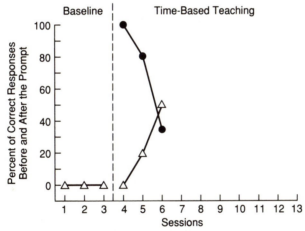

Baseline | Time-Based Teaching

Key: △ = correct response to target stimulus alone,
● = correct response to target stimulus plus prompt

Figure 8.8. This data collection form for transition-based teaching includes columns describing when the instructional trial took place, whether the transition was adult- or child-directed, and the words the student was asked to read. In the student responses columns a " + " indicates a correct response, a " – " indicates an incorrect response, and an "0" indicates no response.

The sample graph below the form shows the percentage of correct responding that occurred both before and after the prompt. Following the daily summary of student performance, correct responses to the target stimulus alone and correct responses to the target stimulus plus the delivery of the prompt are graphed.

SAMPLE TRANSITION-BASED TEACHING PROCEDURE

The following example illustrates the steps in the transition-based teaching procedure.

Ryan, a 12-year-old with hydrocephaly and moderate mental retardation, is in a self-contained classroom for students with multiple disabilities. Ryan expressively identifies photographs, counts to 20, sorts a variety of materials, and performs simple self-care skills. Ms. Rice, his teacher, decides that Ryan needs a more functional curriculum. She wants to begin by teaching him to identify expressively survival words he finds in and around the school building. However, Ms. Rice does not have the time or the available staff to add another one-on-one or small-group instructional session to the scheduled classroom activities. Therefore, she will use the transition-based teaching procedure to teach Ryan to read sight words.

Ms. Rice decides to teach Ryan two words during the transitions. She randomly selects the order in which she will present the words. Ms. Rice decides to conduct an instructional trial during transitions between regularly scheduled morning activities or when Ryan initiates a request. She identifies a total of ten transitions for ten instructional trials each morning. To conduct an instructional trial, she interrupts Ryan at the beginning of a transition or when he initiates an interaction to her. For example, after he puts his coat away but before he moves to an activity, Ms. Rice approaches Ryan; secures his attention; and presents the task direction, "Read the word." She then provides a response interval of 4 seconds. When Ryan reads the word correctly, Ms. Rice delivers descriptive verbal praise—"Good, that is (the word)."—and allows him to continue the transition. If Ryan does not read the word correctly or if he makes no response, she delivers a model of the correct response by reading the word. After he correctly imitates the model, she praises him and allows him to continue in the transition.

SUMMARY COMMENTS

- The naturalistic teaching procedures have been used effectively to teach a variety of language and functional communication skills to students with varying disabilities.
- Instruction occurs in the natural environment (i.e., a setting where the skill will be used), thereby increasing the probability that the behavior will be used when needed.
- The use of student initiations, adult initiations during child-directed activities, natural routines, and transitions increases teacher and classroom efficiency because instruction is conducted at times when instruction does not normally occur.
- Although instruction occurs in the natural environment, each procedure is implemented in a systematic, step-by-step manner.
- The procedures are similar: (a) It is possible with each procedure to teach language or functional communication behaviors; (b) each procedure is implemented in the natural environment; (c) each involves teacher planning of some

type of environmental manipulation; (d) each has a well-defined target stimulus and prompt to ensure correct responding; and (e) each has the same type of student responses. The differences between the procedures are seen in the type of target behavior, who initiates the communicative interaction, the type of teacher behavior involved in the environmental change, and the selection of the target stimulus and prompt.

Chapter 3–8 described 11 widely used instructional procedures, defined the steps for the effective use of each procedure, and provided examples to illustrate each procedure. The following chapter offers a brief overview of additional instructional procedures and general guidelines for selecting the most appropriate procedure for an instructional purpose.

EXERCISES

1. Discuss the ease of using naturalistic procedures, as described in this chapter, within the context of typical instructional activities that occur in the classroom.
2. Design an incidental teaching program with a student who is using a type of picture augmentative communication system.
3. Discuss the differences between transition-based teaching episodes and those episodes that occur with the other naturalistic teaching procedures. Design a program using transition-based teaching for a severely disabled student using both a skill related to and a skill not related to the transition.
4. Discuss how mand-model differs from traditional methods used to teach language skills in terms of the instructional format.
5. Define the differences between increasing language with adult-directed versus child-directed initiations in terms of acquisition, generalization, and maintenance. Design a program using one of the naturalistic procedures for each type of initiation.

REFERENCES

Cavallaro, C. C. & Bambara, L. M. (1982). Two strategies for teaching language during free play. *Journal of the Association for the Severely Handicapped, 7,* 80–93.

Cavallaro, C. C., & Poulson, C. L. (1985). Teaching language to handicapped children in natural settings. *Education and Treatment of Children, 8*(1), 1–24.

Fabry, B. D., Mayhew, G. L., & Hanson, A. (1984). Incidental teaching of mentally retarded students within a token system. *American Journal of Mental Deficiency, 89,* 29–36.

Halle, J., Baer, D., & Spradlin, J. (1981). Teachers' generalized use of delay as a stimulus control procedure to increase language use in handicapped children. *Journal of Applied Behavior Analysis, 141,* 389–409.

Halle, J., Marshall, A., & Spradlin, J. (1979). Time delay: A technique to increase language use and facilitate generalization in retarded children. *Journal of Applied Behavior Analysis, 12*(3), 431–439.

Hart, B., & Risley, T. (1968). Establishing use of descriptive adjectives in the spontaneous speech of disadvantaged preschool children. *Journal of Applied Behavior Analysis, 1,* 109–120.

——— (1974). Using preschool materials to modify the language of disadvantaged children. *Journal of Applied Behavior Analysis, 7*(2), 243–256.

——— (1975). Incidental teaching of language in the preschool. *Journal of Applied Behavior Analysis, 8,* 411–420.

——— (1980). In vivo language intervention: Unanticipated general effects. *Journal of Applied Behavior Analysis, 13,* 407–432.

Kaiser, A. (1987). *Teaching Functional Language Skills.* Distinguished lecture series, Department of Special Education, University of Kentucky, Lexington.

Kaiser, A. P., Alpert, C. L., & Warren, S. F. (1987). Teaching functional language: Strategies for language intervention. In M.E. Snell (Ed.), *Systematic instruction of persons with severe handicaps* (3rd ed.) (pp. 247–272). Columbus, OH: Charles Merrill.

McGee, G., Krantz, P., & McClannahan, L. (1985). The facilitative effects of incidental teaching on preposition use by autistic children. *Journal of Applied Behavior Analysis, 18*(1), 17–31.

Miller, J., & Allaire, J. (1987). Augmentative communication. In M. E. Snell (Ed.), *Systematic instruction of persons with severe handicaps* (3rd ed.) (pp. 273–297). Columbus, OH: Charles Merrill.

Neef, N., Walters, J., & Egel, A. (1984). Establishing generative yes/no responses in developmentally disabled children. *Journal of Applied Behavior Analysis, 17*(4), 453–460.

Rogers-Warren, A., & Warren, S. (1980). Mands for verbalization: Facilitating the display of newly trained language in children. *Behavior Modification, 4,* 361–382.

Schwarts, I. S., Anderson, S. R., & Halle, J. W. (1989). Training teachers to use naturalistic time delay: Effects on teacher behavior and on the language use of students. *Journal of the Association for the Severely Handicapped, 14,* 48–57.

Warren, S., & Kaiser, A. P. (1987). Research in early language intervention. In S.L. Odom & M.B. Karnes (Eds.), *Early intervention for infants and children with handicaps* (pp. 89–108). Baltimore: Paul Brookes.

Warren, S., McQuarter, R., & Rogers-Warren, A. (1984). The effects of mands and models on the speech of unresponsive socially isolated children. *Journal of Speech and Hearing Disorders, 49*(4), 43–52.

Wolery, M., Doyle, P. M., Gast, D. L., Ault, M. J., & Lichtenberg, S. (1991). *Comparison of progressive time delay and transition-based teaching with preacademic behaviors and preschoolers who display developmental delays.* (Manuscript submitted for publication.)

CHAPTER 9

Selecting Response Prompting Procedures

Chapter Overview

General Comments about Selecting Instructional Procedures
General Guidelines for Selecting Instructional Procedures
Summary Comments
Exercises
References

Key Terms

Response Shaping
Stimulus Modification Procedures
Stimulus Shaping
Stimulus Fading
Stimulus Superimposition
Error Correction Procedures
Effectiveness

Efficiency
Primum Non Noscere
Least Dangerous Assumption
Intrusiveness
Restrictiveness
Principle of Parsimony
Social Validity

Questions to Be Answered by This Chapter

1. What are the potential instructional procedures from which to select?
2. What specific guidelines should a teacher follow when selecting instructional procedures and practices?

Chapters 3–8 described various response prompting procedures—including constant time delay, progressive time delay, the system of least prompts, most-to-least prompting, antecedent prompt and test, antecedent prompt and fade, graduated guidance, and naturalistic strategies (incidental teaching, mand-model procedure, naturalistic time delay, and transition-based teaching). A teacher may well ask these questions: "Why are there so many procedures?" "Which procedure is best?" "When should I use each procedure?" These are legitimate questions. This chapter presents a few guidelines for selecting from among these procedures, but first it comments on the selection process.

GENERAL COMMENTS ABOUT SELECTING INSTRUCTIONAL PROCEDURES

This section provides three general comments about the selection of instructional strategies. The guidelines presented later in the chapter should be applied with these general considerations in mind.

A Broad Array of Strategies Exist

As noted in Chapter 1, teaching is the process of organizing student experience so that target behaviors come under the control of new and different stimulus conditions. The process involves establishing or transferring stimulus control. A stimulus acquires control of behaviors (i.e., behaviors reliably and predictably occur when the stimulus is present) by a simple arrangement: The behavior is reinforced when the stimulus is present and not reinforced when the stimulus is not present. There are a number of different procedures to establish stimulus control. The response prompting procedures listed above represent a primary set of options. Other strategies include response shaping, stimulus modification procedures, and error correction. Before these procedures are described, it is important to note the similarities of the response prompting strategies described in this text.

Response Prompting Strategies.   All the response prompting procedures are designed to establish stimulus control, and they share three characteristics for accomplishing this task. First, each of these procedures relies heavily on positive reinforcement. Positive reinforcement, of course, is any event that follows a behavior and maintains that behavior's occurrence or increases its rate of occurrence. Several things about reinforcement are well known but important to remember (see Baer, 1978; Cooper, Heron, & Heward, 1987; Wolery, Bailey, & Sugai, 1988). Reinforcers are idiosyncratic to each individual—a stimulus that is a reinforcer for one student may not be a reinforcer for another. Reinforcers have different value that may vary with time. Some reinforcers are stronger than others, and the strength may vary depending on the states of the student, the extent to which the reinforcer is used, and other factors. Reinforcers increase the behaviors they follow; therefore, they should be delivered contingently and clearly.

Second, each of these procedures uses teacher assistance (prompts) to get the student behavior to occur in the presence of the stimulus. This is done so that the teacher has opportunities to reinforce the behavior when the stimulus is present. Although it is the reinforcement of the behavior in the presence of the stimulus that causes it to acquire control, it is horribly inefficient to wait for the behavior to occur naturally or "by chance" when the stimulus is present. Therefore, the teacher prompts the student to do the behavior when the stimulus is present and immediately provides reinforcement for doing the behavior.

Third, each of these procedures is designed to remove or fade the use of prompts. Prompts are simply used to get the behavior to occur so that it can be reinforced. However, when they are used, a danger exists that the prompt *and* the stimulus will acquire control of the behavior's occurrence. If this occurs, then the student will not display the behavior when only the stimulus is present. Thus, each of these procedures is designed to eliminate the prompt. With progressive, constant, and naturalistic time delay, the prompts are faded on a time dimension, and the student has opportunities to respond independently or wait for assistance; however, to access reinforcers quickly, they must respond before the prompt. With the system of least prompts, incidental teaching, mand-model procedure, and transition-based teaching, the student is provided with the opportunity to respond independently on each trial. If the student does not do the behavior, the teacher provides prompts; however, if the student does the behavior, the teacher quickly provides reinforcement. With the most-to-least prompting procedure, the student is provided with assistance that is systematically decreased each time he reaches the criterion at more intrusive prompt levels. With the antecedent prompt and test procedures, the teacher abruptly removes the prompts and provides the student with opportunities to respond independently; however, if independent performance is not forthcoming, the teacher reinstates prompted trials. With the antecedent prompt and fade procedures and with graduated guidance, the teacher makes decisions about when and how to decrease prompts. With antecedent prompt and fade procedures, the decisions are made between trials or sessions, and with the graduated guidance procedure the decisions are made moment by moment as trials progress.

In summary, each of these procedures provides reinforcement for the target behavior being performed in the presence of the stimulus. The student then learns that reinforcement is probable if the stimulus is present. Each procedure uses prompts to help the student perform the behavior so that the teacher does not have to wait for the behavior to happen naturally in the presence of the stimulus. However, since a student should learn to perform only when the stimulus is present and not when the stimulus *and* the prompt are present, the procedures are designed for the teacher to remove the prompts in some way.

Although the response prompting procedures are widely used, effective with multiple skills and tasks, and well represented in the literature, there are other instructional strategies that are not described in this text. Two types of these other procedures are particularly noteworthy because of their rich tradition in behavioral instruction and because they are definite alternatives and supplements to the response prompting procedures: response shaping and stimulus modification procedures. In addition, a third type of strategy, error correction, deserves note because it is used frequently. Although a thorough discussion of these procedures is beyond the scope of this text, these strategies are described briefly below as potential procedures from which a teacher may select.

Response Shaping.   **Response shaping** is the teacher reinforcing successive approximations of the target behavior (Cooper et al., 1987; Panyan, 1980). As the definition suggests, the procedure relies heavily on positive reinforcement. The teacher defines the target behavior for a given student and generates a series of steps by using task analysis (see Wolery, 1989). These steps build from the student's current behavior to the target behavior. The teacher begins by reinforcing the student for doing the most basic form of the response when the appropriate stimuli are present. After the student consistently does this most basic form, the teacher reinforces a slightly more complex or advanced variation of the response. The behavior that the teacher previously reinforced no longer receives reinforcement. This process of reinforcing successive approximations of the response continues until the student consistently performs the target behavior. For example, if a preschool child does not play with toys, her teacher might initially reinforce the child for looking at the toys; when looking is well established, the teacher would provide reinforcement for touching the toys; when touching is well established, the teacher would provide reinforcement for moving the toys; when moving is well established, the teacher would provide reinforcement for particular types of movements that are related to particular toys. As is evident, stimulus control is established for each of the skills (i.e., looking, touching, moving, and manipulating in particular ways); that is, the presence of the toys signals the child that reinforcement is possible if these behaviors are displayed. Response shaping requires considerable skill on the teacher's part, careful implementation of differential reinforcement, and skillful task analysis of the target behavior. For more information on response shaping, read Cooper et al. (1987) and Panyan (1980).

Stimulus Modification Procedures.   Stimulus modification procedures may be useful strategies for some situations. **Stimulus modification procedures,** as their name suggests, allow the teacher to manipulate the stimulus gradually as instruction progresses (Cooper et al., 1987; Wolery, Bailey, & Sugai, 1988). Initially, the stimulus must be one that currently has control of the student's behavior. As instruction progresses, the teacher gradually changes the stimuli so that they approximate and finally represent the target stimulus. For example, Bob is learning to read his name. Initially, he cannot say "Bob" when shown the written word "Bob," but he does say "Bob" when shown a picture of himself. His teacher will gradually change the picture to the word "Bob." During the first phase of instruction, the teacher will show the picture of "Bob" without the word "Bob." In the next phase, the teacher will write the word "Bob" lightly on the picture. In the next phase, the teacher will write the written word darker; in the next phase, she would write it even darker. She will then gradually decrease the picture; for example, she will make the picture part of the card lighter by placing a layer of semiclear plastic over it—so that the word would remain unobstructed. In the next phase, she will put another layer of plastic over it. This will continue until she totally obstructs the picture and the word "Bob" is present. This process is quite different from that used with the response prompting strategies described in this text. With the response prompting strategies, the stimulus remains constant and the student's behavior is prompted until it can be performed independently; however, with the stimulus modification procedures, the behavior is constant and the stimulus conditions under which it is displayed are gradually changed.

Three major types of stimulus modifications procedures exist: stimulus shaping, stimulus fading, and superimposition (Cooper et al., 1987; Etzel & LeBlanc, 1979). These types are different from one another concerning how the stimulus is modified as instruction progresses. **Stimulus shaping** involves the teacher changing the critical or relevant dimension of the stimulus. **Stimulus fading** involves the teacher changing some noncritical or irrelevant dimension of the stimulus. For example, if a student is learning to name the letters of the alphabet, the shape of each letter is the critical dimension; however, the color, size and print type of the letters are irrelevant. For example, if a student's favorite color is red and he is learning to point to letters named by his teacher, the color of the target letters could be red and the color of the distractor letters could be black. Over the phases of instruction, his teacher could gradually change the color of the target letters to black. This is an example of stimulus fading. If stimulus shaping was used, then the teacher would change the actual shape of the letters. Generally, stimulus fading programs are easier to design than stimulus shaping ones. However, fading requires the student to shift from the nonrelevant stimulus dimension to the relevant stimulus dimension to make the final discrimination. In the example above, the initial discrimination could be made on the basis of the color of the letters; however, at the end of instruction, the discrimination would need to be made on the basis of the shape of the letters. Some students will have difficulty making this shift. **Stimulus superimposition,** another stimulus modification procedure, involves the teacher placing one stimulus over another and gradually changing the salience or intensity of one stimulus. For example, in the earlier example of the teacher teaching "Bob" to read his name, if the teacher wrote the word "Bob" across the picture, then this would be an example of superimposition.

Stimulus modification procedures have both positive and negative features. On the positive side, some research indicates that they may be more effective in some situations than the response prompting strategies (Ault et al., 1989). Also, stimulus shaping programs have been used to teach fine discriminations. There are two primary disadvantages, however. First, some stimuli are impossible or at least difficult to manipulate, and the costs involved in manipulating some stimuli are extensive. Second, stimulus modification procedures require considerable material preparation time (LeBlanc, Etzel, & Domash, 1978). These two factors make stimulus modification less desirable than many of the response prompting strategies. However, the use of computer-assisted instruction may be an avenue for teachers to employ the stimulus modification strategies in a more efficient manner. At present, though, the utility of the stimulus modification procedures is limited.

Error Correction Procedures.   Error correction procedures are used frequently when teachers instruct students with moderate and severe disabilities. **Error correction procedures** are relatively straightforward and involve the teacher presenting the student with an opportunity to respond independently; if the student's response is correct, the teacher provides reinforcement; if the response is incorrect, then the teacher provides a prompt. Error correction is technically a response prompting procedure because the student is prompted to perform the correct response; however, the timing of the prompt occurs after the student makes an error. The information about how to do the behavior is presented after the student has attempted to do it and done so incorrectly. Although error correction procedures are relatively easy to implement, their use is generally not recommended for two reasons. First, error correction procedures are generally less efficient than response prompting and stimulus modification procedures (Ault et al., 1989). Second, a student must demonstrate some level of failure before receiving the response prompt. While some students can tolerate frequent errors, other students tend to display problem behavior when they make errors in difficult tasks (O'Neill et al., 1990).

Teachers can select instructional strategies from response prompting, response shaping, stimulus modification, and error correction procedures. The guidelines presented later in this chapter apply to all of these procedures; they are not unique to the response prompting strategies. Teachers of students with moderate to severe disabilities should understand each of these strategies and should be able to use each when it is needed.

Teachers Should Be Skilled in Using a Broad Array of Procedures

Two purposes of this text are (a) to describe strategies in detail so that teachers can learn to use them and (b) to list references that will allow teachers to learn more about the strategies. However, a teacher's reading and hearing about how to do something will not always result in his knowing how to do it skillfully. A teacher learning to use the procedures described in this text is similar to that teacher teaching students with disabilities to learn particular skills. First, the teacher must learn how to use the procedures; second, she must become fluent in using them; third, she must maintain her fluency; and, finally, she must apply or generalize its use across children and skills. Clearly, using the guidelines presented later in this chapter for selecting instructional strategies will be a relatively meaningless activity if the teacher cannot implement the procedure she selects.

To learn to use the procedures, the teacher should follow four general practices. First, he needs to read the chapters and other sources about the procedures, which will probably require more than one reading. He must understand each step of each procedure.

Second, the teacher should develop a plan for using the procedure he chooses by using the flow charts presented in each chapter as a checklist of the things to attend to when he uses the procedure. Some parts of the flow charts describe prerequisite skills, other parts describe planning decisions, and other parts describe how the procedure is actually implemented with a student or group of students.

Third, the teacher needs to practice the procedure. Frequently he can try the procedure out with his own children, his spouse or companion, a team teacher or teaching assistant, or some other friend or that friend's children. Although this is probably not necessary, considerable research has documented the positive benefits of role-playing when a teacher is learning to use a new procedure. When learning to use these procedures, the teacher starts with a student or group of students that are relatively easy to teach. Frequently, when attempting a new procedure, a teacher makes decisions more slowly, makes some initial errors, and tends not to be smooth in his presentation. Thus, when working out the "bugs" of the new procedure, the teacher will find it helpful to have students who do not require constant attention.

Fourth, the teacher needs feedback on the use of the procedure. This feedback can come from a variety of sources, such as a practicum or student teaching supervisor, another teacher, videotapes of the teacher using the procedures, and the students being taught. This latter source is particularly important. Research on staff development and the use of innovations indicates that teachers will adopt new procedures that have positive benefits for their students (Guskey, 1986). Feedback can be received from a student in two ways: (a) data collected on whether she has learned what is being taught and (b) her comments and affect related to the use of the procedure. With the response prompting procedures, it is critical for the teacher to collect data on whether the student is learning. If more information on how to collect and analyze data are needed, the teacher should review the data collection sections of the chapters on each procedure and consult Cooper et al. (1987), White and Haring (1980), and Wolery et al. (1988). In addition to collecting data on the student's performance, several things can give the teacher feedback about how well he is teaching. Examples include the student's affect during instruction, the extent to which she pays attention, and her comments (if verbal) during and about instruction. Ideally, instruction and learning should be fun for the student. If she seems to be enjoying the instruction, then it may mean that the teacher is implementing it correctly. Also, if she is attending during instruction, then correct implementation is likely. Finally, sometimes a student will make comments about an instructional procedure. For example, when progressive time delay was used in a study with mildly disabled children, they frequently commented during the early parts of instruction that their teacher did not give them enough time to respond.

After learning how to use a procedure, the teacher needs to practice it with sufficient regularity to become fluent. This means that his implementation will become smooth, fast, and easy to do. It will require less thought and concentration on his part. However, such proficient performance can be accomplished only through repeated use—i.e., practice. After becoming fluent in using the procedure, the teacher can begin to apply it with more difficult students, with different types of behaviors, and in different contexts. In other words, the teacher should program his behavior for maintenance and for generalization.

All Selections Should Be Viewed as Tentative

Another issue that the teacher should consider when selecting instructional strategies is that no selection should be seen as a permanent choice. The purpose of any instructional procedure is to establish stimulus control. If a procedure is not working, then the teacher must analyze the instructional situation and determine what changes are needed. To do this, the teacher must collect data on the student's performance and analyze that data as described in Chapter 1. One possibility when a student is not making acceptable progress is that the teacher should change the instructional strategy. The chapters presenting each response prompting strategy described procedures for dealing with some patterns of performance. If these procedures are not effective quickly, then the teacher should consider changing instructional procedures.

Summary

Before the guidelines for selecting instructional strategies can be useful, the teacher must recognize that there is a broad array of procedures from which to select. These include response prompting procedures as described in this text, response shaping, stimulus modification procedures, and error correction. Further, when selecting a procedure, the teacher must not assume that he knows how to use it effectively. He must acquire the basic steps of implementing the procedure, practice it to become fluent, maintain it over time, and generalize it to other situations. Finally, after he selects a strategy, he should not consider it a permanent choice; if it does not work, he should select another procedure.

GENERAL GUIDELINES FOR SELECTING INSTRUCTIONAL PROCEDURES

As described above, there are a number of viable instructional strategies. From the authors' review of the instructional research with students who have moderate to severe disabilities (Wolery et al., 1986), two relevant findings have emerged. First, there is a relatively limited set of defined and studied instructional strategies. This text has described 11 different strategies. Also, there are three stimulus modification strategies and error correction. Thus, fewer than two dozen direct instructional strategies have been described in the literature. Second, many of these strategies have been used effectively across a broad range of skills, ages, and disabilities. The findings seem to indicate that it is possible for a given teacher to be skilled in implementing each of these procedures. Further, a teacher's learning to use these strategies is probably worth the effort because they are so generalizable (i.e., can be used across skill domains).

This section presents seven general guidelines. These guidelines are based on logic and experience; there is little, if any, research describing how a teacher should select from the instructional strategies listed above. In the past, teachers were expected to select strategies based on their preferences rather than on some logical choice between potential options. These guidelines are presented to encourage teachers to think carefully about which procedures they will use for given situations. Each of these guidelines presents some information that should be considered in the selection decision. The relative value of each is difficult to determine; in short, each guideline is important, and the teacher must ultimately determine the amount of emphasis to place on any single guideline. However, several of the guidelines are based on the assumption that the selection or choice is being made between strategies with demonstrated effectiveness. A procedure that is not likely to be effective should not be chosen over procedures that are effective.

Consider the Research Base of Potential Options

A major emphasis in this text and in many teacher training programs is that a teacher's behaviors should be based on the research literature (Heward, Heron, & Cooper, 1990; Kaiser & McWhorter, 1990). This guideline assumes that a teacher of students with moderate and severe disabilities will be a consumer of the research literature. Therefore, in selecting any instructional strategy or practice, a teacher must determine whether there are any research reports that focus on students similar to hers being taught skills similar to the ones she wants to teach. Preference would then be given to the strategies that were used in the research reports, if, of course, those strategies were effective.

In each of the chapters of this text that describe specific strategies, a section was devoted to describing the skills and the students taught with the particular procedures. The teacher should recognize that the precise skill she is teaching may not match that in the published literature. However, in many cases, the various strategies have been used with discrete responses and chained tasks. Frequently, procedures that have been used with one such skill can be applicable to other skills that require a similar format or mode of presentation.

A teacher's analysis of the literature in this way can result in at least four general outcomes. First, the teacher can search the literature and fail to find instructional research reports focusing on skills similar to his target skill which students similar to his students have been taught. In such a case, the teacher should rely on his experiences with his students and similar skills and on the information from the other guidelines.

Second, the teacher may find reports in which the target or similar skill was taught to some subjects with a single strategy. In such cases, if the procedure was effective, then the teacher should consider it for teaching the students and skills in question. If it was not effective in the research report, then he should avoid it.

Third, the teacher can find reports in which the target skills were taught with several different procedures. In most cases, these reports will not compare instructional strategies but will demonstrate that given certain subjects in specified contexts, the use of a particular procedure was effective. This suggests that the teacher can use the other selection guidelines for determining which procedure to use.

Fourth, occasionally, the teacher will find reports in which the target skills were taught to similar subjects and two or more strategies were compared directly. These types of studies are perhaps the most useful in selecting instructional strategies. Usually, the strategies are compared on at least two dimensions: effectiveness and efficiency. **Effectiveness,** as defined generally, refers to "the actual production of or the power to produce an effect" (Mish, 1988, p. 397). In terms of instruction, the definition of effective is that children learn what they are taught (Wolery & Gast, 1990). Teaching is effective when students can eventually perform skills that they could not do before instruction. **Efficiency,** as defined generally, is the "quality or degree of being efficient" (Mish, 1988, p. 397)—which is defined as the potential or power of causing effects without loss of or waste of energy. Efficiency implies effectiveness (power of causing effects), but only a certain type of effectiveness—that which is done with less energy. In terms of instruction, procedures are efficient if they are effective and require less energy or time than other procedures. Instructional procedures must be effective to be efficient; however, effectiveness does not ensure efficiency. Efficiency is relative, implying a comparison either to some established standard or to another procedure. To be found efficient, an instructional procedure must demonstrate that it is effective *and* that it results in better learning than does some other procedure. The manner in which efficiency is conceptualized is discussed in Chapter 10.

Although additional research comparing the efficiency of instructional procedures continues to be disseminated, there are a number of general statements based on the literature that can be made [for additional discussion of this issue, consult Ault et al. (1989)]:

- Procedures using antecedent prompts (e.g., incidental teaching, progressive time delay, system of least prompts, and stimulus modification procedures) appear to produce fewer errors and lower error percentages than does error correction (Haught, Walls, & Crist, 1984; Walls, Zane, & Thvedt, 1980).

- Stimulus shaping and stimulus fading appear to produce fewer errors than do most-to-least prompting, the system of least prompts, progressive time delay, and error correction (Richmond & Bell, 1983; Mosk & Bucher, 1984; McGee & McCoy, 1981).

- Direct comparisons of most-to-least prompting and the system of least prompts have produced mixed results; however, most-to-least prompting appears to produce fewer errors (Day, 1987). The amount of instructional time required may vary depending on the specific criterion used with most-to-least prompting and the frequency with which less intrusive prompt and independent levels are probed.

- Integrated instructional strategies (e.g., stimulus modifications and the system of least prompts) may be more efficient than are the strategies used alone (Mosk & Bucher, 1984).

- Progressive time delay appears to be more efficient than the system of least prompts for students who (a) have moderate to severe mental retardation, (b) have intact sensory systems (with appliances or adaptations such as manual signs), (c) have identified reinforcers, (d) are imitative, and (e) are learning discrete responses (Bennett et al., 1986; Godby, Gast, & Wolery, 1987). "More efficient" means that progressive time delay will require fewer sessions, trials, errors, and minutes of direct instructional time to criterion.

- Constant time delay is more efficient than the system of least prompts for students who (a) have mild to moderate mental retardation or autism, (b) have intact sensory systems (with appliances or adaptations such as manual signs), (c) have identified reinforcers, (d) are imitative, and (e) are learning discrete *or* chained responses (Ault, Wolery, Gast, Doyle, & Eizenstat, 1988; Doyle et al., 1990; Gast et al., 1988; McDonnell, 1987; Wolery et al., 1990).

- Constant and progressive time delay appear about equal in terms of efficiency for students who (a) have moderate mental retardation or learning disabilities, (b) have intact sensory systems, (c) have identified reinforcers, (d) are imitative, and (e) are learning discrete behaviors. Measures included the number of sessions, trials, minutes of direct instructional time, and percent of errors (Ault, Gast, & Wolery, 1988; Precious, 1985; Thomas, 1989). However, for some students, constant time delay appears to be more efficient. No variables could be identified to determine which students would learn more readily with constant time delay.

- Most-to-least prompting and constant time delay have been compared with chained tasks in two studies—however, the findings were mixed. Miller and Test (1989) found constant time delay to be more efficient; McDonnell and Ferguson (1989) found most-to-least prompting to be more efficient.

- Transition-based teaching and progressive time delay appear to be equal in terms of efficiency for preschoolers who (a) have mild disabilities, (b) have intact sensory systems, (c) have identified reinforcers, (d) are imitative, and (e) are learning discrete tasks (Wolery, Doyle, Gast, Ault, & Lichtenberg, 1991).

Consider the Potential Harmfulness of the Procedures

Although instructional strategies are generally risk free, it is possible for a teacher to unwittingly devise instructional programs that are harmful to children. Two principles apply: *primum non noscere* ("first, not to injure") (Zigler & Sietz, 1975, p. 490) and the **least dangerous assumption** (Donnellan, 1984). The *primum non noscere* principle suggests that the minimal acceptable criteria for any practice or treatment is that it do no harm to those who experience it. The principle of the **least dangerous assumption** suggests that when two or more procedures are equally effective and efficient or when there is no research base with the strategies under consideration, then the teacher should select the procedure that has the smallest potential for causing harm. Harm can be conceptualized as physical injury, social stigmatization, and maintaining states or conditions of dependency. Thus, the teacher should select procedures that will not physically injure students, that will not cause social ridicule or belittling, and that will result in students learning to be more independent and self-sufficient.

Although most instructional procedures are harmless, in some cases a teacher may use physical prompts. The manner in which physical prompts are applied can in some cases cause harm to students. The teacher should ensure that any physical prompts he administers are done in a safe and harmless manner. Two other times when these principles are particularly important with students who have moderate to severe disabilities are when a teacher is using community-based instruction (Sailor et al., 1986) and when the teacher is teaching safety skills (Collins, Wolery, & Gast, 1991). When children are taught in the community, they are potentially exposed to dangerous situations; thus, careful attention must be given to scheduling supervising, transporting, and other concerns. When teaching safety skills, the teacher should design her instruction to minimize danger. For example, when teaching students to clean up broken glass, Winterling, Gast, Wolery, and Farmer (in press) used simulated materials (e.g., small pieces of rubber and plastic) and errorless teaching procedures. After the students learned to clean up the simulated materials accurately and independently, the researchers introduced actual broken glass into the training procedures.

Consider the Intrusiveness and Restrictiveness of Procedures

Intrusiveness and restrictiveness are closely related terms. **Intrusiveness** refers to the extent to which a procedure impinges on a student's being, and **restrictiveness** refers to the extent to which a student's freedom is constricted or curtailed. Some strategies or prompts are both intrusive and restrictive; for example, a full physical manipulation impinges on a student's body (i.e., a teacher has his hands on the student's hands and moves them as desired) and restricts the student's ability to move her hands independently. Other prompts are restrictive but not intrusive; for example a 10-second, in-seat time-out delivered for errors is not intrusive, but it restricts the student's access to reinforcers. Thus, a teacher should evaluate the intrusiveness and the restrictiveness of the potential instructional strategies and practices.

These notions, of course, each occur on a continuum from very to not at all intrusive or restrictive. As much as possible, the teacher should select instructional strategies and practices that are minimally intrusive and restrictive. Strategies that are not intrusive and are not restrictive are described as being "natural" or more normative—similar to those used with students without disabilities. Generally, more natural instructional arrangements and procedures should be used. However, the criteria of least intrusive, least restrictive, and most natural must be applied only to strategies that are effective; that is, given that there are multiple effective strategies, then these criteria can be used to make choices about which procedure to use. Clearly, there is no justification for using ineffective strategies simply because they are minimally restrictive and intrusive but appear natural. (Axelrod, 1990).

Consider the Student's Response Patterns and Learning History

When selecting instructional strategies, the teacher needs to consider the student's performance in past instruction. For example, relevant aspects include how well the student attends to instruction, what reinforcers appear effective, what prompts are controlling, what prompts appear ineffective, does the student learn from observing other students, do problem behaviors occur when errors are present, do problem behaviors occur when particular prompts are used, how have similar behaviors been taught in the past, and what strategies appear to be effective.

When implementing instruction, the teacher should collect and analyze data on the student's response patterns. The previous chapters presented decision rules and recommendations for particular types of performance patterns. These should be considered by a teacher when selecting instructional strategies and in modifying instruction after it has been initiated. Although few rules exist about selecting instructional strategies based on the student's response patterns, some suggestions are provided in Table 9.1.

Consider the Phase of Performance

Although much of this text focuses on teaching a student to perform new behaviors, teaching also involves getting a student to use the new behaviors he has been taught. Performance during instruction, as described in Chapter 1, can be conceptualized as occurring in four overlapping phases: (a) acquisition—learning the basic requirements of a skill; (b) fluency—performing the skill quickly and smoothly; (c) maintenance—continuing to perform the skill after instruction has stopped; and (d) generalization—performing the skill in situations other than training. Also, as noted in Chapter 1, each of these phases of performance appears to be influenced by slightly different instructional procedures or arrangements. Thus, when selecting instructional strategies, the teacher must be aware of the purpose of instruction—that is, is it to promote acquisition, fluency, maintenance, generalization, or some combination of these.

Acquisition appears to be promoted by the teacher providing the student with information (assistance) related to how to perform the target behavior. Thus, instructional strategies for promoting acquisition should provide the student with additional information. However, such strategies will not be helpful in building fluency, which is promoted by practice. Thus, strategies selected to promote fluency should increase the student's motivation to engage in practice sessions. Strategies for promoting maintenance are thinning reinforcement schedules, delaying reinforcers, using natural

TABLE 9.1. "If . . . Then" Recommendations About Students' Response Patterns

Student Behavior	Teacher Behavior
If physical contact with the teacher is a strong positive reinforcer,	Then instructional strategies that involve physical prompts may be less successful than those that do not rely on such prompts.
If students withdraw from or react negatively to physical contact,	Then physical prompts should be avoided.
If students respond quickly to task directions without attending to the instructional stimuli or waiting for teacher assistance,	Then use of (a) procedures that delay assistance may be contraindicated, (b) specific attentional responses (e.g., repeating the task direction or acting on the stimulus before responding) are warranted, and (c) wait training is needed and appropriate.
If students have a history of learning particular types of responses with a given procedure,	Then use of similar procedures is indicated.
If students have a history of one-on-one instruction,	Then they may need specific instruction in group formats before new instructional procedures in group formats are attempted.
If students become disruptive or work more slowly when errors occur,	Then errorless teaching procedures should be used.
If students become disruptive when required to wait for prompts,	Then the system of least prompts may not be appropriate because the controlling prompt is presented at the end of the prompt hierarchy.
If the students have generalized imitative repertoires,	Then models should be considered as controlling prompts.
If students are not imitative,	Then model prompts should not be used as controlling prompts.
If natural contingencies, differential reinforcement, and error correction are ineffective or inefficient,	Then response prompting strategies should be used.
If response prompting strategies are ineffective or inefficient,	Then stimulus modification procedures should be considered.
If students display overselective attention,	Then stimulus shaping should be considered.
If students performance is variable or deteriorates,	Then changes in the reinforcers and reinforcement schedules should be attempted.
If students remain prompt dependent,	Then alternative methods of fading prompts should be considered.

[Adapted from Wolery, Doyle, Alig, Ault, Gast, and Morris (1988).]

reinforcers and reinforcement schedules, and teaching children to perform skills fluently. Thus, if a student is in the maintenance phase of instruction, then her teacher should select strategies on this basis. Generalization is promoted by carefully selecting instructional materials and behaviors; varying materials, teachers, teaching formats, and instructional settings; teaching in the natural environment; and using self-control procedures. Thus, when attempting to promote generalization, the teacher must select strategies that allow this type of flexibility.

Consider the Principle of Parsimony

When all other factors—such as the effectiveness and efficiency of two or more procedures—appear to be equal, the teacher should select instructional strategies based on the principle of parsimony (Etzel & LeBlanc, 1979). The **principle of parsimony** states that when there are two or more solutions for a problem, the simpler/est solution should be adopted. In other words, when two or more instructional strategies are likely to be equally effective and efficient, then the teacher should use the simpler/est procedure. Two rationales exist for this recommendation. First, simpler procedures are likely to result in fewer procedural errors. In other words, the teacher is more likely to implement simpler procedures accurately. Second, simpler procedures require less work and effort on the teacher's part. Teaching, as described in this text, is not an easy endeavor, so when the task can be simplified without loss of effectiveness or efficiency, it should be.

Consider the Social Validity of the Options

Social validity refers to the value assigned by experts and consumers to the goals, procedures, and outcomes of an educational practice (Wolf, 1978). The social validity of the goals for a student with a moderate and severe disability should be addressed by the teacher through the assessment and instructional planning process. The social validity or acceptability of the procedures or strategies, however, also should be addressed. Clearly, procedures should be used that are viewed as acceptable to the students' families, teachers, and other team members. If procedures are viewed as acceptable (i.e., socially valid), then it is thought that they will be more readily used. Social validity, however, is similar to some of the other guidelines. It is not a criterion for selecting from the full array of strategies; it is only a criterion for selecting from strategies that have been identified as effective and efficient. As with restrictiveness, intrusiveness, and parsimony, the teacher should not select and use ineffective procedures just because they are acceptable to team members.

SUMMARY COMMENTS

- Instructional options include response prompting strategies, response shaping, stimulus modification procedures, and error correction strategies.
- Because of the generalizability of these strategies, a teacher should learn to use all of the strategies described in this text.
- Selection of an instructional procedure should not be viewed as a permanent decision, but should be reviewed if the student does not readily learn.
- Guidelines for selecting instructional strategies include the following: the research base on the effectiveness and efficiency of various procedures, the potential harmfulness of the procedures, the intrusiveness and restrictiveness of the procedures, the student's learning history and patterns of responding, the phase of performance that is the focus of instruction, the complexity of the procedures, and the acceptability of the procedures.

This chapter discussed some issues for a teacher to consider when selecting the instructional strategies described earlier in the book. The final chapter addresses issues for increasing the efficiency of instruction. This notion of efficiency was introduced in this chapter, but it is explained in detail in the next. Chapter 10 also describes the issue of structuring small-group instruction to emphasize the need to apply the instructional strategies described in this book in the context of groups rather than in the contexts of one-on-one instruction.

EXERCISES

1. Ask an experienced teacher how he or she decides which strategies to use.
2. For a given student and a given skill, attempt to apply the guidelines for selecting instructional strategies.
3. Observe a teacher providing instruction, identify which strategy he or she is using, and attempt to determine whether you would use that strategy by following the guidelines.

REFERENCES

Ault, M. J., Gast, D. L., & Wolery, M. (1988). Comparison of progressive and constant time delay procedures in teaching community sign-reading. *American Journal of Mental Retardation, 93,* 44–56.

Ault, M. J., Wolery, M., Gast, D. L., Doyle, P. M., & Eizenstat, V. (1988). Comparison of response prompting procedures in teaching numeral identification to autistic subjects. *Journal of Autism and Developmental Disabilities, 18,* 627–636.

Ault, M. J., Wolery, M., Doyle, P. M., & Gast, D. L. (1989). Review of comparative studies in instruction of students with moderate and severe handicaps. *Exceptional Children, 55,* 346–356.

Axelrod, S. (1990). Myths that (mis)guide our profession. In A. C. Repp & N. N. Singh (Eds.), *Perspectives on the use of nonaversive and aversive interventions for persons with developmental disabilities* (pp. 59–72). Sycamore, IL: Sycamore Publishing.

Baer, D. M. (1978). The behavioral analysis of trouble. In K. E. Allen, V. A. Holm, & R. L. Schiefelbusch (Eds.), *Early intervention—a team approach* (pp. 57–93). Baltimore: University Park Press.

Bennett, D., Gast, D. L., Wolery, M., & Schuster, J. (1986). Time delay and system of least prompts: A comparison in teaching manual sign production. *Education and Training of the Mentally Retarded, 21,* 117–129.

Collins, B. C., Wolery, M., & Gast, D. L. (1991). A survey of safety concerns for students with special needs. *Education and Training in Mental Retardation, 26,* 305–318.

Cooper, J. O., Heron, T. E., & Heward, W. L. (1987). *Applied behavior analysis.* Columbus, OH: Charles Merrill.

Day, H. M. (1987). Comparison of two prompting procedures to facilitate skill acquisition among severely mentally retarded adolescents. *American Journal of Mental Deficiency, 91,* 366–372.

Donnellan, A. M. (1984). The criterion of the least dangerous assumption. *Behavior Disorders, 7,* 531–556.

Doyle, P. M., Wolery, M., Gast, D. L., Ault, M. J., & Wiley, K. (1990). Comparison of constant time delay and system of least prompts in teaching preschoolers with developmental delays. *Research and Intervention in Developmental Disabilities, 11,* 1–22.

Etzel, B. C., & LeBlanc, J. M. (1979). The simplest treatment alternative: Appropriate instructional control and errorless learning procedures for the difficult-to-teach child. *Journal of Autism and Developmental Disorders, 9,* 361–382.

Gast, D. L., Ault, M. J., Wolery, M., Doyle, P. M., & Belanger, S. (1988). Comparison of constant time delay and the system of least prompts in teaching sight word reading to students with moderate retardation. *Education and Training in Mental Retardation, 23,* 117–128.

Godby, S., Gast, D. L., & Wolery, M. (1987). A comparison of time delay and system of least prompts in teaching object identification. *Research in Developmental Disabilities, 8,* 283–306.

Guskey, T. R., (1986). Staff development and the process of teacher change. *Educational Researcher, 15,* 5–12.

Haught, P., Walls, R. T., & Crist, K. (1984). Placement of prompts, length of task, and level of retardation in learning complex assembly tasks. *American Journal of Mental Deficiency, 89,* 60–66.

Heward, W. L., Heron, T. E., & Cooper, J. O. (1990). The masters thesis in applied behavior analysis: Rationale, characteristics, and student advisement strategies. *The Behavior Analyst, 13,* 205–210.

Kaiser, A. P., & McWhorter, C. M. (Eds.) (1990). *Preparing personnel to work with persons with severe disabilities.* Baltimore: Paul Brookes.

LeBlanc, J. M., Etzel, B. C., & Domash, M. A. (1978). A functional curriculum for early intervention. In K. E. Allen, V. A. Holm, & R. L. Schiefelbusch (Eds.), *Early intervention—a team approach* (pp. 331–381). Baltimore: University Park Press.

McDonnell, J. (1987). The effects of time delay and increasing prompt hierarchy strategies on the acquisition of purchasing skills by students with severe handicaps. *Journal of the Association for the Severely Handicapped, 12,* 227–236.

McDonnell, J., & Ferguson, B. (1989). A comparison of time delay and decreasing prompt hierarchy strategies in teaching banking skills to students with moderate handicaps. *Journal of Applied Behavior Analysis, 22,* 85–91.

McGee, G. G., & McCoy, J. F. (1981). Training procedures for acquisition and retention of reading in retarded youth. *Applied Research in Mental Retardation, 2,* 263–276.

Miller, U. C., & Test, D. (1989). A comparison of constant time delay and most-to-least prompting in teaching laundry skills to students with moderate retardation. *Education and Training in Mental Retardation, 24,* 363–370.

Mish, F. C. (Ed.), (1988). *Webster's Ninth New Collegiate Dictionary.* Springfield, MA: Merriam-Webster.

Mosk, M. D., & Bucher, B. (1984). Prompting and stimulus shaping procedure for teaching visual-motor skills to retarded children. *Journal of Applied Behavior Analysis, 17,* 23–34.

O'Neill, R. E., Horner, R. H., Albin, R. W., Storey, K., & Sprague, J. R. (1990). *Functional analysis of problem behavior: A practical assessment guide.* Sycamore, IL: Sycamore Publishing.

Panyan, M. (1980). *How to use shaping.* Austin, TX: Pro-Ed.

Precious, C. J. (1985). *Efficiency study of two procedures: Constant and progressive time delay in teaching oral sight word reading.* Unpublished master's thesis, University of Kentucky, Lexington.

Richmond, G., & Bell, J. (1983). Comparison of three methods to train a size discrimination with profoundly mentally retarded students. *American Journal of Mental Deficiency, 87,* 574–576.

Sailor, W., Halvorsen, A., Anderson, J., Goetz, L., Gee, K., Doering, K., & Hunt, P. (1986). Community intensive instruction. In R. H. Horner, L. H. Meyer, & H. D. Fredericks (Eds.), *Education of learners with severe handicaps* (pp. 251–288). Baltimore: Paul Brookes.

Thomas, P. L. (1989). *A comparison of constant and progressive time delay in teaching oral sight reading.* Unpublished master's thesis, University of Kentucky, Lexington.

Walls, R. T., Zane, T., & Thvedt, J. E. (1980). Trainers' personal methods compared to two structured training strategies. *American Journal of Mental Deficiency, 84,* 495–507.

White, O. R., & Haring, N. G. (1980). *Exceptional teaching* (2nd ed.). Columbus, OH: Charles Merrill.

Winterling, V., Gast, D. L., Wolery, M., & Farmer, J. A. (in press). Teaching safety skills to high school students with moderate disabilities. *Journal of Applied Behavior Analysis.*

Wolery, M. (1989). Using assessment information to plan instructional programs. In D. B. Bailey & M. Wolery (Eds.), *Assessing infants and preschoolers with handicaps.* Columbus, OH: Charles Merrill.

Wolery, M., Ault, M. J., Doyle, P. M., & Gast, D. L. (1986). *Comparison of instructional strategies: A literature review.* (U. S. Department of Education, Grant No. G008530197). Lexington, KY: Department of Special Education.

Wolery, M., Ault, M. J., Gast, D. L., Doyle, P. M., & Griffen, A. K. (1990). Comparison of constant time delay and the system of least prompts in teaching chained tasks. *Education and Training in Mental Retardation, 25,* 243–257.

Wolery, M., Bailey, D. B., & Sugai, G. M. (1988). *Effective teaching: Principles and procedures of applied behavior analysis with exceptional students.* Boston: Allyn & Bacon.

Wolery, M., Doyle, P. M., Alig, C., Ault, M. J., Gast, D. L., & Morris, L. L. (1988). *Selecting instructional strategies: Issues and recommendations.* Unpublished instructional manual, Department of Special Education, University of Kentucky, Lexington.

Wolery, M., Doyle, P. M., Gast, D. L., Ault, M. J., & Lichtenberg, S. (1991). *Comparison of progressive time delay and transition based teaching with preacademic behaviors and preschoolers who display developmental delays.* (Manuscript submitted for publication.)

Wolery, M. & Gast, D. L. (1990). *Efficiency of instruction: Conceptual framework and research directions.* (Manuscript submitted for publication.)

Wolf, M. M. (1978). Social validity: The case for subjective measurement or how applied behavior analysis is finding its heart. *Journal of Applied Behavior Analysis, 11,* 203–214.

Zigler, E., & Sietz, V. (1975). On "an experimental evaluation of sensorimotor patterning": A critique. *American Journal of Mental Deficiency, 79,* 483–492.

CHAPTER 10

Using Instructional Strategies

Chapter Overview

Increasing the Efficiency of Instruction

Using Small-Group Instruction

Summary Comments

Exercises

References

Key Terms

Effectiveness	General Attentional Responses
Efficiency	Chained Tasks
Acquired Equivalence	Total Task Format
Transfer Mediational Paradigm	Choral Responding
Observational Learning	Intrasequential Arrangement
Incidental Learning	Intersequential Arrangement
Attentional Cues	Tandem Arrangement
Attentional Responses	One-on-one Supplement
Specific Attentional Cues	Arrangement
Specific Attentional Responses	Choral Responses
General Attentional Cues	Group Contingencies

Questions to Be Answered by This Chapter

1. Why should the efficiency of instruction be studied?
2. How can the efficiency of instruction be measured?
3. How can observational learning be promoted?

4. How can incidental learning be promoted?
5. What issues should the teacher consider when designing small-group instruction?

A primary goal of educational programming with students who have moderate to severe disabilities is to ensure their adaptive performance and participation in the community. In the past, this goal was seen as desirable but largely unobtainable; currently, it is becoming a reality for many students. This change has occurred because of policy initiatives, more teacher training programs, and better instructional technology. The procedures described in this text are effective in teaching students a broad array of useful skills.

Despite these advances, three major tasks related to instructional programming remain unsolved: (a) increasing the efficiency of instruction, (b) ensuring that every teacher of students with moderate and severe disabilities can fluently use the most effective and efficient instructional procedures (Kaiser & McWhorter, 1990), and (c) developing instructional procedures for the most profoundly involved students (Sailor et al., 1987). This chapter addresses the issue of instructional efficiency and addresses the issue of using the response prompting procedures in small-group arrangements. This latter issue is included because one-on-one instruction is rarely possible in most school classrooms. Also, as recent research indicates, there are some distinct advantages of group over one-on-one instruction.

INCREASING THE EFFICIENCY OF INSTRUCTION

As defined in Chapter 2 and 9, **effectiveness** of instructional procedures refers to whether a student learns what she is taught. If, as a result of teaching, a student can do behaviors that she previously could not do, then the instruction was effective. **Efficiency,** however, refers to an instructional procedure that results in learning (i.e., is effective) *and* is better than some other instructional procedure. However, a legitimate question is, "How is 'better' measured?" Recently, Wolery and Gast (1990) proposed five ways of conceptualizing, or measuring, "better" as it relates to instructional efficiency. These conceptualizations are useful ways for a teacher to think about improving and evaluating his instructional practice. This section presents the rationale for improving instructional efficiency, describes the five conceptualizations, and includes suggestions for improving the efficiency of the response prompting procedures described earlier in this text.

Rationale for Maximizing Instructional Efficiency

There are benefits of increasing the efficiency of instruction for the student, the teacher, and the field. For the student, Wolery and Gast (1990) proposed three benefits: (a) The student will learn more in less time; (b) the student will receive more frequent positive reinforcement; and (c) the student will have larger skill repertoires at the end of the schooling. For the teacher, two major benefits accrue: (a) The teacher is able to teach the same amount of behaviors in less time and thus have more time for teaching other skills or engaging in other important activities; and (b) since the student is learning better, there are increased opportunities for positive interactions with the student. The primary benefit for the field of studying instructional efficiency is that the instructional procedures will become more refined.

Conceptualizations of Instructional Efficiency

The following five conceptualizations deal with how the teacher can measure instructional efficiency. However, as will be obvious, there is relatively little research that has addressed each of these.

Efficiency Conceptualized as Rapid Learning.   As described in Chapter 9, many response prompting strategies have been compared to one another, and conclusions about their relative efficiency have been drawn. For example, constant time delay and the system of least prompts have been compared directly with discrete skills for preschoolers with developmental delays (Doyle, Wolery, Gast, Ault, & Wiley, 1990), for elementary-aged students with moderate mental retardation (Gast et al., 1988), and for elementary-aged students with autism (e.g., Ault et al., 1988); the two procedures also have been compared in teaching chained tasks to elementary-aged students with moderate mental retardation (Wolery, Ault, Gast, Doyle, & Griffen, 1990a) and older students with severe retardation (McDonnell, 1987). In those studies, data were collected on how many sessions, how many trials, and how many minutes of instructional time were required with each procedure to teach behaviors to criterion. Also, the number and percent of errors that occurred were measured for each procedure. As described in Chapter 9, in these studies with these measures, the constant time delay procedure was judged to produce more rapid learning; that is, students learned behaviors in fewer sessions, trials, and minutes of direct instruction and with lower error percentages. Constant time delay appears to be more efficient than the system of least prompts. Conclusions about the efficiency of other strategies in terms of the rapidity of learning were made in Chapter 9 and are described by Ault et al. (1989).

Efficiency Conceptualized as Greater Generalization.   The ultimate test of the benefit of instruction is whether a student uses the skills she learns when and where those skills are needed. Two procedures could be compared for the rapidity of learning they produce and would be found to require an equal number of sessions, trials, and minutes of instruction. However, one procedure might result in more generalization and use of the skills than the other. The strategy that results in greater generalization would be considered more efficient because additional programming would not be needed to establish skill use.

As described in Chapter 1, many procedures appear to increase the probability that generalization of skills will occur (see Horner, Dunlap, & Koegel, 1988; Haring et al., 1989; Liberty & Billingsley, 1988; Wolery, Bailey, & Sugai, 1988). There are procedures for analyzing cases where generalization does not occur (Horner, Bellamy, & Colvin, 1984) and data decision rules for promoting generalization (Liberty, 1988). However, almost no research evaluates the efficiency of the procedures for establishing generalization.

The implications of this conceptualization for practice and for research are clear. In terms of practice, the teacher should use the procedures and decision models that have been described for establishing generalization of skills. Also, when possible, she should evaluate the relative efficiency of the generalization promoting procedures. In terms of the implications for research, more studies are needed in two areas: (a) Investigators should continue to evaluate how to establish greater generalization; and (b) investigators should evaluate the efficiency of the procedures that they study (Wolery & Gast, 1990). This will lead to more strategies for promoting generalization and strategies that do so more readily.

Efficiency Conceptualized as the Emergence of Relationships.   This conceptualization of efficiency also is relatively unstudied in the applied research literature; however, there is a large volume of research in more basic areas under the titles of **acquired equivalence** and the **transfer mediational paradigm.** A repeated finding in many areas has been that a student can learn that certain stimuli are related (i.e., are equivalent) despite the fact that those relationships have not been taught directly. A student could be taught to select a blue circle from a choice of a blue, red, green, and yellow circles in response to the direction, "Find blue." Subsequently, the child could be taught to select the written word *blue* from a choice of four words (*blue, red, green,* and *yellow*) in response to the direction, "Find blue." The student could then be presented with an opportunity to match the written word *blue* to a choice of four different-colored circles. If the student matches correctly, then he has demonstrated that the written word *blue* and the blue circle have an equivalent relationship. This relationship was not taught directly but was mediated by the task direction, "Find blue." Instruction that is structured to take advantage of the emergence of the untrained relationships would be more efficient than instruction not so designed. However, at this time, relatively little applied research has studied this possibility.

In terms of implications for practice, a teacher can do two things. He can analyze the content of the skills he is teaching to identify the potential for these relationships. Also, after he has identified such potential relationships, he should assess the student to see if the relationships are established without direct training.

Efficiency Conceptualized as Broader Learning.   Theoretically, it is possible for two procedures to produce equally rapid acquisition, equal generalization, and equal emergence of relationships; however, differences could exist. It is possible that one procedure could cause the student to learn *only* the skills she is taught directly; the second procedure could cause the students to learn the skills that are taught directly *and* other related nontarget skills. The procedure that would teach the targeted skills *and* other related skills would be considered more efficient than the procedure that caused the child to learn only the target skills.

Two types of learning may allow students to acquire skills that they are not taught directly: observational learning and incidental learning. **Observational learning** is the acquisition of behaviors performed by, or taught to, others for which there are no programmed contingencies for the observer (Bandura, 1971). If David and Phil are being taught separate skills in the same setting, then it is possible that David will learn his own skills and will also learn the skills taught to Phil. Clearly, if a student can learn his own behaviors and the behaviors taught to his peers, then instruction would be more efficient than if he learned only what was taught to him.

Incidental learning is the acquisition of nontarget information that is present in the instructional context and for which there are no programmed contingencies for the learner to acquire that information (Stevenson, 1972). If Cassie is learning to shop in a grocery store, her teacher might use a response prompting strategy (e.g., constant time delay) to teach Cassie to read the words on a grocery list (e.g., *milk, corn, hamburger,* and *soap*). The teacher could present the words and needed prompts and, when Cassie is correct, could praise her and also state where in the store that particular item is found. For *milk,* the teacher could say, "Great reading, milk is in the dairy section"; for *hamburger,* he could say, "Good reading, hamburger is in the meat section." The word reading is being taught directly and the location of the food is being presented, but Cassie is not required to say where the food is found or respond to it at all. That information is simply added to the trial sequence. If Cassie learns to read the words and learns where each food is located, then she has learned the target behaviors (word reading) and incidentally learned the nontarget information (location of the food in the store). A procedure that results in the student's learning the target and nontarget behaviors is more efficient than a procedure where only the target behaviors are acquired.

Below are recommendations for increasing the amount of observational and incidental learning. These procedures can be integrated into many of the response prompting strategies described earlier in this book. By combining these arrangements with the response prompting procedures that result in rapid learning, the teacher can further increase the efficiency of instruction.

Findings and Recommendations for Increasing the Amount of Observational Learning. Observational learning is a phenomenon that has been widely studied in the child development literature. However, much of that literature has focused on the development of imitative behaviors, the characteristics of models that increase the probability of imitation, and the role of observational learning in acquiring social behavior (Bailey & Wolery, 1984). This section primarily discusses observational learning that is programmed to teach students specific skills.

For a student to learn through observational learning, four factors are desirable: (a) that student must be capable of imitating others, (b) she must have the opportunity to observe others doing or being taught behaviors different from her own, (c) she must attend to the stimuli presented to her peers and her peers' performance, and (d) she should have opportunities to see her peers being reinforced for doing the modeled behavior. To ensure that the student has opportunities to observe her peers being taught different behaviors, the teacher should use small-group instruction (see the last section of this chapter). To ensure that a student attends to the stimuli and behavior of her peers, the teacher should use specific attentional responses, teach each student different but similar behaviors, call the attention of all students in the group to the stimuli for each student, and assess all students on all the behaviors taught to the group. Further, the teacher should ensure that each student observes his or her peers being reinforced.

Several conclusions can be stated about observational learning from the direct instruction literature. First, students with mild, moderate, and severe disabilities who imitate others appear to learn some behaviors taught to their peers in small-group instruction (Alig-Cybriwsky, Wolery, & Gast, 1990; Doyle, Gast, Wolery, Ault, & Farmer, 1990; Farmer et al., 1991). However, not all students with moderate to severe retardation will imitate. Therefore, a legitimate goal for them is to learn to imitate others. Several strategies have been devised for teaching students to imitate (see Bailey & Wolery, 1984; Cooper, Heron, Heward, 1987).

Second, a large part of observational learning appears to occur while a student is learning his own behaviors (Ault et al., 1990; Doyle, Gast, Wolery, Ault, & Farmer, 1990; Wolery, Alig-Cybriwsky, Gast, & Boyle-Gast, 1991). When learning in small groups, some students may reach criterion before others. The teacher is then faced with the choice of teaching the student who reached criterion new behaviors or providing review trials on acquired behaviors until his group members meet criterion thus giving him more opportunity to focus attention on the behaviors taught to his peers. However, it appears that a majority of the behaviors a student learns observationally he will learn by the time he reaches criterion on his own behaviors. Thus, when possible, it makes sense for the teacher to add new behaviors for group members as each member reaches criterion.

Third, a student may learn when her sole role in the group is observation (Shelton et al., 1991). Since observational learning occurs when the student is in a small group and each student is being taught, Shelton et al. were interested in whether being taught was necessary for observational learning to occur. Therefore, in some conditions, they taught all members of the group except one. This student simply came to the group but was not given teaching trials. Interestingly, when students were not required to learn in the small group, they still learned what was taught to their peers. This suggests that when a teacher has difficulty providing supervision and coverage to all students in her class, she can allow a student to be in the instructional group and not be taught directly and can assume that this student may learn new behaviors observationally. This finding deserves much more study. For example, legitimate questions for further research are these: (a) Does the amount of attendance in the group predict how much students will learn observationally? (b) Will students learn observationally if they are never taught directly in the group, but when their role is observation throughout all instructional conditions? (c) Will the observer-only student learn more observationally, if the teacher gives him some role in the group, such as holding up the stimulus item, praising his peers for correct responses, or recording his peers' behaviors?

Fourth, specific attentional cues and responses appear to increase the amount of observational learning and the maintenance of observational learning (Wolery, Alig-Cybriwsky, Gast, & Boyle-Gast, 1991). **Attentional cues** are the teacher statements, questions, or actions that signal to a student that she should attend to the instructional stimuli. **Attentional responses** are the behaviors a student uses to show the teacher that she is attending. Attentional cues and responses are particularly important in small-group instruction, because they are one way to increase the probability that the student will attend to the stimuli and behaviors being taught to her peers, thereby increasing the probability of observational learning. Attentional cues and responses can be divided into many categories. However, there are two broad groupings: general and specific attentional cues and responses. **General attentional cues** and **general attentional responses** do not require a very specific interaction with the target stimulus; the teacher might say, "Are you ready?" and the student might nod or say, "Yes"; or the teacher might hold up the stimulus and say, "Look," and the student might simply look toward the teacher. **Specific attentional cues** and **specific attentional responses** require the student to interact more directly with the target stimulus. The teacher might hold up a word to be read and say, "Say these letters with me"; the student might be required to name the letters of the word, then might be given the task direction to read the word. Other specific attentional responses are matching the target stimuli, touching it, and repeating the task direction. Specific attentional cues frequently call the student's attention to the critical dimensions of the target stimulus. As a result, specific attentional cues have been added to the trial sequences when students are not making sufficient progress with the response prompting procedures (see Doyle, Wolery, Gast, Ault, & Wiley, 1990). Direct comparisons of specific attentional cues and responses to general attentional cues and responses have produced some interesting findings. Specific and general attentional cues did not differentially influence the rapidity of learning; however, students learned more behaviors taught to their group members (observational learning) and maintained those behaviors at higher levels when specific attentional cues were used (Alig-Cybriwsky, Wolery, & Gast, 1990; Wolery, Alig-Cybriwsky, Gast, & Boyle-Gast, 1991). Although more research is needed, it seems reasonable for a teacher to use specific rather than general attentional cues.

Fifth, a student with a moderate disability can learn both discrete and chained tasks observationally (Doyle, Gast, Wolery, Ault, & Farmer, 1990; Griffen, Wolery, & Schuster, in press; Farmer et al., 1991; Schoen & Sivil, 1989). Although the teaching of discrete tasks in small groups is a relatively common practice and the teacher decisions necessary to implement these groups are described later in the chapter, teaching chained tasks is more problematic.

Chained tasks involve a student performing a number of behaviors in sequence to form a more complex skill. Many of the skills needed by students with moderate to severe disabilities are chained tasks; examples include putting on and taking off clothing, making a bed, cooking, making a snack, doing janitorial tasks, and performing many vocational skills. Best practice and some research suggest that teachers should teach chained tasks in a total task format, in context, and at naturally occurring times (Kayser, Billingsley, & Neel, 1986). The **total task format** involves the teacher teaching all the behaviors of the chain at one time rather than one skill at a time, as in backward and forward chaining. Using total task formats, teaching in context, and providing instruction at naturally occurring times places some interesting demands on the teacher. If the student task is cooking a casserole for lunch, then the teaching should be done just before lunch, in a kitchen, for only one trial on most steps per day. Further, it is difficult to provide such instruction to a group of students at once. Recently, researchers began to address these issues and problems.

Schoen, Lentz, and Suppa (1988) compared most-to-least prompting and graduated guidance in teaching preschoolers chained tasks by providing instruction in dyads (i.e., in pairs of students). One student was taught the chain, and the second student was an observer. The teacher cued the observer to watch the instruction and reinforced him or her for watching the other student being taught. Interestingly, the observer and the student being taught both acquired the chains. Later, Schoen and

Sivil (1989) used the same arrangement to compare time delay and the system of least prompts. Again, both students, the observer and the student who was taught directly, learned the chains. Wolery, Ault, Gast, Doyle, and Griffen (1991) also taught chains in a total task format to dyads of students. However, both children served as the student being taught and as the observer. Student 1 was taught the first half of the chain while Student 2 observed the instruction; they then switched roles. The teacher did not instruct the observer to watch and did not reinforce the observer; however, at the beginning of the chain, she prompted the instructed student to tell the observer to watch. The students learned the parts of the chain they were taught directly and also the parts they observed. Hall et al. (in press) also taught chained skills to dyads, but they arranged the instruction in a slightly different manner. On the first day, Student 1 was taught the first half of the chain and Student 2 was taught the second half. On the second day, Student 2 was taught the first half of the chain and Student 1 was taught the second half. Both students observed the parts of the chains being taught to their peer each day. This alternation was continued throughout the study. Again, the students learned all parts of the chain. Although it was not possible to identify the effects of direct instruction and observational learning, it was a useful way of teaching two students to do a response chain that would occur only once per day. Griffen, Wolery, and Schuster (in press) taught chained tasks in triads (three students). One student was taught the chain (a snack-making task with a picture recipe book), and the other two students observed. The instructed student cued the observers to turn the pages of the picture recipe book, and the teacher praised the observers for turning the pages and watching the instruction. The student who was taught and the two observers learned each chain.

Several conclusions can be drawn from these studies on observational learning and chained tasks. An imitative student with a moderate to severe disability can learn to perform chains taught in total task format with single trials per day (or a few trials per day) when she is taught directly and when she is allowed to observe her peers being taught. In these studies, the observers were told to observe and the instructed student or the teacher provided reinforcement to each observer. The role of these cues and the reinforcement have not been evaluated. Thus, in such arrangements, the teacher should include cues and reinforcement for the observer.

In summary, an imitative student with a moderate or severe disability can learn observationally when taught in a small group. The skills that she learns observationally appear to be acquired when the student is learning her own skills rather than after she has learned her own skills. The student appears to learn observationally when her sole role in the group is to observe—that is, when she is not being taught directly. In small-group instruction, specific attentional cues appear to facilitate observational learning and maintenance of behaviors learned observationally. Finally, observational learning has occurred for both chained and discrete behaviors.

Findings and Recommendations for Increasing the Amount of Incidental Learning. Incidental learning, as defined above, is the student's acquisition of information that is present in the instructional context but for which there are no programmed contingencies and which is not taught to the student directly. Additional related information has been inserted into instructional trials in three places: in antecedent events that occur before the student is to respond, in prompt hierarchies (e.g., with the system of least prompts), and in consequent events that occur after the student responds. The teacher can present this additional information orally or through pictures, cards, or paper. Other presentations, although possible, have not been studied.

Several conclusions can be made from the research related to increasing the efficiency of instruction by adding extra information into instructional trials. First, when a student is presented with additional information in antecedent events, he frequently learns some of this information (Alig-Cybriwsky et al., 1990; Wolery, Ault, Gast, Doyle, & Mills, 1990). In these studies, students were taught to read words. In the attentional cue prior to reading the words, they were asked to name the letters of the word. This indicated to the teacher that they were attending to the word on the card. However, it also resulted in students learning to spell the words without direct instruction.

Second, when additional information is presented in consequent events (after the student responds), the student also learns some of that information (Doyle, Gast, Wolery, Ault, & Farmer, 1990; Gast, Doyle, Wolery, Ault, & Farmer, 1991; Gast, Wolery, Morris, Doyle, & Meyer, 1990). In many instructional programs, the teacher provides praise after the student's correct responses. In these studies, the students were praised *and* additional information was provided. For example, in the Gast, Wolery, Morris, Doyle, and Meyer (1990) study, students read words and were then told the meaning of those words. This resulted in students learning to define some of the words.

Third, when additional information is presented in the antecedent and the consequent events, the student learns both types of information (Shelton et al., in press). In the Shelton et al. study, students also were taught to read words. Prior to each trial, they named the letters of the words to indicate that they were attending to the stimulus. After correct responses, the teacher's praise statements included a definition of the word. As a result, students learned to read the words, spell some of them, and define most of them.

Fourth, when additional information is presented in the consequent event in the context of small-group instruction, the student will also learn some of the additional information presented for his peer's target behaviors (Doyle, Gast, Wolery, Ault, & Farmer, 1990; Stinson et al., 1991). As noted above, when students are taught in small groups and each student has his own behaviors, they frequently learn some of the behaviors taught to their peers. When the additional information—such as the definition of words—is added to the praise statements following correct responses, the student learns to read his own words, learns to read some of the words taught to his peers, learns the definition of some of his own words, *and* learns the definitions of some of his peers' words.

Fifth, when additional information is presented for some behaviors in the consequent event and for other behaviors in the antecedent event, that information is acquired about equally (Gast, Doyle, Wolery, Ault, & Baklarz, 1991). In this study, three conditions were compared: (a) additional information was presented in the antecedent events for some behaviors, (b) additional information was presented in the consequent events for other behaviors, and (c) no additional information was presented. Students learned the additional information regardless of where the additional information was presented.

Sixth, when two pieces of additional information are presented in the consequent events, the student appears to learn both bits of information if they are of the same type (Gast, Doyle, Wolery, Ault, & Baklarz, 1990). In this study, students were given two pieces of information for each behavior. When those pieces were of the same type, the students learned both; however, when the two pieces of information were of different types, they learned only one. Much more additional research is needed to understand what types of additional information are more readily learned incidentally. However, an interesting finding was that in some conditions, students were learning their target behavior and both additional pieces of information.

Seventh, when additional information is presented in the antecedent events, the teacher having all students in the group respond may result in more learning than if having only the target student respond (Wolery, Ault, Gast, Doyle, & Mills, 1990). In the Wolery et al. study, students were taught in a small group, with each child learning to read his or her own words. Prior to reading their words, students were to name the letters in the word as an attentional response. The naming of letters, however, occurred in two ways. In one condition, only the target child named the letters; in the second condition, all the students in the group named the letters but only the target child read the word. This latter condition resulted in students learning to spell more of their peers' words.

Eighth, when the system of least prompts is used, the prompt levels can include information that is unknown but useful to learn. When this occurs, the student can learn that additional information from the prompt levels (Doyle, Gast, Wolery, Ault, & Meyer, 1990). While this is not technically incidental learning, it is a means of getting a student to acquire additional information.

In summary, these studies suggest that the student can learn additional information that is not taught directly. The teacher can add that information to the antecedent events (i.e., attentional cues and responses) and/or to the consequent events. When the teacher does this, the student is likely to learn at least some of this information. In nearly all of the above studies, instructional strategies such as progressive or constant time delay were used. Thus, procedures that have been found to cause rapid learning can be made even more efficient by including additional information in trial sequences.

Efficiency Conceptualized as Promoting Future Learning. The final conceptualization of efficiency is based on the idea that some ways of structuring current instruction may influence how rapidly a student learns behaviors that are taught in the future. It is possible that two procedures produce equally rapid acquisition, equal amounts of generalization, equal emergence of untrained relationships, and equal acquisition of related information; however, differences could still exist. If one procedure results in more rapid acquisition of behaviors taught in the future than the other, then it is the more efficient.

There has been very little research on this issue, but what little does exist is encouraging. Wolery, Doyle, Ault, Gast, Meyer, and Stinson (1991) taught students with moderate mental retardation to name pictures; some pictures were of local fast-food restaurants and others were of people performing various vocations. For half of the pictures, students were shown the word for the restaurant or vocation depicted in the picture while being praised for correct responses; for the other half of the pictures, they received only praise. After students achieved the critrion on all the pictures, they were taught to read the words for all the pictures (those they had been shown and those they had not been shown). The results indicated that showing the words for the pictures in the first condition resulted in much faster total learning. Thus, a manipulation of the current instructional condition caused more rapid learning in the future. Clearly, more research along these lines is needed. However, in the meantime, the teacher should identify what he will teach the student next and include that in the current instruction in some manner.

In summary, the efficiency of instruction can be measured in at least five ways: the rapidity with which acquisition occurs, the extent to which generalization is established, the emergence of untrained relationships, the amount of additional nontarget behaviors that are learned, and the effects of current instruction on later learning. Clearly, a teacher should use strategies that have been shown to cause more rapid learning than other procedures (see Chapter 9), use procedures that are likely to cause her students to generalize and apply their skills in other contexts, analyze the curriculum for possible relationships that could emerge without training, teach in small groups to increase the probability of observational learning, insert additional information into the antecedent and consequent events of trial sequences, and include future target behaviors in the trial sequences of current instruction. The combination of these manipulations should result in her providing the most efficient instruction possible.

USING SMALL-GROUP INSTRUCTION

Although considerable instructional research with students who have disablties has been done in the context of small groups, relatively little research has focused on the procedural issues related to group instruction. Little research, for example, has examined the best way to structure groups and present instruction in them. The following section discusses decisions and issues the teacher faces if he uses small-group instruction. This information is taken largely from Collins et al. (1991).

Rationale for Using Small-Group Instruction

There are at least four rationales for using small-group instructional arrangements as compared to one-on-one formats. First, small-group arrangements may prepare the students for other settings, such as general education classrooms (Fink & Sandall, 1978). Much of the instruction in non-special education classrooms requires group presentation of content. Thus, the student's learning to be a group member and learning to learn in a group may allow him to move to less restrictive placements. Second, the teacher's using small-group arrangements is a more efficient use of her time because she can provide instruction to more than one student at a time. Third, small-group instruction may provide opportunities for the student to learn interaction skills (Alberto et al., 1980; Lefebvre & Strain, 1989; Odom et al., 1986). Fourth, the student may acquire skills that are taught to other students through observational learning (Doyle,

Gast, Wolery, Ault, & Farmer, 1990; Westling, Ferrell, & Swenson, 1982). As discussed above, small-group instruction can make instruction more efficient if each student learns the skills targeted for him or her and for the peers.

Decisions Related to Small-Group Instruction

Collins et al. (1991) identified four major types of decisions teachers must make when using small-group instruction: (a) determine the group composition, (b) determine the instructional procedures, (c) determine the monitoring system, and (d) determine how to manage group behavior.

Determine the Group Composition.   A teacher faces several issues when determining the composition of instructional groups: the group size, whether to have heterogenous or homogenous groups, the nature of the skills being taught, the entry level skills needed, and the nature of the group arrangement. The number of students in the group is highly dependent on their previous experience with group arrangements and their skills related to group memberships (e.g., presence of interfering problem behaviors, ability to attend during group instruction, and presence of reinforcers). Some students, especially those who are young and those with severe disabilities, may have relatively little experience with group instruction. For such students, smaller group size may initially be necessary, but they should be included systematically and progressively in larger groups (Koegel & Rincover, 1974). Certain skills, such as sitting or staying in place and attending to the teacher, are necessary for most types of one-on-one and group instruction; they must be displayed more consistently in group instruction. However, there are no clear criteria. These skills can be taught through differential reinforcement in group contexts. Therefore, when constructing groups, the teacher must be aware of the extent to which her students need assistance in performing the "group behaviors."

The use of homogenous and heterogenous groups is an issue that relates directly to how these terms are defined. For example, *homogeneous* can mean students of the same age, same general functioning level, and same type of disability. Clearly, there is evidence that students can learn well in both types of groups (Alberto et al., 1980; Doyle, Gast, Wolery, Ault, & Farmer, 1990; Favell, Favell, & McGimsey, 1978). In reality, decisions about the degree of heterogeneity in groups depend on the skill being taught and the practical concerns of providing adequate coverage or supervision of the students in the classroom.

The skills being taught is a critical issue when groups are constructed. As noted above, a variety of discrete skills and chained tasks have been taught in group formats. However, when planning a group, the teacher has several choices. Students can be taught (a) the same task with the same stimuli (Doyle, Gast, Wolery, Ault, & Meyer, 1990), (b) the same task with different stimuli (Kohl, 1981), (c) different tasks with the same stimuli (Horst et al., 1981), and (d) different tasks with different stimuli (Brown & Holvoet, 1982). *Task* as defined here refers to the *type* of behaviors being taught (e.g., reading words, receptively identifying objects, and cooking); *stimuli,* of course, are things to which students respond. For example, in a same task/same stimuli format, all students could learn to name objects expressively and to name the same objects; in a same task/different stimuli format, all students could learn to name objects, but the objects for each student could be different. Three comments are important. First, if the same behaviors are being taught to each group member, then the opportunity for learning additional skills observationally is lost. The use of the different behaviors with the same or different stimuli provides the student with an opportunity to learn other students' skills. Second, the ease of conducting group instruction is probably related to the amount of difference within the session across students. Therefore, the same task/same stimuli format is probably the easiest for the teacher to conduct and the different task/different stimuli format is probably the most difficult. Third, relatively little research has evaluated this issue. Doyle, Gast, Wolery, Ault, and Farmer (1990) compared same task/same stimuli to same task/different stimuli. The data suggests that the same task/different stimuli condition resulted in more rapid learning, but the same task/same stimuli resulted in students learning more behaviors. Because little research exists, the teacher should decide what format to use based on the skills that are most important for each student, the amount of imitative skills each student displays, and his own ability to conduct the group without making errors in the presentation of the trials.

There are four different group arrangements, and the teacher needs to plan which type he will use: intrasequential, intersequential, tandem, and one-on-one supplement (Brown et al., 1980). In the *intra*sequential arrangement, the teacher provides instruction to each member individually and does not program interactions between group members (e.g., Alig-Cybriwsky, Wolery, & Gast, 1990). In the *inter*sequential arrangement, the teacher provides instruction and programs interactions between group members; for example, students praise one another, cue each other to observe, or help present the stimuli to the other members (e.g., Wolery, Ault, Gast, Doyle, & Griffen, 1990). In the **tandem arrangement,** instruction starts in a one-on-one arrangement and additional students are systematically added to the group (see Koegel & Rincover, 1974). In the **one-on-one supplement arrangement,** instruction is provided in a group and some or all students also receive additional instruction in a one-on-one arrangement (Faw et al., 1981).

The research literature does not provide information about which of these arrangements promotes the best learning. Therefore, the teacher should select an arrangement based on her preference and her students' performance. For chained tasks, the literature and logic suggest that the intersequential arrangement may be important. For a student who has little or no experience in group instruction, the tandem arrangement can teach him to learn from group instruction. For a student who is not making adequate progress in group instruction, the one-on-one supplement provides additional flexibility.

Determine the Instructional Procedures.   After specifying the group composition and arrangement, the teacher must select an instructional strategy and specify the trial sequence. The selection of instructional strategies, reviewed in Chapter 9, is not discussed here. The specification of the trial sequence involves several decisions—such as determining whether to use attentional cues and responses, identifying the type of student responding, selecting the schedule of trial presentation, specifying the consequences for each potential response, and stating a criterion.

As noted earlier, the teacher can use general attentional cues and responses (i.e., the teacher says, "Everyone look," and students look) or specific attentional cues and responses (e.g., the teacher says, "Jamie, name the letters in this word," and Jamie names the letters). The use of specific attentional responses appears to facilitate observational learning of additional information (Wolery, Alig-Cybriwsky, Gast, & Boyle-Gast, 1991). However, specific attentional responses can increase the length of sessions slightly.

In group instruction, two general types of student responses are possible: individual responses and **choral responses** (entire group responds in unison). With individual responding, the student has the opportunity for observational learning; with choral responding, she does not. Comparisons of these two types of responding indicate little difference in total learning (Sindelar, Bursuck, & Halle, 1986; Wolery, Ault, Doyle, Gast, & Griffen, 1990b). However, choral responding to attentional cues and individual responding to target stimuli appears to result in more learning of additional information presented in attentional responses than individual responding to both attentional cues and target stimuli (Wolery, Ault, Gast, Doyle, & Mills, 1990). With individual responding, the student must be cued to respond only when it is his turn; with choral responding, the student must be cued to respond in unison with other students. In either case, the presentation of the target stimuli should be such that all students in the group can see and hear it.

When using individual responding, the teacher must determine the schedule of trial presentation. One issue for the teacher to consider is whether a student can predict when it is her turn. Although teachers frequently believe that unpredictable trial presentation is superior to predictable trial presentation, the research suggests that minimal, if any, differences exist for experienced learners (Ault et al., 1990). Another issue is the number of behaviors to be taught. It appears that teaching a minimum of two behaviors to a student results in his more rapid learning than teaching one behavior at a time (Doyle et al., 1989). However, the number of behaviors taught to each student can be more than two and should depend on how rapidly the student learns and the difficulty of the skills being taught.

Other issues include the number of trials presented for each behavior, the number of trials presented to each student, and the number presented in each session. Again, the teacher should make such decisions on the basis of knowledge of the student's learning history. Three general rules should be considered. First, the teacher should keep the sessions as short as possible—two 10-minute sessions are probably preferable to one 20-minute session; four 5-minute sessions may be preferable to one 20-minute session. Second, rapid acquisition of behaviors is preferable to slower acquisition. Rapid acquisition results in the student being correct more often and thus receiving more reinforcement. Thus, teaching two behaviors that can be learned in one week is probably preferred over teaching four behaviors that would take two weeks. Third, the teacher should present as many trials as possible in as short a time as possible. Students appear to learn more quickly when the pace of instruction is rapid (Sainato, Strain, & Lyon, 1987).

Another decision focuses on the teacher selecting the consequences for each potential response. Three general rules apply here. First, the student should initially receive continuous reinforcement followed by more intermittent reinforcement as she demonstrates acquisition (Cooper et al., 1987). Second, the teacher's delivery of reinforcers can be made more manageable and can be more individualized if he uses tokens during the group session. Those tokens could then be exchanged for backup reinforcers at the end of the session or at some other point in the day. Third, the student should be allowed to choose her reinforcers (Mason et al., 1989).

As with all instruction, the teacher must specify a criterion for determining when a student has learned and when instruction can move on to other skills. With group instruction, the teacher must decide whether each student moves to new behaviors when he or she reaches criterion on his or her own behaviors or when the entire group reaches criterion. The individual criterion allows the student to move more quickly through the needed content but increases the complexity of operating the group. If students are learning at about the same pace, a group criterion is probably defensible; if they are not, an individual criterion should be used.

Determine the Monitoring System.   The purpose of monitoring student performance is twofold: (a) to determine when the student has acquired the skills and can move on to learning other behaviors or other phases of performance, and (b) to determine when progress is not being made and to make needed changes in instruction as indicated by the student's performance. For this latter purpose, the teacher should use the data decision rules described in Chapter 1. Two considerations are important with group instruction. First, if students are responding chorally (in unison), then the teacher must regularly probe each student to determine whether he or she is learning. Second, when students are responding individually, the teacher should regularly assess whether they are learning the behaviors taught to their peers. In both individual and choral responding, however, the teacher should regularly assess whether the student is maintaining behaviors that were taught previously and whether he is using (generalizing) the skills that were taught.

Determine How to Manage Group Behavior.   By teaching needed skills, using response prompting strategies, presenting instruction at a brisk pace, and providing frequent reinforcement for correct performance, the teacher will help most students behave appropriately in group instruction. However, on occasion, some students will display disruptive, inattentive, or noncompliant behaviors; such students will need additional programming. There are three general strategies for this. First, throughout instruction, the teacher can reinforce these students with individually determined reinforcers on an intermittent schedule for attending to the stimuli and behaving appropriately in the group (Mason et al., 1989). Second, the teacher can use group contingencies (Kerr & Nelson, 198; Litow & Pumroy, 1975). Although a variety of **group contingencies** exist, the notion is that the group is reinforced based on other students' behavior as well as their own. Third, the teacher can devise and implement individualized behavior control programs in the context of group instruction (Wolery, Bailey, & Sugai, 1988).

In summary, a teacher providing group instruction involves more than teaching a couple of students at the same time. The teacher must make decisions about the composition of the group, the instructional procedures she uses, the system for monitoring students' learning, and the management of group members' behavior.

SUMMARY COMMENTS

- Increasing the efficiency of instruction holds benefits for the learner, the teacher, and the field.
- Efficient instruction can be conceptualized as increasing the rapidity of the student's learning, increasing the amount of generalization, increasing the likelihood that untrained relationships will be acquired, increasing the opportunities for observational and incidental learning, and increasing the probability that current instruction will help the student learn future behaviors more rapidly.
- Small-group instruction is preferred over one-on-one instruction because it is more efficient in terms of teacher time, matches the next most probable placements for the student, allows the student to learn interactional skills in a group, and sets the stage for observational learning to occur.
- When implementing small-group instruction, the teacher must make decisions about the composition of the group, the instructional strategies and procedures he uses, the means for evaluating students' performance, and procedures for controlling student behavior.

EXERCISES

1. Observe an instructional session and, using the discussion in this chapter, try to identify ways to increase the efficiency of that program.
2. Observe a group of students being taught and determine what type of group arrangement the teacher is using.
3. Plan an instructional program to increase maximum efficiency and to address the issues related to using small-group instructional arrangements.

REFERENCES

Alberto, P., Jobes, N., Sizemore, A., & Doran, D. (1980). A comparison of individual and group instruction across response tasks. *Journal of the Association for the Severely Handicapped, 5,* 285–293.

Alig-Cybriwsky, C. A., Wolery, M., & Gast, D. L. (1990). Use of a constant time delay procedure in teaching preschoolers in a group format. *Journal of Early Intervention, 14,* 99–116.

Ault, M. J., Wolery, M., Doyle, P. M., & Gast, D. L. (1989). Review of comparative studies in instruction of students with moderate and severe handicaps. *Exceptional Children, 55,* 346–356.

Ault, M. J., Wolery, M., Gast, D. L., Doyle, P. M., & Eizenstat, V. (1988). Comparison of response prompting procedures in teaching numeral identification to autistic subjects. *Journal of Autism and Developmental Disorders, 18,* 627–636.

Ault, M. J., Wolery, M., Gast, D. L., Doyle, P. M., & Martin, C. P. (1990). Comparison of predicatble and unpredictable trial sequences during small group instruction. *Learning Disability Quarterly, 13,* 12–29.

Bailey, D. B. & Wolery, M. (1984). *Teaching infants and preschoolers with handicaps.* Columbus, OH: Charles Merrill.

Bandura, A. (1971). *Social learning theory.* New York: General Learning Press.

Brown, F., & Holvoet, J. (1982). Effects of systematic peer interaction on the incidental learning of two severely handicapped students. *Journal of the Association for the Severely Handicapped, 7*(4), 19–28.

Brown, F., Holvoet, J., Guess, D., & Mulligan, M. (1980). The individualized curriculum sequencing model (III): Small group instruction. *Journal of the Association for the Severely Handicapped, 5*(4), 352–367.

Collins, B. C., Gast, D. L., Ault, M. J., & Wolery, M. (1991). Small group instruction: Guidelines for teachers of students with moderate to severe handicaps. *Education and Training in Mental Retardation, 26,* 18–32.

Cooper, J. O., Heron, T. E., & Heward, W. L. (1987). *Applied behavior analysis.* Columbus, OH: Charles Merrill.

Doyle, P. M., Gast, D. L., Wolery, M., Ault, M. J., & Farmer, J. A. (1990). Use of constant time delay in small group instruction: A study of observational and incidental learning. *Journal of Special Education, 23,* 369–385.

Doyle, P. M., Gast, D. L., Wolery, M., Ault, M. J., & Meyer, S. (1990). *System of least prompts and related non-target learning in small group instruction.* (Manuscript submitted for publication.)

Doyle, P. M., Wolery, M., Ault, M. J., Gast, D. L., & Wiley, K. (1989). Establishing conditional discriminations: Concurrent versus isolation-intermix instruction. *Research in Developmental Disabilities, 10,* 349–362.

Doyle, P. M., Wolery, M., Gast, D. L., Ault, M. J., & Wiley, K. (1990). Comparison of constant time delay and the system of least prompts in teaching preschoolers with developmental delays. *Research in Developmental Disabilities, 11,* 1–22.

Farmer, J. A., Gast, D. L., Wolery, M., & Winterling, V. (1991). Small group instruction for students with severe handicaps: A study of observational learning. *Education and Training in Mental Retardation, 26,* 190–201.

Favell, J. E., Favell, J. E., & McGimsey, J. F. (1978). Relative effectiveness and efficiency of group versus individual training of severely retarded students. *American Journal of Mental Deficiency, 83,* 104–109.

Faw, G. D., Reid, D. H., Schepis, M. M., Fitzgerald, J. R., & Welty, P. A. (1981). Involving institutional staff in the development and maintenance of sign language skills with profoundly retarded persons. *Journal of Applied Behavior Analysis, 14,* 411–423.

Fink, W. T., & Sandall, S. R. (1978). One-to-one versus group academic instruction with handicapped and nonhandicapped preschool children. *Mental Retardation, 16,* 236–240.

Gast, D. L., Ault, M. J., Wolery, M., Doyle, P. M., & Belanger, S. (1988). Comparison of constant time delay and the system of least prompts in teaching sight word reading to students with moderate retardation. *Education and Training in Mental Retardation, 23,* 117–128.

Gast, D. L., Doyle, P. M., Wolery, M., Ault, M. J., & Baklarz, J. L. (1990). *Acquisition of incidental information: Amount and type of information.* (Manuscript submitted for publication.)

———— (1991). Acquisition of incidental information during small groups. *Education and Treatment of Children, 14,* 1–18.

Gast, D. L., Doyle, P. M., Wolery, M., Ault, M. J., Farmer, J. A. (1991). Assessing the acquisition of incidental information by secondary-age students with mental retardation: A comparison of response prompting strategies. *American Journal on Mental Retardation, 96,* 63–80.

Gast, D. L., Wolery, M., Morris, L. L., Doyle, P. M., & Meyer, S. (1990). Teaching sight word reading in a group instructional arrangement using constant time delay. *Exceptionality, 1,* 81–96.

Griffen, A. K., Wolery, M., & Schuster, J. W. (in press). Triadic instruction of chained food preparation responses: Acquisition and observational learning. *Journal of Applied Behavior Analysis.*

Hall, M. G., Schuster, J. W., Wolery, M., Gast, D. L., & Doyle, P. M. (in press). Teaching chained skills using a divided half format. *Journal of Behavioral Education.*

Haring, T. G., Breen, C., Laitinen, R., Weiner, J., Bednersh, F., Bernstein, D., & Kennedy, C. (1989). *Complex models of generalization: Extending repertoires of critical skills.* Santa Barbara: School of Education, University of California, Santa Barbara.

Horner, R. H., Bellamy, G. T., & Colvin, G. T. (1984). Responding in the presence of non-trained stimuli: Implications of generalization error patterns. *Journal of the Association for Persons with Severe Handicaps, 9,* 287–295.

Horner, R. H., Dunlap, G., & Koegel, R. L. (Eds.) (1988). *Generalization and maintenance: Life-style changes in applied settings.* Baltimore: Paul Brookes.

Horst, G., Wehman, P., Hill, J. W., & Bailey, C. (1981). Developing age-appropriate leisure skills in severely handicapped students. *Teaching Exceptional Children, 14,* 11–15.

Kaiser, A. P., & McWhorter, C. M. (Eds.) (1990). *Preparing personnel to work with persons with severe handicaps.* Baltimore: Paul Brookes.

Kayser, J. E., Billingsley, F. F., & Neel, R. S. (1986). A comparison of in-context and traditional instructional approaches: Total task, single trial versus backward chaining multiple trials. *Journal of the Association for Persons with Severe Handicaps, 11,* 28–38.

Kerr, M. M., & Nelson, C. M. (1989). *Strategies for managing behavior problems in the classroom* (2nd ed.). Columbus, OH: Charles Merrill.

Koegel, R. L., & Rincover, A. (1974). Treatment of psychotic children in a classroom environment: I. Learning in a large group. *Journal of Applied Behavior Analysis, 7,* 45–49.

Kohl, F. L., (1981). Effects of motoric requirements on the acquisition of manual sign responses by severely handicapped students. *American Journal of Mental Deficiency, 85,* 396–403.

Lefebvre, D., & Strain, P. S. (1989). Effects of a group contingency on the frequency of social interactions among autistic and nonhandicapped preschool children: Making LRE efficacious. *Journal of Early Intervention, 13,* 329–241.

Liberty, K. (1988). Decision rules and procedures for generalization. In N. G. Haring (Ed.), *Generalization for students with severe handicaps: Strategies and solutions* (pp. 177–204). Seattle: University of Washington Press.

Liberty, K., & Billingsley, F. F. (1988). Strategies to improve generalization. In N. G. Haring (Ed.), *Generalization for students with severe handicaps: Strategies and solutions* (pp. 143–176). Seattle: University of Washington Press.

Litow, L., & Pumroy, D. K. (1975). A brief review of classroom group-oriented contingencies. *Journal of Applied Behavior Analysis, 8,* 341–347.

Mason, S. A., McGee, G. G., Framer-Dougan, V., & Risley, T. R. (1989). Practical strategy for ongoing reinforcer assessment. *Journal of Applied Behavior Analysis, 22,* 45–68.

McDonnell, J. (1987). The effects of time delay and increasing prompt hierarchy strategies on the acquisition of purchasing skills by students with severe handicaps. *Journal of the Association for Persons with Severe Handicaps, 12,* 227–236.

Odom, S. L., Strain, P. S., Karger, M. A., & Smith, J. D. (1986). Using single and multiple peers to promote social interaction of preschool children with handicaps. *Journal of the Division for Early Childhood, 10,* 53–64.

Sailor, W., Gee, K., Goetz, L., & Graham, N. (1987). Progress in educating students with the most severe disabilities: Is there any? *Journal of the Association for Persons with Severe Handicaps, 13,* 87–99.

Sainato, D. M., Strain, P. S., & Lyon, S. R. (1987). Increasing academic responding of handicapped preschool children during group instruction. *Journal of the Division for Early Childhood, 12,* 23–30.

Schoen, S. F., Lentz, F. E., & Suppa, R. J. (1988). An examination of two prompt fading procedures and opportunities to observe in teaching handicapped preschoolers self-help skills. *Journal of the Division for Early Childhood, 12,* 349–358.

Schoen, S. F., & Sivil, E. O. (1989). A comparison of procedures in teaching self-help skills: Increasing assistance, time delay, and observational learning. *Journal of Autism and Developmental Disorders, 19,* 57–72.

Shelton, B., Gast, D. L., Wolery, M., & Winterling, V. (1991). The role of small group instruction in facilitating observational and incidental learning. *Language, Speech, and Hearing Services in Schools, 22,* 123–133.

Sindelar, P. T., Bursuck, W. D., & Halle, J. W. (1986). The effects of two variations of teacher questioning on student performance. *Education and Treatment of Children, 9,* 56–66.

Stevenson, H. W. (1972). *Children's learning.* New York: Appleton-Century-Crofts.

Stinson, D. M., Gast, D. L., Wolery, M., & Collins, B. C. (1991). Acquisition of nontarget information during small group instruction. *Exceptionality, 2,* 65–80.

Westling, D. L., Ferrell, K., & Swenson, K. (1982). Intraclassroom comparison of two arrangements for teaching profoundly mentally retarded children. *American Journal of Mental Deficiency, 86,* 601–608.

Wolery, M., Ault, M. J., Gast, D. L., Doyle, P. M., & Griffen, A. K. (1990a). Comparison of constant time delay and the system of least prompts in teaching chained tasks. *Education and Training in Mental Retardation, 25,* 243–257.

———— (1990b). *Choral and individual responding during small group instruction: Identification of interactional effects.* (Manuscript submitted for publication.)

———— (1991). Teaching chained tasks in dyads: Acquisition of target and observational behaviors. *Journal of Special Education. 25,* 198–220.

Wolery, M., Ault, M. J., Gast, D. L., Doyle, P. M., & Mills, B. M. (1990). Use of choral and individual spelling attentional responses in teaching sight word reading during small group instruction. *Remedial and Special Education, 11*(5), 47–58.

Wolery, M., Bailey, D. B., & Sugai, G. M. (1988). *Effective teaching: Principles and procedures of applied behavior analysis with exceptional students.* Boston: Allyn & Bacon.

Wolery, M., Alig-Cybriwsky, C., Gast, D. L., & Boyle-Gast, K. (1991). Use of constant time delay and attentional responses with adolescents. *Exceptional Children, 57,* 462–474.

Wolery, M., Doyle, P. M., Ault, M. J., Gast, D. L., Meyer, S., & Stinson, D. (1991). Effects of presenting incidental information in consequent events on future learning. *Journal of Behavioral Education, 1,* 79–104.

Wolery, M., & Gast, D. L. (1990). *Efficiency of instruction: Conceptual framework and research directions.* (Manuscript submitted for publication.)

Glossary

Acquired Equivalence.   When two or more stimuli produce the same response—that is, fulfill the same functions.

Acquisition.   "The period of learning when, if performance falters, changes designed to provide information to the learner about how to perform the desired response have a higher probability than other strategies of promoting pupil progress" (Haring, Liberty, & White, 1980, pp. 171–172).

Adult-directed Interaction.   An approach made by an adult toward a student paired with a request for information to increase the probability that the student will emit a communicative interaction.

Aim Line.   A projection of the amount of learning that is needed each day to reach the criterion set in the objective by a previously identified date; used to judge the adequacy of a student's progress.

Antecedent.   The stimulus or event that occurs immediately before a student response.

Antecedent Prompt and Fade.   A response prompting procedure involving the presentation of a prompt that controls a student's behavior followed by the gradual removal of the prompt.

Antecedent Prompt and Test.   A response prompting procedure involving the initial, simultaneous presentation of the target stimulus and a prompt that controls a student's behavior, followed by the total removal of the prompt.

Antecedent Prompt Trials.   Instructional trials used with the antecedent prompt and test procedure, in which the controlling prompt is presented simultaneously with the stimulus that cues the student's response.

Attentional Cues.   The teacher's statements, questions, or actions that signal to the student that he should attend to the instructional stimuli.

Attentional Responses.   The behaviors a student uses to show the teacher that she is attending to the instructional stimuli.

Augmentative Communication.   Any alternative form to the speech mode of communication—such as sign, photographs, or computers—that results in the exchange of information between individuals.

Backward Chaining.   A type of instructional format used in teaching a chained task, in which each step is taught individually to criterion, beginning with the last step and progressing toward the first step of the task analysis.

Behavior. A repeatable motor response that has a beginning and end and can be reliably measured by two or more individuals.

Chained Tasks/Responses. A number of discrete behaviors sequenced together to form a more complex skill.

Child-Directed Interaction. An approach made by a student toward an adult to initiate a communicative interaction.

Choral Responses. Involves all members of the group responding to the stimulus in unison.

Community-Based Instruction. Instruction that is conducted outside of the confines of schools—that is, instruction that occurs in the natural environment when and where the skill is needed.

Consequent Event. A stimulus that contingently follows a student's response.

Constant Delay Trials. Instructional trials used with the constant time delay procedure in which a fixed, unchanging amount of time is inserted between the presentation of the stimulus that cues the student to perform a task and the delivery of the controlling prompt.

Constant Time Delay. A response prompting procedure characterized by inserting a fixed amount of time between a stimulus that cues a student to perform a task and the controlling prompt.

Controlling Prompts. Teacher behaviors that, when used, will ensure that the student performs the target behavior.

Correct Response. Accurate performance of the target behavior by the student within the specified response interval.

Criterion. Specification of minimum acceptable performance for determining continuation of instruction (acquisition of target skill) or movement within the instructional program, such as correct responding at each prompt level.

Curriculum-Based Assessment. A process of gathering information for the purpose of determining what skills should be taught.

Curriculum Catalogs. Listings of common skills or activities by curriculum area.

Differential Reinforcement. Reinforcement that is delivered under certain conditions (e.g., when a given behavior occurs) and not delivered under other conditions.

Discrete Task Response. A single behavior having a distinct beginning and end.

Discriminative Stimulus Relationship. The stimulus cues the student that reinforcement is probable if the target behavior is performed.

Ecological Inventories. Individualized assessments of (a) the demands or requirements of specific activities within current and future environments and (b) the student's ability to complete those activities successfully.

Effectiveness. Whether students actually acquire the targeted behaviors as a result of an instructional procedure; if they do, instruction is said to be effective.

Efficiency. The relative amount of time and effort required to learn a skill.

Error Correction Procedure. An instructional strategy where the response prompt is provided in the consequent event after error responses.

Fade. The gradual removal of a prompt.

Fluency. The "speed or ease with which a child performs a movement or series of movements" (White & Haring, 1980, p. 312).

Focus. To orient toward, or give attention to, a stimulus—such as the student, task materials, or an action.

Form. The actual behaviors used to complete a skill or activity or cause an effect.

Forward Chaining. A type of instructional format used in teaching a chained task, in which each step is taught individually to criterion, beginning with the first step and progressing toward the final step in the task analysis.

Full Physical Prompts. Teacher behaviors that allow the teacher to manipulate the student's hands and body; are used to cause the student to perform the correct response.

Function.   The effects fulfilled by behaviors (forms).

Functional Communication.   Specific language behaviors that can be immediately used by the student to increase independent functioning and convey to others individual wants and needs.

General Attentional Cues.   Nonspecific teacher behaviors that call the attention of a student to the instructional stimuli.

General Attentional Responses.   Nonspecific student behaviors that inform the teacher that attention is being given to the instructional target.

Generalization.   Correct responding in situations other than the training situation (e.g., across persons, across materials, across natural consequences, across stimuli, across setting, and across time).

Gestural Prompts.   Nonverbal behaviors, such as hand movements and facial expressions, that "tell" the student how to perform the correct response.

Graduated Guidance.   A response prompting procedure involving presentation of a prompt that controls a student's behavior followed by its removal based on immediate, moment-to-moment decisions during instruction.

Group Contingencies.   Providing reinforcement to a group for the performance of individual members or of the group as a whole.

Hierarchy.   Used to denote the presence of a group of prompts arranged in some order of amounts of assistance.

Incidental Learning.   The acquisition of nontarget information that is present in the instructional context and for which there are no programmed contingencies for the learner to acquire that information.

Incidental Teaching.   A naturalistic response prompting procedure that involves a teacher arrangement of the environment to encourage child-directed initiations of communicative exchanges.

Incorrect Response.   Inaccurate performance of the target behavior by the student within the specified response interval.

Intensity.   One method of prompt removal involving changing the strength or force of a prompt.

Intersequential Arrangement.   A method of providing group instruction that involves the teachers delivering trials and programmed interactions between group members.

Intrasequential Arrangement.   A method of providing group instruction that involves the teacher delivering trials to each member individually and not programming any interactions between group members.

Intrusiveness.   The extent to which an instructional procedure impinges or intrudes on the student's body.

Learning.   A relatively permanent change in performance as a result of experience; does not refer to changes in performance that occur as a result of excitement, fatigue, or maturation.

Least Dangerous Assumption.   Principle related to selecting interventions that states when two or more alternatives exist and a research base is absent, then the procedure that has the smallest potential for causing harm should be selected.

Least Intrusive-to-Most Intrusive.   The arrangement of prompts or stimuli within a hierarchy progressing from the minimum to the maximum amount of assistance.

Level.   The position or rank of a stimulus within a hierarchy that provides assistance to the student.

Locus of Control.   One method to remove physical assistance involving changing the position of physical guidance on the student's body.

Maintenance.   Continued performance of a target behavior after teaching has stopped.

Mand.   A type of verbal request or command (non-yes/no) used in the mand-model instructional procedure, in which the teacher requests that the student emit a verbal response (includes nonverbal communication), resulting in a reinforcer specific to the response.

Mand-Model.   A naturalistic response prompting procedure involving an adult-directed initiation toward a student that interrupts the student activity, requests that the student emit a response related to the activity, and allows the student to resume the activity after a correct response is made.

Maximum Prompt Delay Interval.   A term used with the progressive time delay procedure to describe the greatest number of seconds that will be inserted between the stimulus that cues a student to respond and the controlling prompt.

Model Prompts.   Demonstrations of the correct behavior.

Models.   Demonstrations of the correct behavior: the teacher does the behavior that the student is learning, and the student is expected to imitate the teacher's model.

Most Intrusive-to-Least Intrusive.   The arrangement of prompts or stimuli within a hierarchy, progressing from maximum to minimum amounts of assistance.

Most-to-Least Prompts (Decreasing Assistance).   A response prompting instructional procedure that progressively fades assistance from the most amount of help needed to ensure correct responding to no help or independent level, of the target behavior.

Natural Environment.   All of the surrounding environments specific to the student's everyday activities.

Naturalistic Time Delay.   A naturalistic response prompting procedure used during existing routines in the natural environment, in which the adult withholds materials or assistance for a specific number of seconds and encourages the student to initiate a communicative exchange.

Naturally Occurring Events.   Events that occur as part of a student's everyday life.

Near Errorless.   A term used to describe instructional procedures that result in the student learning new skills with very few errors.

Negative Reinforcement.   The process by which an aversive event is removed contingent on the occurrence of a behavior and produces an increase or maintenance in the occurrence of that behavior.

Noncontrolling Prompts.   Teacher behaviors that increase the probability of the student responding correctly but do not ensure that correct responses will occur.

Nonverbal Request.   A nonspeech initiation made by a student toward an adult—such as a point, cry, or look at an object—in order to gain access to a toy or activity, receive assistance, seek information, or ask permission.

No Response Errors.   Failure to emit any response within the specified response interval following delivery of the target stimulus or a prompt.

Observational Learning.   The acquisition of behaviors performed by, or taught to, others for which there are no programmed contingencies for the observer.

One-on-one Supplement Arrangement.   A method of providing group instruction that involves the student participating in a group and also receiving one-on-one instruction.

Parsimonious.   Relatively simple to use.

Partial Physical Prompts.   Teacher behaviors that involve touching the student but not controlling her movements; they are provided to cause the student to perform the correct response.

Pictorial Prompts (Two-Dimensional Prompts).   Pictures or written messages that tell the student how to perform the correct response.

Positive Reinforcement.   The process by which an event follows (occurs contingently on) a behavior and produces an increase in the occurrence or the maintenance of that behavior.

Primum Non Noscere.   A principle related to selecting interventions stating that the minimal acceptable criteria for any practice or treatment is that it does no harm to those who experience it.

Principle of Parsimony.   When two or more solutions exist for a problem, then the simpler/est solution should be adopted.

Principle of Partial Participation.   A process for devising adaptations to assist the student in taking part in activities despite the fact that he cannot perform each component of the activity independently.

Probes (Test Trials).   Trials in which the stimulus that cues a response is presented without a prompt to test for transfer of stimulus control.

Progressive Delay Trials.   Instructional trials conducted with the progressive time delay procedure, in which gradually increasing increments of time are inserted between the stimulus that cues a student to respond and delivery of the controlling prompt.

Progressive Time Delay.   A response prompting procedure characterized by inserting progressively increasing amounts of time between the stimulus that cues a student to perform a task and the controlling prompt.

Prompt Delay Interval.   A term used in the constant and progressive time delay procedures to define the amount of time between delivery of the stimulus that cues the student to respond and delivery of the controlling prompt.

Prompted Correct.   Accurate performance of the target response by the student following delivery of the prompt within the specified response interval.

Prompted Error.   Inaccurate performance of the target behavior by the student following delivery of the prompt within the specified response interval.

Request for an Elaboration.   A form of target stimulus used in the incidental teaching procedure that signals the student to respond with a more complex communicative behavior.

Response Interval.   The amount of time a student is allowed to respond following presentation of a prompt or the stimulus that cues the response.

Response Prompts.   Teacher behaviors presented to increase the probability of correct responding (assistance provided by the teacher).

Response Prompting Strategies.   Procedures that provide and fade extra teacher assistance (prompts) to students so that the behavior will occur when the stimulus is present, thus allowing reinforcement to be provided to build stimulus control.

Response Shaping.   Reinforcement of successive approximations of the target behavior.

Restrictiveness.   The extent to which an instructional procedure inhibits or restrains a student's freedom.

Routine.   Events that occur regularly in the student's natural environment.

Shadowing.   A technique used with the graduated guidance procedure in which the teacher's hands follow closely with the student's hands without actually touching them.

Simultaneous Prompting.   A systematic antecedent prompt and test procedure.

Social Validity.   The value assigned by experts and consumers to the goals, procedures, and outcomes of an educational practice (Wolf, 1978).

Specific Attentional Cues.   Teacher behaviors that call the attention of a student to particular elements of the instructional stimuli.

Specific Attentional Responses.   Behaviors that indicate the student is attending to particular elements of the instructional stimuli.

Stimulus Conditions.   The situations, others' behaviors, environmental variables, materials, and so forth under which behaviors occur or should occur.

Stimulus Control.   The reliable or predictable performance of a behavior when particular stimulus (stimuli) is (are) present and the absence of that behavior when that stimulus (those stimuli) is (are) absent.

Stimulus Fading.   Changing some noncritical or irrelevant dimension of the stimulus from a currently controlling stimulus to the target stimulus.

Stimulus Modification Procedures.   Strategies that involve gradual changes in the instructional stimuli from some current level of stimulus control to some desired level of stimulus control.

Stimulus Shaping.   Changing the critical or relevant dimension of the stimulus from a currently controlling stimulus to the target stimulus.

Stimulus Superimposition.   Placing one stimulus (a controlling one) over another (target stimulus) and gradually changing the salience or intensity of the stimuli.

System of Least Prompts.   A response prompting procedure that delivers assistance based on student responding in order of the least amount of help to the maximum amount of assistance needed to ensure correct performance of the target behavior.

Systematic Instruction.   A series of steps to identify the behaviors to be taught, plan instructional activities, implement those activities, evaluate their effects, and determine whether the student's behavior changes as desired.

Tandem Arrangement.   A method of providing group instruction that involves initially presenting one-on-one instruction and systematically adding children to the group.

Target Behaviors.   Any responses that have been identified by a team of professionals and the student's family as being an important focus of instruction.

Target Stimulus.   The antecedent stimulus that cues the student to respond.

Task Direction.   A type of target stimulus, such as a command or question, that signals the student to respond but does not tell the student how to respond.

Teaching.   The process of organizing experience so that the student performs behaviors under new and/or different stimulus conditions.

Total Task Format.   Method of teaching chained tasks that involves teaching all steps of the sequence at once.

Transfer Mediational Paradigm.   A structure of organizing instruction that allows acquisition of untrained relationships to emerge.

Transfer of Stimulus Control.   The predictability of a student's response shifts from one stimulus (i.e., a prompt) to another (i.e., the target stimulus).

Transition.   The time that exists between ongoing activities embedded in a student's schedule when transition-based teaching trials are conducted.

Transition-Based Teaching.   A naturalistic response prompting procedure in which instructional trials across any skill area are conducted during transitions between ongoing activities.

Two-Dimensional Prompts (Pictorial Prompts).   Pictures or written messages that tell the student how to perform the correct response.

Unprompted Correct.   Accurate performance of the target response by the student before delivery of the prompt within the specified response interval.

Unprompted Error.   Inaccurate performance of the target behavior by the student before delivery of the prompt within the specified response interval.

Verbal Prompts.   Vocal statements by teachers that give students information about how to perform the correct response.

Verbal Request.   An initiation made by a student toward an adult using speech or some form of augmentative communication to gain access to a toy or activity, receive assistance, seek information, or ask permission.

Verify.   Adult confirmation of the accuracy of a stimulus or event.

Wait Training.   A procedure used before implementing a constant or progressive time delay program that involves teaching the student to wait for a prompt from the teacher before responding.

Zero-Second Delay (0-Second).   A term used with constant or progressive time delay procedures describing no amount of time being inserted between the stimulus that cues a student to respond and a controlling prompt.

Zero-Second (0-Second) Delay Trials.   Instructional trials presented when using the constant or progressive time delay procedures that involve presenting a stimulus that cues a student to respond and then immediately presenting a controlling prompt.

Index